SOCIOLOGY AND SOCIAL WELFARE SERIES

edited by Paul Halmos

Exercises in Social Science

IN THE SAME SERIES

Social Science and Social Purpose
T. S. Simey

A Reader in Social Administration
edited by A. V. S. Lochhead

Industrial Democracy
Paul Blumberg

Exercises in
Social Science

John Liggett

Senior Lecturer in Psychology,
University College of South Wales and Monmouthshire

and

Raymond Cochrane

Research Assistant, Department of Psychology,
University College of South Wales and Monmouthshire

Constable London

First published in 1968
by Constable and Co Ltd
10 Orange Street London WC2
Copyright © 1968 by John Liggett & Raymond Cochrane
All rights reserved
Printed in Great Britain
by Butler & Tanner Ltd, Frome and London
SBN 09 455820 5 (hardback)
SBN 09 455821 3 (paperback)

Acknowledgments

This book could not have been written without the devoted care and skilled assistance of Arline Liggett to whom the authors wish to express their sincere gratitude.

They would also like to thank Mary Cochrane whose understanding and cooperation was a constant source of encouragement, Mrs Margaret Stacey of University College, Swansea, Mr Ivor B. Davies and Mr John Harper, also Mr J. Wakeford for his interest in the early planning stages of the book and Miss Mary Lace for her original drawings for the Exercise on Human Personality and Miss Elfreda Powell for her editorial help.

The authors also thank The Institute of Practitioners in Advertising for use of material from the *IPA National Readership Survey, 1967*, Her Majesty's Stationery Office for material from *Criminal Statistics for England and Wales, 1965*, and from the *Annual Abstract of Statistics*, Penguin Books Ltd for use of material from *Sense and Nonsense in Psychology* by H. J. Eysenck, The American Psychological Association for use of Heidbreder's Introversion Questionnaire which appeared in *The Journal of Abnormal Psychology*, I.B.M. United Kingdom Ltd, and The Social and Economic Archive Committee.

University College   J.L.
Cardiff   R.C.

Contents

Preface

This book of exercises is intended for use by students who are beginning their studies in social science. Its aim is to introduce them to some of the practical methods used in the collection and analysis of many distinct varieties of data, to enable them to appreciate some of the practical problems facing social scientists and to give them the right level of informed scepticism in reading accounts of research work. It may also be useful to those working in social administration by enabling them to see the limitations of data of various kinds and also perhaps by helping to suggest new lines of analysis and enquiry which they may find of practical value in their future work. It may be helpful too in bringing to the attention of specialists in one discipline techniques more usually employed by specialists in another.

Thirty-six exercises are described in detail and these cover a very wide range of subject matter and techniques. All of the data and materials needed to undertake these exercises will be found within the covers of this book and it is not necessary therefore to purchase additional material of any kind. Each of the exercises can be completed within a three-hour practical period and each of them makes an important 'design' point or an illustration of the use of a well-known statistical procedure in a way which, it is hoped, will stimulate the student's interest in the *techniques* involved, as well as in the specific content which usually has high intrinsic interest anyway.

The exercises are divided into four sections. In Section A the concern is with the handling and use of data *which already exist*, either in a statistical or documentary form. Section B deals with a selection of widely-used techniques of *observation*, and the collection, recording and processing of such observational data. Section C covers a variety of techniques of *measurement*, such as the survey techniques used by sociologists and the mental measurements made by psychologists. In Section D the concern is less with data collection and scoring but rather with problems of *design of investigations* and the propriety of drawing conclusions from apparent relationships between variables. The authors' intention has been to provide not only detailed instructions for 36 specific exercises but also a compact collection of data and materials for use by instructors in practical teaching procedures of the kind which have long been used in the teaching of psychology but which are, as argued elsewhere, (Liggett, J. & Wakeford, J., 'Sociology as a laboratory subject', *Sociological Review*, 1964, 12: pp. 203–7), equally appropriate to other areas of social science. Much of the test material and data supplied—such as the case histories in the first three exercises and the detailed descriptions of the population of a small town given in Exercise 20—may thus be used for a variety of additional exercises, under the guidance of an instructor.

In order to take some of the drudgery, and perhaps some of the terror, from the statistical computations special charts have been included wherever possible to indicate the procedural steps in the calculations. For the sake of uniformity the symbols and terminology used in one particular statistical text have been employed throughout (*Statistics for the Social Sciences* by Connolly & Sluckin, Cleaver-Hume Press, 18s.). A number of alternative statistical texts are listed in Appendix 1. Instructors will no doubt wish to specify their own texts for background reading. For the sake of the student working on his own, however, specific references to supplementary reading are given with each exercise. For those specially interested in research, *Research Methods in Social Relations* by Selltiz, Jahoda, Deutsch & Cook (Holt, Rinehart and Winston), is particularly recommended. No special importance attaches to the sequence in which the exercises appear in this book and the student should not feel it necessary to undertake them in this particular order. The fourfold division of the book is intended simply to facilitate the initial orientation of the student beginning his studies of social science and implies no sacred inviolate boundaries either of content or of method.

Section A

The Use of Existing Documentary Evidence

Introduction (A)

Some writers, such as Harrisson, have suggested that society is much too subtle and complex to admit of numerical analysis. They suggest that the most, and the best, we can do is to make careful intensive study of the individuals (or the groups of people) we are interested in and, after a good deal of thoughtful consideration of these single people (or single societies), draw our conclusions about them. The advocates of this 'case study' approach insist that individuals cannot be adequately represented by mere numbers and argue that conclusions based on methods and experiments akin to those of the physical sciences are bound to be misleading. While this argument between the advocates of 'statistical' and 'case study' approaches has been going on, some very valuable records of individuals have been collected, as for example in social work and medicine. In these fields case history-taking has long been accepted as a standard procedure. *Exercises 1* and *2* consider respectively the case records of an individual and a family and illustrate the great range and variety of factors which must be taken into account. At the same time these two exercises show the possible inferential pitfalls of the case study method. How far can we, in fact, justifiably generalise from an individual case?

In *Exercise 3* a comparison is made of three primitive communities—and an attempt is made to decide whether their very different social and physical environments have influenced their personalities and customs in any important ways. A comparison is made, too, with modern western society. The case study method has been used, of course, to great effect in societies nearer home—such as the studies by Young and Willmott of the people of East London, and in studies of communities such as the gang in Whyte's *Street Corner Society* (Chicago University Press, 1943).

A great deal of valuable information about society is readily available in documents of various kinds—in literary works, in directories, year books and in official archives and statistics. The British Government publication *Annual Abstract of Statistics* (H.M.S.O.), for example, contains a wealth of information on subjects as diverse as family expenditure and immigration.

Exercises 5, 6 and *7* are concerned with the analysis of government statistics—in this case relating to crime and punishment. The last two exercises in this section are also concerned with drawing conclusions from official statistics, but require certain elementary calculations to be performed—such as the computation of average family expenditures on certain types of products. *Exercise 9* shows how two variables may be related to each other and some interesting predictions made. A statistical glossary will be found in Appendix 1 which may be helpful in dealing with the calculations. Throughout the exercises in the book, charts have been provided to assist in these calculations. A note explaining the use of these charts will be found in Appendix 2.

Exercise 1. Individual Case Study

Introduction

A great deal of factual data on social processes already exists in the form of detailed accounts of particular *societies*, of particular *organisations*, and most commonly of all, of particular *individuals*. All of these accounts have in common the fact that they are concerned with the sum-total of what has been observed. They are not concerned with the analysis of sub-groups within the whole. Studies of whole societies in many different parts of the world have been made by cultural anthropologists—such as Mead's study of the peoples of New Guinea reported in *Sex and Temperament in Three Primitive Societies*. There are also many well-known case studies of smaller communities such as Young and Willmott's study, *Family and Kinship in East London*, and the Lynd's study, *Middletown*. Case studies have also been made of industrial communities where the investigator's interest has often been in the efficiency of the *whole* group as a function of different types of management technique. By far the most numerous, however, are case studies of individual persons, and these are often based on evidence as diverse as personal documents, biographical interviews or repeated observations by an investigator employing standard 'test' procedures.

The term 'case study' is occasionally used, however, in a quite different sense—to describe the analysis—by all available means—of an event or a decision (e.g., in industrial or political settings). Such case studies are usually concerned with real events but may occasionally involve imaginary situations constructed for pedagogical purposes (e.g. imaginary law cases). This exercise is not concerned with 'case study' in this latter sense.

Many writers, such as G. W. Allport (referring to individuals) and T. Harrisson (referring to groups) have eloquently argued the importance of the study of individual instances. The case study approach is, of course, central in psychiatry and medicine.

Case studies may be undertaken for scientific as well as for purely practical purposes however. Science proceeds by inductive inferences based on observation—and case histories may contain much sound observation. They may also contain much unsound and misleading

4

material, which is not more than subjective interpretation. It is the purpose of this exercise to underline the importance of the distinction between observation and interpretation, though it will become evident during the exercise that the distinction is sometimes very hard to draw.

It is characteristic of supporters of the case study approach that they frequently stress the essential 'uniqueness' of the individual or the society they are studying. They sometimes imply that there is no point in looking for general laws common to all cases. As Argyle (*The Scientific Study of Social Behaviour*, 1957) and Eysenck (*The Scientific Study of Personality*, 1952) declare, however, this approach is mistaken. The uniqueness, as Eysenck declares, resides not in the laws but in the individual's unique pattern of values which must be inserted in the general laws. Eysenck readily agrees that each individual is unique— but this uniqueness derives solely from his differing quantitatively from every other individual on many variables. General laws will eventually be found which will accommodate all possible combinations of these individual variables.

By far the most commonly occurring case studies are those concerning individuals who are believed to have some form of social 'abnormality' whether this be:

a. a behavioural abnormality (e.g., delinquent, chronically unemployed), or
b. a situational abnormality (e.g., orphaned, crippled, blind, old), or
c. an emotional abnormality (e.g., severe depression, neuroticism or alcoholism),

and where it is hoped that some *modification* can be introduced by therapy or by other means.

The main purpose of case studies or case histories in such circumstances is often quite practical—to establish a rational basis for action which will successfully modify the abnormality. The first purpose of a case history is often diagnostic, i.e. to decide on the particular nature of the abnormality. The second is often to enable a decision to be taken about the relevance and probable success of a particular type of therapy.

The precise form of the case history and the concepts it employs are inevitably determined by the particular needs and methods of the social agency initiating it. Usually, however, a case history attempts to describe, in as objective terms as possible, the present situation of the patient or 'client'. An attempt is made to summarise the salient features of the client's environment (necessarily involving some degree of interpretation by the case worker) and the way in which the client appears to be reacting to his environment. The report often contains reference to the main events and significant persons in the client's life from early childhood to the present time. Work history and medical history are often summarised too since these are clearly important in understanding the present personality and behaviour of the client. A well-written case history has great utility in that it helps to organise the facts about the client in a systematic and economical way. The facts may be derived from many sources—from the patient's family, from various social agencies, hospitals, schools, courts—or from the results of special examinations and tests (for example, tests of personality or intelligence). In addition to clear statements of factual information a case history inevitably contains statements which represent the investigator's opinion or interpretations of the client's situation and these are inevitably coloured by the particular theoretical preconceptions of the investigator (and to some extent also of the organisation concerned). Frequently case histories also include an account of presumed pressures on the client—from housing or neighbourhood conditions, low income or unsatisfactory employment or domestic stress, or from friends, neighbours or religious groups. Particular attention is often given to apparent sources of anxiety, guilt and feelings of inadequacy (as reported by the patient or his family). Attitudes and defence mechanisms which seem characteristic of the client are sometimes included in psychiatric case histories as also are the ways in which he deals with his libidinal and aggressive impulses.

Though it is easy to see why theoreticians have misgivings about the scientific value of case history data, there is little doubt, however, that a well-written report by a skilled observer can make a considerable contribution to the understanding and good management of social problems.

Objective

To study Case Histories 1 and 2, to attempt to summarise their information in tabular form, to separate factual from interpretative material, and to consider alternative methods of recording and analysis of case study data.

Materials

Case histories 1: Mrs Ellen (Item 1.1), and 2: The Lincoln family (Item 2.1).

Method

1. Case History 1 (Mrs Ellen) should be studied carefully until the student feels well acquainted with the case.

2. He should then attempt to draw up a list of the 'classes of information' in the case history. Thus, items of purely 'biographical' information will be found (e.g., 'age when married').

Again, there is information relating to 'physical disorders' (e.g., anaemia).

This is a difficult and important part of this exercise and should be undertaken with care.

3. When the six or eight or more categories have been decided upon, a simple scoring or marking system should be devised, e.g., P or 'Phys' for physical symptoms, B or 'Biog' for biographical data.

(One such suggested list is contained in Item 1.2 and may be referred to if in serious difficulty.)

Each unit of information in the case record should then be marked or scored appropriately by entering the agreed symbol alongside the statement in the case history.

4. An attempt should then be made to construct a synoptic chronological chart which shows in tabular form the very approximate sequence in time of the various events discussed in the case history.

An example of such a tabular treatment of Case 1 will be found in the Item 1.2. It is best not to examine this until an unaided attempt has first been made.

Discussion

1. Why *was it* so difficult to 'score' the information in the case history?

2. Could you envisage and describe a set of Instructions to Case History Writers which would have made your task easier?

3. What ill-effects might possibly follow the use of such a formal procedure?

4. How far is it possible to separate fact from interpretation on the part of the case worker?

Quote two examples from Case History 1 where the distinction was particularly hard to draw.

5. Does this case worker appear to be committed to one *particular* theory of human experience and behaviour? Illustrate by quoting verbatim.

ESS—B

6. To what extent do you feel Mrs Ellen's difficulties have been due to factors outside herself (external deprivation, frustration, or provocation) and to what extent are her difficulties due to her own personality inadequacies or excessive needs and demands.

7. Do you agree with the conclusions and action plan reached by the case worker? What further objectives would you consider might be achieved and how would you set about the task?

8. Do you accept the notions of normality and abnormality implied in the case worker's account? What is the most *useful* way of employing these terms? Is there any essential conflict between commonsense and statistical notions of abnormality?

9. Did any feature of the case history suggest a new line of enquiry which might profitably be followed up in future research?

10. What further information, if any, would be needed before active therapy could begin?

References

For a discussion of the validity of conclusions drawn from case study material see:

ARGYLE, M., *The Scientific Study of Social Behaviour* (Methuen, London 1957).

Case study as a mode of *therapy* (as distinct from *investigation*) is discussed in:

HOLLIS, F., *Case work: Psychosocial therapy* (Random House, N.Y. 1964), and in

HAMILTON, G., *Theory and Practice of Social Case work* (Columbia University Press 1951).

ITEM 1.1: CASE HISTORY OF MRS ELLEN, AGED 43

Mrs Ellen was a patient on Ward E1 for two weeks, two years ago, when her condition was diagnosed as reactive depression.

Her stay in hospital revealed the existence of problems in the family situation. Social investigation following her discharge and subsequent family orientated case work has disclosed multifarious psycho-social problems of a chronic pattern.

Background

Mr and Mrs Ellen were married 13 years ago when both were aged thirty. Mr Ellen is a Jamaican, very black, and of obvious negroid parentage. He was nineteen when he left Jamaica to take up a sea-faring career, and remained a sailor until about five years ago. Mrs Ellen comes from the North of England and has disclosed that she married against the wishes of her father.

There are five children of the marriage: Lorraine, 12; Patricia, 10; Colleen, 9; Daniel, 8; and David, 6. All the children have negroid features either in skin colour, frizzy hair, broad noses and/or thick lips. Danny, the 8 year old, is the darkest. For his age he is small-boned and very much 'a little chap' in comparison with the others who are well-built children. The five children are interesting to talk to and hold their own scholastically. At home they are lively and yet by and large, well behaved and seemingly well within the control of both parents. They are pleasant and likeable children and yet, it would seem, cer-tainly not without their own problems and anxieties in the neighbour-hood. The family unit is close knit. The psycho-social problems are inextricably interwoven and knowledge of the family from study so far is limited. Some of the dominant problems have been isolated and understood to some extent.

Firstly, there is Mrs Ellen's health. She is a chronically sick woman, and one might be inclined to feel that there is an endogenous element in this depression. Her husband has described her as 'having always suffered from a weak chest and bad heart'. Although in the main her general health before marriage—and according to Mr Ellen, until about five years ago—was 'good', 'she was always a plump healthy woman'. However, for some years now she has been suffering acutely from chest conditions, bronchitis type. She is anaemic and two years ago refused hospitalisation offered by her G.P. for treatment for her anaemia. She has cysts and polypi of the womb requiring minor opera-tive treatment. These cause increasing discomfort—prolonged men-struation and other persistent discharges, causing her much mental anxiety, particularly because of the strong smell and the fear of cancer. Mrs Ellen quickly succumbs to inclement weather and has recently had pneumonia. She has a fear of hospitalisation and puts off treatment for her womb trouble. In part this fear derives from her physical experience shortly after David's birth when she was sterilised without anaesthetic. She relives this experience in her mind over and over. Psychologically she seems to carry anxieties and guilt from this time.

Secondly, an area giving rise to anxieties in both parents for similar and different reasons, and undoubtedly affecting psycho-social develop-ment of the children, is the preoccupation with the question of colour, mixed marriage, etc. It has already been mentioned that Mrs Ellen's marriage was against her family's wishes and probably without their blessing. Her guilt about this is partly seen in her anxieties about the children and their status in the neighbourhood and school, for example. Her admission to hospital was triggered off by an incident where Danny cried about going to school with a torn pullover, saying that the other children would call him a 'ragged blacky'. Mrs Ellen, probably already in a very depressed state, at that time with additional problems of rent arrears, County Court Debts, her husband's unemployment, amongst others, reacted to Danny's pleas by 'going berserk'. She lost control completely of her pent-up emotions and smashed the T.V. etc. It is interesting that much later, Mr Ellen said in an interview that on many occasions he would like to see his wife lose her temper, but that she tends to keep control of herself.

Could it be that perhaps psychologically her 'bad smell' and her 'fear of cancer'—that is, the rottenness within her—symbolise for Mrs Ellen her badness and her unworthiness. She is certainly not a dull woman and has been found to have a sensitivity in spite of her ability to manipulate and to know her way about. She seems to have deep-rooted guilt about her marriage in its total context among other recognised and non-recognised factors. To understand Mrs Ellen more it would be desirable to know much more about her early life, her attitudes towards her family and her parental history within her family or origins, e.g., her relationship to her father and what it meant to defy him in this way. Mrs Ellen has an obsessive need to be cleaning by decorating frequently and in her new home this has certainly been without a real practical need. This decorating is often achieved, it seems, at hardship both financially and physically to herself; e.g., she insisted on papering the living-room this Christmas in spite of very bad health and there seemed something almost masochistic about it, and certainly it seems to have a purging element.

This colour problem or awareness, is seen in Mr Ellen in one way in his attitude to work and to authority. He left seafaring about four or five years ago after the birth of David which, followed by Mrs Ellen's sterilisation, is recurrently presented by both spouses as the cause of their present psycho-social family problems. From this time, they hold, can be traced Mrs Ellen's deterioration in health. Since this time Mr Ellen's work pattern has become sporadic. He has been unemployed for lengthy periods, and has alienated himself from authoritative agencies, e.g., Min. of Labour and the National Assistance Board. He

interprets their attitudes to him as stemming from his colour, and therefore their low estimation of him as a human being. Being unemployed
undermines his self-confidence and helps to perpetuate a vicious circle.
He introjects what he believes other people feel about him and sees
himself as valueless: 'I'm no value, so people let me down.'

These three factors: Mrs Ellen's health, the colour problem, and
Mr Ellen's unemployment seem linked in some way in another dimension. Mrs Ellen when depressed, fears to be left alone. Although on the
surface she may encourage her husband to get work and even criticises
him and nags because he is about the house unemployed, in fact she
colludes with his unemployment. She said of a neighbour who is depressed: 'She keeps her husband home because she needs him.' Mr Ellen
described how, when his wife was once taken ill, he was called down
by the foreman from a high scaffolding. He felt anxious and worried
to death and so fears leaving her. Mr Ellen recognises that his only
work that he knows and understands and likes is seafaring. He has a
wish to return to the sea but sees himself as holding himself back because of his fear that something might happen to Mrs Ellen while he is
away, and his love for his children, and his recognition of day to day
practical responsibility in caring for them. I wonder how much Mrs
Ellen's health factor is a means of keeping her husband tied to home
and her country. And on the other side of this coin, her absolute
dependence upon him.

Mr Ellen is known to have had isolated incidents of *delinquency*. The
first dates, in fact, from *nine months* before David's birth, when he was
imprisoned for larceny for nine months. This indicates the existence of
problems *before* David's birth. More recently he has had motoring
offences causing disqualification from driving for about one year, and
this ends in January 1967. An additional factor contributing to a work
antipathy attitude on the part of both Mr and Mrs Ellen is that although
the wage stop is operating, the financial incentive is dubious. Border-
line poverty brings practical daily problems. The cost of clothing the
children is high, especially as they all are hard on shoes. Partly because
of her ill health, mending and washing sometimes get beyond Mrs
Ellen.

Help has been given by various social agencies: ourselves, and
W.V.S., as well as N.A.B. Mr Ellen supports her a great deal in
housework, e.g., will get children to school in the morning, clean, etc.
The children are aware of their colour and anxious not to stand out
in school by being badly dressed. I have the feeling that there is some

resentment—especially with Colleen, Patricia and Danny. Colleen has attended Child Guidance following disturbed behaviour accredited to a sexual assault but certainly more deeply lying. She is described by both parents as a difficult child and 'different from the others'. She tries to straighten her frizzy hair. I wonder if she is in some way a family scapegoat? Although this is not so in any obvious way.

Plan

I feel a social worker, through a warm relationship which is accepting of colour, and sensitive to both the more obvious presented practical problems (e.g., regular need of renewal of clothes for children), and the submerged problems in the family, may help to bring about a reversal of declining confidence and self value of both Mr and Mrs Ellen. If Mrs Ellen's health can improve and one need here is her minor gynaecological operation, then she may be more able to let go a little of Mr Ellen, enough perhaps to enable him to begin to build up a more positive attitude to work. I believe he is capable of a good work record but must first free himself to some degree of anxieties, especially irrational ones. Mrs Ellen will need much support to go into hospital. I feel that she might find help in talking about her fears carried over both physically and psychologically from her sterilisation. She refers, at least in passing, to this at every interview, and I feel she has much guilt about this, and, that this is bound up with the meaning of her marriage from several aspects—guilt brought over from her relationship to her parents, the fact of being mother of coloured children, and fears about herself as a wife and a woman.

ITEM 1.2: MRS ELLEN

Biographical Milestones and Conspicuous Environmental Events and Pressures

WIFE	HUSBAND
White	Negro
Children born:	
1. Lorraine	Left home for
2. Patricia	seafaring career
3. Colleen	
4. Daniel	Imprisoned for
	larceny (9 months)

WIFE		HUSBAND
5. David	Financial hardship e.g., clothing children	
	Daily mending and cleaning difficult	
	due to bad health	Unemployed
Sterilised		
	Rent arrears	Gave up
	County Court debts	sea career
Hospitalised for 2 weeks 'depression'		

Emergent Abnormalities

BEHAVIOURAL	PHYSICAL	EXPERIENTIAL
Delinquency and H. imprisoned for larceny	MARRIAGE	W. married against the wishes of her father
	'W. has always suffered from weak chest and weak heart' (H.)	Children aware of colour—try to straighten hair
W. went beserk outburst—smashed T.V.		
	W. has suffered acutely from chest conditions bronchitis	H. feels 'he would like to see his wife lose her temper'
H. alienated self from agencies, e.g., N.A.B. and Min. of Labour (blames 'colour prejudice')	W. anaemic—GP suggested hospitalisation	Children worried re clothing—being called 'ragged blacky'
	W. refused	
	Cysts removed	W. feels she smells badly—cancer phobia
	Diagnosis for W. 'reactive depression', hospital, sterilised without anaesthetic	W. depressed
		Relives sterilization operation 'over and over again'
		Both H. and W. feel that deterioration in health dates from sterilisation

Comments by Case Worker

INTERPRETATION	ACTION SUGGESTED
I would like to know much more about her early life, her attitudes towards her family, and her personal history within her family	Further enquiry
I would like to know about her early relationship to her father and what it meant to defy him in this way	Further enquiry
I feel she has deep-rooted guilt about her (coloured) marriage against her father's wishes	'A warm relationship accepting of colour'
W. is certainly not a dull woman	
W. guilty about being mother of coloured children	Discuss guilt feelings
I wonder if Child Colleen is a family scapegoat?	An approach sensitive to the obvious practical needs, e.g., clothing renewal
W. will not 'let go' of H.	Get W. to 'let go' of H. so H. can make more positive approach to work
It has occurred to me that perhaps psychologically her 'bad smell' and her fear of cancer (i.e., rottenness within her) symbolise her badness and her unworthiness	
There is a serious decline of confidence and self-value in both	Attempt reversal of declining confidence
'There is an endogenous element in her depression'	Support W. so can go to hospital for minor gynaecological operation
'The financial incentive is dubious'	
'I believe H. is capable of good work record'	Encourage talk about fears and guilt from sterilisation

Exercise 2. Family Case Study

Introduction

The case study approach is often used to gain an understanding of groups of people as well as for the study of individuals. This exercise focuses on one disturbed family and the next exercise on whole societies. Much useful knowledge is gained by taking into careful account the social relationships of the individuals in the group. In the particular case presented here, none of the people might have been socially inadequate given strong support from a stable family and from a relatively normal environment. But the weakness of each individual can be seen here to cumulate and to put the whole family in distress.

The issues raised in our discussion of the previous case history exercise apply equally here and the same pattern of work should be undertaken. The student may care to consider the prognosis in this complex case; what is the eventual outcome likely to be?

ITEM 2.1: CASE HISTORY OF THE LINCOLN FAMILY

This family came to the attention of the authorities when the parents made application for three of the children to be taken into care. Mr Lincoln, an Airman in the R.A.F., was separated from his wife three years ago and has been living with Mrs Mottram for nearly two years. (Mrs Mottram has now changed her name to Lincoln by deed poll.) Mr Lincoln had two sons (Tony and Paul) and a daughter by his marriage and the two boys were living with their father at the time of this crisis. The daughter, aged 11, is with her mother somewhere in Australia. Mrs Mottram is also separated from her husband and receives a small amount of maintenance from him for the only child of their marriage (Mark) who lives with her and Mr Lincoln. One child has come from her cohabitation with Mr Lincoln, a baby boy, Michael. The family consists of: Mr Lincoln, aged 33; Mrs Mottram (now Lincoln), aged 27; Tony Lincoln, aged 8 (adopted); Paul Lincoln, aged 6; Mark Mottram, aged 6; Michael, aged 6 months.

Shortly after beginning the cohabitation with Mrs Mottram Mr Lincoln discharged himself from the R.A.F. and was given notice to quit married quarters. Mrs Mottram threatened suicide and Mr Lincoln accused her of not allowing him to go to work at the job he had found. They obtained a flat and the N.A.B. helped with the furniture but Mrs Mottram refused to move. Mr Lincoln lost his job and the land-lord re-let the flat leaving the family with no home and with very weak finances. The R.A.F. allowed the family to stay until the birth of the baby Mrs Mottram was now expecting. The two Lincoln boys went to stay with their grandmother during the confinement but Mrs Mottram insisted that they be returned as soon as the child was born. A few months later the R.A.F. obtained a possession order on the married quarters and Mr Lincoln and Mrs Mottram applied for three children (Tony and Paul Lincoln and Mark Mottram) to be taken into care while they looked for accommodation for themselves and baby Michael.

Mrs Mottram insisted that Mark should be with the two Lincoln boys, and said that they must never be parted as they are all part of the same family. This appears to be her means of keeping a hold on Mr Lincoln. She has great feelings of guilt about her cohabitation, and needs to hold on to Mr Lincoln in the hope that he will marry her and help her to overcome this.

Mark looks upon the two Lincoln boys (who are not in any way related to him) as his brothers, and Mrs Mottram encourages these attitudes. He is also very fond of his baby brother, and finds it hard to understand why this child is at home, and he is not. She wants Mark to feel that he is a member of the Lincoln family and wants him to forget that he had any other family. Mark remembers his own father and describes him as a 'nice man'.

Personality and Attitudes of the Parents
MR LINCOLN

A very weak character. Professed interest in his children, but is very easily influenced by the behaviour of his co-habitee. His wife left with another man and went to live in Australia taking their daughter. Mr Lincoln had a period of depression during the break-up of his mar-riage, and was seen by a psychiatrist. Appears to be work-shy but is full of excuses why he cannot work. Material care of children good. He is firmly opposed to their joining their mother in Australia or to his mother having them, as he thinks she turns them against him. He needs constant support if he is to establish a secure home for his children.

MRS MOTTRAM

Materially an excellent mother. A very disturbed personality and was probably damaged by her own childhood experiences (her parents parted and she was put into care) but she is less disturbed now than she was. Very attached to Mark, but professes as much love for Mr Lincoln's children, whom she considers to be a part of the same family. Is very determined to give her children the secure home that she was denied, but is not emotionally able to do this. Is making a more realistic approach now, e.g., had seen a solicitor about her divorce. Needs the support of Mr Lincoln and becomes hysterical if she feels he has deserted her. The maternal care which she gives her children is excellent. Quite unable to see the future realistically, but improving in her capacity to do so. Wants to marry Mr Lincoln and has a very strong hold on him. Very accepting of the children and looks on them as part of her family.

She has obviously been mentally ill in the past but has consistently refused to see a doctor. She has threatened suicide on several occasions. She appears to exhibit attention-seeking behaviour in an effort to establish a hold on Mr Lincoln. She has improved considerably since she came to this town, and can now look at things more realistically and can accept that Mr Lincoln needs work to support his family, and can bear him out of her sight. Was treated for depression after the birth of Mark.

Family Relationships

THE PARENTS

Very strained and emotionally explosive relationship. They want to get a divorce and marry each other, but are constantly frustrated. Mrs Mottram constantly threatens to leave him unless he makes a greater effort to divorce his wife and marry her, but he says he cannot do so until he is financially secure, and that she is so jealous she will not allow him out of her sight to go to work. Mrs Mottram becomes hysterical if Mr Lincoln is missing even for a few minutes, and immediately thinks he has left her. There had been constant friction because she had forced him into refusing to let his mother have the two boys by saying she will leave him, if he divides the family and splits his two boys from her boy. Mr Lincoln needs Mrs Mottram because she mothers him.

SIBLINGS

The two boys are very attached to each other, and to Mark, the son of their father's co-habitee. They are fond of their baby brother, and perhaps jealous that he is living with his parents and they are not. They show no particular caring about their mother and sister who are living in Australia. Were apparently happy when staying with paternal grandparents. Tony knows he is adopted, and is rather sensitive about it, but does not yet fully understand the meaning of adoption.

Parents maintain that he has a lot of feeling, but finds it hard to show emotion.

Name of child: *Anthony Frederick Lincoln*: Age 8 yrs.

Pen Picture

Speech defect very noticeable. A friendly child not at all shy. Had alopecia when admitted, but hair is growing again now. Wears a knitted cap, and is not at all self-conscious about this. Has quite a good understanding of his situation, and sees himself in elder brother role. Is anxious to talk about his family, and appears to have a good relationship with all his relatives.

Now legally adopted at County Court. Formerly Anthony Jones. Placement made through an Adoption Society. Child was not related.

History and Development

a. Pregnancy and Birth. Adopted child. Not known. Was born in Wessex General Hospital. Father was told that birth was normal.

b. Early feeding. Immediately after birth his mother placed him with private foster parents who physically ill-treated him and deprived him of food and comfort. He came to the Lincolns at the age of 1 year, was physically undeveloped and underweight. Fed with bottle and soft foods. Within six months he had attained normal development.

c. Milestones. Holding head up, not known. Sitting unsupported 15 months. Eruption of 1st tooth 1 year. Talking (babble) 1 year. Standing 18 months, walking 20 months, talking—words—18 months, bowel control 19–20 months, bladder control 4 or 5 years, talking— sentences, speech defect.

When placed at 1 year old could only sit up supported by straps. Was starting to cut his first tooth at the age of 1 year. Within a few weeks of placement began to say a few words, then stopped after two or three weeks. Did not talk again for about two months.

d. Toilet training. Bowel training caused no difficulty, but child had frequent accidents with his bladder, and was wetting the bed and occasionally wetting during the day up to the age of 5 years.

e. Changes of environment. Private foster mother until 9 months old. Then an L.C.C. foster mother for 3 months, before placement with the Lincolns. Together as a family there until he was 5 years old. Three years ago parents separated and father took him to R.A.F. Camp. Spent three months with paternal grandparents, then returned to father until coming into care.

f. Child's pre-admission health. Has always been quite healthy. Father cannot remember any illnesses. In the summer had a severe cut to his head from a derelict car. Had anti-tetanus injection.

g. School/Employment. Attended Airfield School. Estimate of intelligence C. Attendance fairly good. Nervous little boy. Now attending special school. Serious speech defect. Lack of concentration. Seems rather backward.

Behaviour, Attitudes and Interests

Rather more insecure than his brother. Is not unhappy at school but is longing to get away from there and back to his family. Although rather slow at school, he enjoys his lessons, but is most emphatic that he does not like painting 'because I get my hands dirty'. Fits in well with the other children at school and is reasonably popular there, but he plays mainly with his one brother and Mark.

Patterns of Reaction to Stress

Stress does not appear to have any outward effect on him. Father says he has never shown any particular reaction to stress. He knows he is adopted, but father has never fully explained to him the meaning of an adoption order, and hesitates to do this as he thinks it will make Tony more insecure.

Was thankful to be admitted to care, and to be relieved of the stress of the home situation. Appears to have settled well at school.

Needs to be with Paul and Mark. Would probably be happiest in a Family Home.

Name of Child: *Paul Raymond Lincoln*: Age 6 years.

Pen Picture

Small witty child, obviously finds concentration difficult. Friendly and cooperative. Likes to brag about his achievements. Aware of the family situation, and would obviously like to return to father and Mrs Mottram (now Lincoln) when the opportunity arises. A very talkative and lively little boy, has a good relationship with adults, and is well behaved when they take him out.

History and Development

a. Pregnancy and birth. Normal pregnancy and normal birth. Mother had been told she was unable to have other children after the birth of Angela, so the coming of Paul was rather a surprise. Weight at birth 5½ lbs.

b. Early feeding. He was a very slow feeder, but took his full feeds. Bottle fed to 11 months of age, was drinking from a cup at 12 months. Not a difficult feeder.

c. Milestones. Holding head up 4 or 5 months, sitting unsupported 6/7 months. Eruption of 1st tooth 7/8 months, talking—babble 7/8 months, standing 11 months, walking 14 months, talking—words 14 months, bowel control Normal, bladder control Normal, talking—sentences 18 months.

Could walk at about 14 months. Normal development. Father says he was able to count in units at 14 or 15 months.

d. Toilet training. Used to wear a nappy as a precaution up to 15 or 16 months. Before this he could ask for his potty. No bother over toilet training; quite Normal.

e. Changes in environment. Remained in the family unit until he was 3. He was then brought to R.A.F. Camp with his father and he remained there until coming into care, except for a period of three months which he spent with paternal grandparents.

f. Child's pre-admission health. Normal Health. Two years ago he fell off an air-raid shelter on to his back; strained tendons and was severely jolted. Kept in the Accident Hospital for one night.

g. School/Employment. Attended Airfield School. Absent very often. Estimate of intelligence D+. Attainment below average. Now attending school with his brother. Seems of average intelligence. Rather solemn.

Behaviour, Attitudes and Interests

It is difficult to hold a conversation with Paul, because he finds concentration on any one subject for more than a minute or so very difficult; he is constantly fiddling with things and changing the subject. Appears fairly happy at school, and likes the variety in the routine there. Enjoys, and looks forward to the visits from his father and Mrs Mottram who visit regularly, at least once a week.

Patterns of Reaction to Stress

Used to be very clinging; easily feels insecure and is afraid of being left. Has settled fairly well at school and is accepted by the other children.

Initial adjustment good. Settled well perhaps because he had known that the home situation would demand his removal from there.

Needs to be with Anthony and Mark. Would probably be happiest in a Family Home.

Name of Child: *Mark Peter Mottram*: Age 6 years.

Pen Picture

Attractive, friendly little boy. Has probably suffered less acutely than the Lincolns. Knows he is of a different family and can accept this. Says he does not like school because the big boys are too rough for him; tends to have fantasies about things his relatives may give him, e.g.: 'My real Daddy is a nice man; he is going to give me a bike, lot bigger than any of the others.' Wants to go and live with his mother and Mr Lincoln. Wants to belong to the Lincoln family, e.g., likes to pretend he was in Singapore with them.

Details of Custody Orders etc.

Mother says she has custody of Mark. This can be verified by solicitor Mr Jones, of Bloggis and Bloggis.

History and Development

a. Pregnancy and birth. Normal pregnancy. Prolonged labour, it was anticipated that she might have to have Caesarian operation, as the baby was so big, but he was delivered normally. Weight at birth 8 lbs $4\frac{1}{2}$ ozs. Had been married three and a half years and very much wanted this baby.

b. Early feeding. Fully bottle fed. Normal feeding. From birth to 5 or 6 months he cried a lot, but this may not have been a hunger cry; may have been reaction to the fact that his mother was caring for eight younger brothers and the household was very noisy.

c. Milestones. Holding head up at 4 or 5 months. Sitting unsupported

7 or 8 months. Eruption of 1st tooth 6 months—talking—babble at 7 months—talking words at 18 months. Walking 13 months. Bowel control and bladder control Normal. Talking sentences 20 months.

d. *Toilet training.* Was out of napkins at about 11 months. No difficulties with toilet training.

e. *Changes of environment.* Mrs Mottram was living at her mother's when Mark was born, as her mother had left home. Family together until Mark was 8 months old, then Mr and Mrs Mottram and Mark moved to a furnished flat. They were there until Mark was 13 months, then parents separated and she returned to her mother with Mark. Stayed there until Mark was 4, and then moved to Mr Lincoln's. Remained there with his mother until coming into care. Mark had never been separated from his mother.

f. *Child's pre-admission health.* Bronchial pneumonia at 6 weeks; was in Hospital for five days. He had tonsillitis three or four times. Suspected Chicken-pox about two and a half years ago. Apparently in normal health.

g. *School/Employment.* Attended Airfield School. Absent very often —not much interest in school. Estimate of intelligence D+. Attainment below average.

Now attends special school. Rather mischievous child. Average intelligence.

Behaviour, Attitudes and Interests

A lively child. On the whole has few behaviour difficulties, and is quite sensible. Likes drawing and creative activities, but not particularly keen on academic side of school work. Fits in well with other children, and is not unhappy in a community environment, but he tends to get very upset if he thinks anyone else is unhappy.

Patterns of Reaction to Stress

Gets upset if he sees anyone hurting his mother, and tries to defend her. He will fight back if anyone attacks him. He will cry if upset.

Reacted well to admission because he had been prepared for this. Seemed thankful to get away from the strained emotional environment of his home. Looks forward to visits from his mother and Mr Lincoln and these mean a great deal to him.

Needs to be with the two Lincoln children. Would probably be happiest in a Family Home.

Name of Child: *Michael*: Age 6 months.

Child of cohabitation. Appears to be well looked after and developing satisfactorily but the insecurity surrounding the family situation may cause difficulties in a year or two.

Exercise 3. Cross Cultural Case Study

Introduction

It is important for us to discover which aspects of human behaviour are culturally determined (and so relatively transient and variable) and which, if any, are truly universal. The case study material collected by cultural anthropologists enables this distinction to be drawn (though it does not allow any conclusions to be drawn as to *causes* of behaviour as Argyle (*The Scientific Study of Social Behaviour*, 1957) has pointed out). Such material varies widely in its usefulness as scientific data (some accounts are little more than anecdotal travellers' tales) but enough careful reports of individual societies are now available for useful comparisons to be drawn.

Objective

To examine two 'primitive' and one western society for similarities and differences, particularly as regards child-rearing practices, sexual and aggressive behaviour patterns, and social behaviour and status—and to relate differences in culture to differences in emergent personality.

Materials

Available anthropological source material and the books mentioned in References.

Method

Detailed accounts of three very different societies should be studied—if possible from original sources. If no original material is available the brief appended material of Items 3.1 to 3.6 should be used. Two of the societies chosen should be 'primitive' and you should assemble relevant material from your own society to make the third case history. An attempt should be made to draw up a list of the ways in which the three societies seem to differ most markedly. One such difference might be 'treatment of children'—another 'beliefs', and another 'conceptions of abnormality'. This is an important and difficult part of this exercise and deserves careful thought. The list may need repeated refinement and modification. A few suggested headings are contained in Item 3.7

which should not be consulted, however, until the student has read original reports carefully and tried to assemble his own list.

When a list of 'aspects' has been collected a blank table should be constructed. This should provide spaces for entries under each of the headings in the list for each of the three chosen societies. An attempt should then be made to complete this 'synoptic table' with brief notes for each society. It is unlikely that all spaces will be filled.

The completed table should be carefully studied before the following questions are considered:

Treatment of Results

1. Select and discuss pairs of observations which might be held by psychoanalysts to support their view that experience in early childhood profoundly affects adult personality.

2. Is it possible to construct a description of the personality of a 'modal' member of each of the three societies you have summarised?

3. What examples can you find of evidence of
    a. ascribed status, and
    b. acquired status in the societies studied?

4. How does aggression vary in
    a. its manifestations, and
    b. its effects?

5. Is there any common content in the conception of anti-social behaviour by the three societies?

6. Is there any common content in conceptions of *abnormality* in the three societies?

7. What is the status of anthropological case material as scientific data?

Are valid non-experimental designs possible using anthropological data? (See Introduction to Section D of this book.)

8. Are any assumptions about the stability of cultures over time being made in this exercise? Are these justified?

9. To what extent does your summarised material indicate the *causes* of behaviour? To what extent is it merely descriptive of behaviour?

10. Are we justified in regarding a culture as relatively homogeneous as we have done here? Have we considered 'sub-cultures' sufficiently?

11. Make a detailed study from these sources, and particularly from Whiting, J. W. M., and Child, I. L., *Child Training and Personality*, of the alleged relationship between the age of weaning and emotional disturbance in adulthood.

Construct from the data in Whiting and Child and from any supplementary sources a frequency-polygon using the age of weaning as abscissa (horizontal axis) and the percentage of cases emotionally disturbed as ordinate (vertical axis). What conclusions may be drawn, if any?

An account of this work will be found in *Handbook of Social Psychology* by G. Lindzey.

12. Does your synoptic table contain material relevant to any of the other cultural variables discussed in Krech, Crutchfield and Ballachey, Chapter 10?

References

ARGYLE, M., *The Scientific Study of Social Behaviour* (Methuen, London 1957).

KRECH, D., CRUTCHFIELD, R. S., and BALLACHEY, E. L., *Individual in Society* (McGraw-Hill, N.Y. 1963), Ch. 10.

YOUNG, KIMBALL, *Handbook of Social Psychology* (Routledge & Kegan Paul, London 1957).

MEAD, M., *Sex and Temperament in Three Primitive Societies* (Morrow, N.Y. 1935).

BENEDICT, R., *Patterns of Culture* (Routledge & Kegan Paul, London 1935).

WHITING, J. W. M., and CHILD, I. L., *Child Training and Personality* (Yale U.P., New Haven 1953).

FRANKENBERG, R., *Communities in Britain: Social Life in Town and Country* (Penguin, Harmondsworth 1966).

HALMOS, P., *Towards a Measure of Man* (Routledge & Kegan Paul, London 1957).

ITEM 3.1: THE MUNDUGUMOR (OF NEW GUINEA)

The Mundugumor live by fishing, agriculture and trading. The social organisation is tribal. There is no cooperation but much conflict. There is an intense sense of possessiveness—and emotional security follows success in acquisition and achievement, e.g., in head-hunting and war. Cannibalism is practised. Children are treated roughly, severely and inconsistently and are often rejected. There is little breast-feeding (and only then to pacify). Weaning is very early. Children are punished severely. There is intense father–son hostility and strong sibling rivalry. Older children are aggressive to younger. There is no orderly training of children (though no demands for work are made on them). Boys tend to help Mother and girls help Father though there is little love for parents or siblings. Virginity has a high value. Polygamy is common. There is no romantic love. In fact the reverse; there is intense husband/ wife conflict for power and status. There is no homosexuality.

There are many taboos and numerous sources of shame and guilt. There is widespread fear of water and drowning. There is high valuation of wealth, prestige and leadership. Conflict and competition are encouraged. There is much jealousy and envy.

ITEM 3.2: THE TCHAMBULI (OF NEW GUINEA)

Women are the property owners; they are the important figures in economic affairs. Organisation is tribal. Descent is patrilineal. Children are treated casually by mothers whose functions are limited to protection and feeding. Breast-feeding tends to be regular and generous. Children are looked after more by the menfolk. Boys are rejected by the womenfolk and are not accepted by the men until older. There is much ceremonial for boys; girls are trained from age 8 by mothers, in self-reliance, as workers, and as mothers. Women are much more aggressive than men. There is a reversal of the more common sexual roles. Girls are taught by mothers to be sexually aggressive. The males are shy, coy, timid and embarrassed, and indulge in rich ceremonial and artistic activity as compensation. These are men's only preserve. Virile and aggressive men are 'abnormal' (though mild women are not so). Male aggression is chiefly disguised as suspicion and injured feelings. The women form a strong solid group and are 'brisk, jovial and patronising'.

ITEM 3.3: THE SAMOANS

The Samoans enjoy an economy of plenty. Life is predominantly agricultural. There is no fear of scarcity or famine. There is no hoarding of property and little accumulation of capital. There is little stealing and lying. The basic economic and social unit is the household which often comprises 15 or 20 members all related by blood, or by marriage or adoption to the 'mata', the male head. Kinship networks extend beyond the household however, and even beyond the village. Children move freely between households and are constantly supervised by any adults or older children. Authority is not vested in the parents. Child groups are strictly divided by sex. There is some mild antagonism between boys and girls between 8 and 14 years. Contact between related children of opposite sex is restricted after the age of 9. Adolescence seems to show few particular stresses. Girls tend to stay within the household and there are few boy/girl contacts. Adults appear to have little specialised sex-feeling, close emotional contacts or romantic love. The women, who tend to be restricted to the household, tend to be more quarrelsome and jealous than the men. Marriage is a purely social and economic arrangement. Adultery is unimportant and common. Divorce is easy—the non-resident partner simply going off taking the family. Moderation is important; one should know one's place and adapt readily. Precocity is bad and there is no need to excel. Dancing is the way to express individuality. Selfishness and violence constitute 'abnormality'.

ITEM 3.4: THE MANUS (OF THE ADMIRALTY ISLANDS)

Life is exacting but starvation is not threatened. There is fishing and trade. Property has great prestige value and respect for property inculcated from earliest years. There is an exacting and continuing exchange system which is of great importance in Manus society. 'One's people are one's property.' Husband/wife ties are less important than kinship ties. Brother/sister and cousin relationships are important. The family unit is allied to the biological family but young couples live in uncle's or brother's house. Children are thoroughly spoilt and made to feel important and there is little training or discipline. Physical perfection is strongly stressed however. After weaning the father becomes the most important parent. The children are sex-segregated but there is little antagonism. They often show the personality of the father. Girls later work in the household and boys are free to canoe and fish. For girls puberty is a ceremony which is followed by training and waiting for marriage. Sex, like elimination, is bad and shameful. Girls tend to avoid youths as potential seducers. The only female relationship allowed young men is a 'tender-respect' bond with sisters. Marriage is arranged, economic issues being paramount. There is no affection between husband and wife—rather is there hostility. Marriage is a time to face the hard realities of life. Ancestor worship and strong belief in spirits is apparent. These spirits are the indulgent fathers of carefree youth. They prosper one's affairs. Economic failure constitutes 'abnormality' as does gentleness and submissiveness. Aggression is encouraged (a child may strike his parents). This aggression is later transferred to individual competition—for example, for more property. The drive to achievement is high.

ITEM 3.5: THE MARQUESANS (OF THE CENTRAL PACIFIC)

The Marquesans are completely dependent on tree crops, sugar cane and fishing, and there is constant danger of famine by drought. There is constant food anxiety in both sexes. All objects are individually owned though the group's needs take priority in emergency. Property has no prestige value. Individuals are members of tribes as well as households. There is tribal warfare. Primogeniture determines social rank. Men are the providers. Women are sexual objects of high status. Polyandry is the rule. The women's job is to attract men to the household. Nursing is short, rough and irregular. Breast-feeding is believed to spoil beauty. Children are never left alone however lest the spirits or (real) cannibals get them. There are no personal attachments. The father is closer than the mother. There is little discipline (especially of eldest child). Boys feel inferior to girls as they get older because of fears of exploitation. Boys consequently form defensive groups (although these tend to be disrupted by differences in rank). There is frequent homosexual activity in males as compensation. Boys gather in gangs fishing, raiding plantations and sleeping out wherever they happen to be. They learn high manual and hunting skills.

There is strong interdependence among males but no strong feeling for females and no romantic love. Sex-play is however quite general from an early age. Intercourse is public and occurs before puberty. The 'Kaioi' are expected sexually to entertain visiting males. They are highly trained in erotic techniques from an early age. There is high sensuality and complete promiscuity. A sexual rebuff is serious (and might lead to suicide). Marriage occurs when the eldest child selects a partner. The younger males then attach themselves to the household. Formal marriage takes place only between chiefs' sons. Only the poorest households are monogamous. Religious rituals are highly organised and there are strange religious beliefs. There are malevolent evil spirits (Vekini-Hai) and dead men's spirits (Tanana) who will operate at call against other women. Priests are very important. There is little adult aggression though there is some sexual jealousy and murder. War is an accepted outlet. There is shame, and guilt-feelings, and sensitivity to ridicule and laughter.

ITEM 3.6: THE MOUNTAIN ARAPESH (OF NEW GUINEA)

Little concern is shown for personal property but there is considerable respect for the property of others. There is no tribal organisation and only a loose kinship system. There is no stress on leadership and no status system. There are strong bonds of affection and dependency in the family. Great indulgence is shown to children and the breast is offered on demand to pacify. Any nursing mother indulges the child. Weaning is late (3rd or 4th year). Children are not hurried to adulthood—they are shielded and kept unaware of adult problems. Girls become betrothed at 10 years and go to live with their future husband's family. There is considerable emphasis on affectionate relationships—upon which the sense of security depends. There is no conflict between the sexes. Strangers tend to be avoided and there is some fear of them and of sorcery. Sorcery can in turn be applied to outsiders. Conflict is feared. Docility is highly prized and leadership avoided. Aggression is felt to lead to loss of health, loss of the cooperation of others and loss of affection. Though aggressiveness is discouraged, there is some slight allowance of anger in boys. Children show a few temper tantrums. Aggression is vented on the outside world rather than on persons.

ITEM 3.7: SOME SUGGESTED HEADINGS FOR A SYNOPTIC
CHART

	A. Primitive	*B. Primitive*	*C. Western*
Childhood Home, family, primary group Child-treatment 　Infant feeding 　Weaning 　Toilet training Early sexual conditions Adolescence 　Rituals 　Stresses			
Maturity Youth special methods 　Stresses 　Social groupings Marriage, nature of Subsistence			
Social Behaviour Social relationships 　Secondary groups Status Cooperation/competition Variety of roles 'Anti-social' behaviour 'Abnormal' behaviour			
Beliefs Beliefs, superstitions Taboos Religious belief Security and morality system 　Its origins and training			

Exercise 4. Content Analysis

Introduction

Forms of 'existing evidence', other than officially published statistics, are usually more difficult to work with for several reasons. The material is rarely if ever in the form most suitable for immediate use and it is often by its very nature difficult to quantify. Often, of course, a *qualitative* analysis is more useful and meaningful (for example, see the Case Study *Exercises 1–3*) but where a *quantitative* analysis *is* possible the extra precision gained may be considered to be worth the corresponding loss of qualitative sensitivity and detail.

In some circumstances the best of both these techniques may be combined and this is illustrated here by the method of 'Content Analysis'.

Content Analysis is a technique which enables the investigator to quantify in a systematic way the content of any form of communication (most frequently a 'mass communication'). The social investigator then usually goes on to attempt to say something about the culture (or sub-culture) from which the material came (as in folk songs or tales etc.) or for which it was intended (as in novels, plays, newspapers). This is a big step and requires not only careful analysis of the material but also extreme caution in generalising from interpretations of specific materials to the culture as a whole. It is easier and safer to compare material intended for different populations. For example, it is known to newspaper proprietors (and advertisers) which sections of the community read their papers, and therefore the content and style of the paper can be analysed, and interpreted, on the basis of the known social composition of the readership. It may also be inferred, of course, that this material reflects, and to some extent moulds, the attitudes and opinions of its readers.

It is obviously much more difficult to assess the cultural significance of other published material such as a play or novel because far less is known about the composition of the audience or the intentions of the author (who may deliberately wish to offend the current sensibilities of his audience).

Objective

To analyse the contents of selected newspapers and to relate differences found in the social composition of the readers of the papers.

Materials

All the editions of the *Daily Mirror, Daily Express* and *Daily Telegraph* for one week.

Method

The total universe of communications to be studied is defined as all the editions of the three papers for one week. Several different types of analysis can be carried out according to the particular objectives of the investigator.

One type of analysis may use the 'item' as its unit of analysis. In this case the paper would be broken down into all its constituent items so that the end-product would take the form of a table which showed (for example) that 12 per cent of the *Daily Mirror's* items were about home politics as compared with 26 per cent of the *Daily Telegraph's* items.

An alternative unit of analysis might be the 'column inch'. In this case the newspaper is broken down into sections one inch long and one column wide and each article, photograph or advertisement is measured in column inches (a separate category could be included for headlines). If this method is used it is of course necessary to take into account the absolute sizes of the papers and standardise the proportions by considering percentages. The categories into which the material is to be analysed can be plain, *descriptive* categories, or *evaluative* categories. If the former is chosen it is necessary to work out as nearly as possible an exhaustive but mutually exclusive set of categories (for example, sport, city, social, home, foreign, pictures, etc.). It would be useful to include a separate set of sub-categories for advertising—based on the type of product (toilet, clothes, food, tobacco, etc.) or the technique (sex, snob-appeal, rational, exaggeration, etc.) or both. The alternative would be to concentrate on one particular aspect and undertake a more detailed evaluative analysis. Let us suppose, for example, that foreign affairs is the chosen topic. The categories then might include: 'for and against the U.S.A.'; 'attitudes to Vietnam'; 'for or against the Common Market'; 'Arab or Israeli'; and other issues which happened to be topical.

Percentages should be used wherever these are more convenient. It is probably most instructive to analyse the total content into broad categories and to select a special area for detailed sorting out and then to attempt to relate the two.

All the results of the foregoing can be interpreted in the light of the information contained in The Institute of Practitioners in Advertising's *National Readership Surveys*. Extracts from the 1966 edition are given below in Item 4.1.

Alternatives: Comparisons may be made between the content of magazines (e.g., *Punch* and *Tit Bits*) or women's periodicals (*Woman* and *Vogue*). Information about their readership can be obtained from the same source.

Treatment of Results

After initial comparison of the total size of the newspapers it is more convenient to convert measures to percentages particularly if column inches are used as the raw data measurement unit.

A graphical profile of each newspaper can be drawn to facilitate direct visual comparison. Use the histogram for this (see, for example, Connolly & Sluckin, pp. 10–12).

Comparisons between two sources on the space devoted to specific topics can be made using a t-Test but N (the number of cases) will be very small (only six editions per paper). (See *Glossary*.)

A more general comparison of two or more papers over several categories can be made by using the simple Chi-squared test (See *Glossary*).

Obviously some of the most interesting results with a technique of this kind are produced by careful inspection and non-statistical interpretation of the data which may produce a more meaningful if less strictly objective account of the results.

Discussion

1. What are the main differences between the content of the three papers?

2. How far can these be explained in terms of the social composition of the respective readerships?

3. What are the implications of differences in readership for advertising and does the actual advertising vary consistently?

4. Does Content Analysis enable you to say anything about the 'style' of the paper and what especial modifications of the technique would be required to do this?

References

BERELSON, B., *Content Analysis in Communication Research* (The Free Press, Glencoe 1952), or in

LINDZEY, G., *Handbook of Social Psychology*, Vol. 1. Ch. 13 (Addison-Wesley Pub. Co. Inc., Cambridge Mass. 1954)

Institute of Practitioners in Advertising *National Readership Survey 1966–1967*

ITEM 4.1: READERSHIP PROFILES OF THREE NEWSPAPERS BY SEX, AGE AND SOCIAL GRADE*

Newspaper	Sex		Age						Social Grade			
	Men	Women	16–24	25–34	35–44	45–54	55–64	65+	AB	C1	C2	DE
Daily Mirror	54	46	23	18	19	18	13	9	4	13	46	37
Daily Express	55	45	15	16	17	19	18	16	12	22	37	29
Daily Telegraph	51	49	18	17	18	18	14	16	40	31	20	9
Total Population (Estimates)	48	52	18	16	17	17	16	16	12	18	37	33

The figures represent percentages of the total readership. Figures in the bottom row indicate estimated percentages in the total adult population. Social Grade is based on head of household *not* income.

AB = Managerial, administrative and professional.

C2 = Skilled working class.

C1 = Supervisory, clerical, junior managerial administrative and professional.

DE = Semi-skilled and unskilled working class and pensioners and widows.

IPA National Readership Surveys, July 1966–June 1967.

Exercise 5
Trends in Crime and Punishment

Introduction

Opinions differ widely as to the 'best' treatment for offenders against society. Little evidence exists as to the relative effectiveness of different forms of punishment (if indeed 'punishment' is what is required). The rationale underlying our treatment of criminals is quite unclear. Though 'retribution' is now rarely spoken of, 'deterrence' and 'protection of the rest of society' are frequently mentioned. The notion of the criminal as a 'sociopath' in need of help and careful therapy is, regrettably, slow to gain acceptance.

A measure of the extent to which this more modern view has been accepted by judges and magistrates would be their preparedness to use probation in sentencing offenders. This exercise attempts to determine from Home Office statistics whether there has been a significant change in the relative use of probation, fining and imprisonment between 1938 and 1965. Only the more serious offences—the so-called 'indictable offences' are considered in this exercise. Non-indictable offences (those not requiring trial by jury) are considered in the next exercise.

Materials

Criminal Statistics for England and Wales for 1965 (Cmnd 3037). (Extracts are given in Item 5.5.)

Method

Prepare Item 5.1, showing the number of persons found guilty of indictable offences in 1938 and 1965 by reference to *Criminal Statistics, 1965* (pp. xii and xiii) as shown in Item 5.5, Table A.

Prepare Item 5.2, showing the number of *males* put on probation after being found guilty of indictable offences. Use Item 5.1 and *Criminal Statistics, 1965* (p. xxvii para 40) as shown in Item 5.5, Table C.

Prepare Item 5.3, showing the number of males *fined* after being found guilty of indictable offences. Use Item 5.1 and *Criminal Statistics, 1965* (p. xxvi para 39) as shown in Item 5.5, Table C.

Prepare Item 5.4, showing the number of males imprisoned after being found guilty of indictable offences. Use Item 5.1 and *Criminal Statistics, 1965* (p. xxv para 38) as shown in Item 5.5, Table D.

Note 1. For the purposes of this exercise, in order to complete Table D, it may be assumed that in 1938 five males between the ages of 17 and 21, and 25 over 21, were sentenced at higher courts after committal for sentence from Magistrates' Courts.

Note 2. The reason for the absence of data for the top two rows in Item 5.4 will be self-evident.

Treatment of Results

Comment on each of the following:

1. Has the ratio of male/female criminals changed since 1938?
2. In which age group has the proportionate increase in crime been most marked?
3. Is the use of *probation* increasing or decreasing
    a. absolutely,
    b. relatively?
In which age group is the change most marked?
4. Is the use of *fining* increasing or decreasing
    a. absolutely,
    b. relatively?
5. Is the use of *imprisonment* increasing or decreasing
    a. absolutely,
    b. relatively?

Discussion

1. What factors possibly influence the change in proportion of cases dealt with by probation?
2. What factors possibly influence the change in proportion of cases dealt with by finings?
3. What factors possibly influence the change in proportion of cases dealt with by imprisonment?
4. Are the data for 1938 and 1965 strictly comparable?
What changes may have occurred in such factors as police efficiency (detection rate), and public attitudes to particular types of crime (and possible consequent changes in police action)? Are you satisfied with the classificatory system employed in the *Criminal Statistics, 1965*?
5. Do you interpret these results as a vote of 'no confidence' in probation?

6. Is it possible that courts are now selecting probationers much more carefully?

If so, where could evidence be found?

7. How likely is it that there has been an increase in the proportion of hardened criminals—for whom probation is unsuitable?

8. Is it possible that courts are trying to avoid overworking the probation services—which they see as heavily overburdened already?

References

WOOTTON, B., *Social Science and Social Pathology* (Allen & Unwin, London 1959).

ST. JOHN, J., *Probation—The Second Chance* (Vista Books, London 1961).

H.M.S.O., *Criminal Statistics for England and Wales for 1965 (Cmnd 3037)*.

ITEM 5.1: PERSONS FOUND GUILTY OF INDICTABLE OFFENCES

Age group	1938		1965	
	Males	Females	Males	Females
Under 14				
14–17				
17–21				
21–30				
30 +				
Total all ages				

ITEM 5.2: MALES PUT ON PROBATION

Age group	1938			1965			Change in % Probationed
	No. guilty	No. on probation	$\frac{Prob. guilty}{\times 100}$	No. guilty	No. on probation	$\frac{Prob. guilty}{\times 100}$	1938–1965
Under 14							
14–17							
17–21							
21 +							
Total all ages							

ITEM 5.3: MALES FINED

Age group	1938			1965			Change in % fined
	No. guilty	*No. fined*	*$\frac{Fined\ guilty}{\times 100}$*	*No. guilty*	*No. fined*	*$\frac{Fined\ guilty}{\times 100}$*	*1938– 1965*
Under 14							
14–17							
17–21							
21 +							
Total all ages							

ITEM 5.4: MALES IMPRISONED

Age group	1938			1965			Change in % im- prisoned
	No. guilty	*No. im- prisoned*	*$\frac{Imp.\ guilty}{\times 100}$*	*No. guilty*	*No. im- prisoned*	*$\frac{Imp.\ guilty}{\times 100}$*	*1938– 1965*
Under 14							
14–17							
17–21							
21 +							
Total all ages							

ITEM 5.5

Table A: Number of Persons Found Guilty of Indictable Offences

MALES

Age group	1938	1963	1964	1965	Percentage variation 1965/64
Under 14*	14,724	27,477	22,786	22,376	− 1·8
14 and under 17	11,645	33,663	32,796	32,818	—
17 „ „ 21	10,131	34,271	35,750	40,486	+13·2
21 „ „ 30	14,321	43,719	42,737	47,099	+10·2
30 and over	17,858	44,981	42,406	44,645	+ 5·3
Total	68,679	184,111	176,475	187,424	+ 6·2

FEMALES

Age group	1938	1963	1964	1965	Percentage variation 1965/64
Under 14*	835	2,699	2,725	2,697	− 1·0
14 and under 17	912	3,945	4,506	4,979	+10·5
17 „ „ 21	1,320	3,547	3,910	4,318	+10·4
21 „ „ 30	2,071	4,981	4,960	5,275	+ 6·4
30 and over	4,646	12,435	12,686	13,742	+ 8·3
Total	9,784	27,607	28,787	31,011	+ 7·7

* S. 16(1) of the Children and Young Persons Act, 1963, which came into operation on 1st February, 1964, raised the age of criminal responsibility from 8 to 10 years. This should be borne in mind when comparisons are being made between figures for different years for the age group 'under 14'.

ITEM 5.5: *Table B: Number of Persons Put on Probation for Indictable Offences*

Age group	MALES				FEMALES			
	1938	1963	1964	1965	1938	1963	1964	1965
Under 14	7,406	9,339	7,997	7,908	470	1,064	1,032	1,000
14 and under 17	5,952	10,775	10,173	10,218	524	1,595	1,760	1,802
17 ,, ,, 21	4,254	7,150	6,892	7,720	826	1,459	1,546	1,701
21 ,, ,, 30	2,552	4,947	4,780	5,035	799	1,370	1,334	1,343
30 and over	1,656	4,072	3,875	4,067	906	1,753	1,801	1,856
Total	21,820	36,283	33,717	34,948	3,525	7,241	7,473	7,702

Table C: Number of Persons Fined for Indictable Offences

Age group	MALES				FEMALES			
	1938	1963	1964	1965	1938	1963	1964	1965
Under 14	709	4,616	3,964	3,987	15	424	535	646
14 and under 17	918	9,113	9,685	9,998	36	950	1,179	1,707
17 ,, ,, 21	1,553	15,480	17,091	19,772	99	1,182	1,465	1,598
21 ,, ,, over	8,557	43,620	44,186	49,891	2,026	9,624	10,098	11,477
Total	11,737	72,849	74,826	83,648	2,176	12,180	13,277	15,528

ITEM 5.5: *Table D: Number of Persons Imprisoned for Indictable Offences*

	MALES				FEMALES			
	1938	1963	1964	1965	1938	1963	1964	1965
Found guilty at magistrates' courts								
Sentenced at magistrates' courts								
Age 17 and under 21	659	839	836	881	43	33	37	42
„ 21 and over	7,774	14,607	13,479	13,765	779	831	682	585
Total	8,433	15,446	14,315	14,646	822	864	719	627
Sentenced at higher courts, after committal for sentence								
Age 17 and under 21	—*	137	154	242	—*	4	1	4
„ 21 and over	—	2,392	3,083	3,120	—	55	73	57
Total	—*	2,529	3,237	3,362	—*	59	74	61
Found guilty at higher courts								
Age 17 and under 21	146	573	509	543	5	16	9	5
„ 21 and over	3,975	8,924	7,811	8,215	247	206	192	187
Total	4,121	9,497	8,320	8,758	252	222	201	192
Total all courts	12,554	27,472	25,872	26,766	1,074	1,145	994	880

* In 1938, 39 persons were sentenced to imprisonment after committal for sentence under s. 10 of the Criminal Justice Act, 1914, but particulars of age and sex are not available.

Exercise 6
Criminal Statistics: Types of Offence

Objective

To consider the relative frequency of different kinds of offence in 1938 and 1965.

Materials

Criminal Statistics for England and Wales for 1965 (Cmnd 3037), H.M.S.O. (Extracts are given in Items 6.3, 6.4 and 6.5).

Method

1. Complete Item 6.1 (Persons Found Guilty of Indictable Offences) for the years 1938 and 1965 by reference to *Criminal Statistics for England and Wales for 1965* (para 55 [Murder] and Appendix 1) as shown in Item 6.3, Tables A, B and C. Note that no allowance is being made here for the increase in the general population between 1938 and 1965 and that the figures for murders are not strictly comparable.

Compute the approximate ratio of the 1965 figures to the 1938 figures for each class of offence.

2. Complete Item 6.2 (Persons Found Guilty of Non-indictable Offences) by reference to *Criminal Statistics, 1965* (para 42) as shown in Item 6.3, Table D. Express frequencies in thousands to the nearest thousand.

Again, compute the ratio of 1965 to 1938 frequencies.

Discussion

1. Comment on the relative increase in different types of offence between 1938 and 1965 and discuss possible contributory causes.

What further evidence does *Criminal Statistics, 1965* contain as to the number of crimes actually committed in these two years (we have considered only those people *apprehended* and found guilty). Note the figures given in Table A on the percentage of offences 'cleared up'.

Is there any evidence of the relative proportion of clearing up of different kinds of crime? What would be the effect of differences here on the statistics?

Do you agree with the use of logarithmic scale in the graphs of 'Indictable Offences Known to the Police' in *Criminal Statistics, 1965* (facing pp. viii and ix). See also Items 6.4 and 6.5.

What is the effect of such a scale?

Does an inspection of the graphs in Items 6.4 and 6.5, taken from *Criminal Statistics, 1965*, support the conclusion that sexual and violent crimes are increasing alarmingly?

Can you find justification in *Criminal Statistics, 1965* for the assertion that 'the greater part of crime committed under 21 is theft committed on the spur of the moment'?

2. Does the method of classification of crimes used in *Criminal Statistics, 1965* appear to be easy to apply?

What, for example, is the dividing line between 'robbery' and 'larceny'? Could it be that different officers or courts have different views on classification?

3. What could be the possible effect of local or regional differences in the compilation of these statistics?

References

WOOTTON, B., *Social Science and Social Pathology* (Allen & Unwin, London 1959).

ITEM 6.1: PERSONS FOUND GUILTY OF INDICTABLE OFFENCES

Offence	1938	1965	Approx. Ratio 65/38
Murder			
Violence against the person			
Sexual Offences			
Receiving, Frauds			
Breaking/entering			
Larceny			
All indictables			

ITEM 6.2: PERSONS FOUND GUILTY OF
NON-INDICTABLE OFFENCES

(In thousands, to nearest thousand)

Offences	1938	1965	Ratio 65/38
Traffic			
Drunkenness			
Revenue Offences			
Railway Offences			
Local Regulations			
Disorderly Behaviour			
Betting/Gaming			
Assault			
Education Act			
Malicious Damage			
Prostitution			
Vagrancy			
Wireless Telegraphy			
Cruelty to Children			

ITEM 6.3:

Table A: Persons Found Guilty of Offences of all Kinds (1965)

Offence	Number of persons found guilty	Percentage of total
Traffic offences (dealt with summarily)	887,128	64·9
Larceny	128,615	9·4
Drunkenness and other offences against intoxicating liquor laws	76,072	5·6
Breaking and entering	44,646	3·3
Revenue law offences (mainly failure to take out licences for dogs or motor cars) (dealt with summarily)	36,183	2·6
Railway offences	19,758	1·4
Breach of local and other regulations	18,469	1·4
Wireless Telegraphy Acts	18,897	1·4
Malicious injuries to property and malicious damage	18,397	1·3
Violence against the person	15,501	1·1
Receiving	11,357	0·8
Assaults (non-indictable)	11,420	0·8
Vagrancy Acts offences (dealt with summarily)	5,964	0·4
Sexual offences (indictable)	5,479	0·4
National Insurance Acts offences	3,480	0·3
Betting and gaming offences (dealt with summarily)	2,278	0·2
Offences by prostitutes	1,532	0·1
All other offences	62,872	4·6
Total	1,368,048	100·0

ITEM 6.3:

Table B: Murder (1932–1965)

Calendar year or period of annual average	Murder of persons aged one year and over			Murder of infants under one year of age		
	Number of known murderers or suspects	Number of victims of persons in column (2)	Total number of victims	Number of known murderers or suspects	Number of victims of column (5) or column (2)	Total number of victims
(1)	(2)	(3)	(4)	(5)	(6)	(7)
1932–35	88	99	102	13	13	27
1936–39	93	102	107	10	12	23
1940–43	105	121	131	4	6	18
1944–47	103	111	124	8	9	28
1948–51	105	115	123	5	6	16
1952	108	126	132	4	7	9
1953	103	127	129	3	4	12
1954	109	130	136	2	5	9
1955	101	121	123	2	2	10
1956	123	137	144	1	2	6
1957*	115	131	142	2	6	12
1958*	97	104	114	5	6	12
1959*	112	127	135	1	3	6
1960*	132	122	126	3	4	9
1961*	110	115	122	6	5	10
1962*	127	126	133	2	4	10
1963*	106	114	124	—	1	9
1964*	127	127	140	2	4	15
1965*	120	131	146	4	4	7

Note.—Where the same person murdered two or more victims, some aged one year or more and some aged less than one year, he is included in colum (2) only.

* The figures for these years are not directly comparable with those for earlier years because, as a result of the Homicide Act, they exclude some cases which would previously have been classified as murder but are not now so classified.

ITEM 6.3: *Table C: Number of Persons Found Guilty of Indictable Offences*

(a) VIOLENCE AGAINST THE PERSON

	Under 17		17–21		21–30		30 and over		Total		Total
	M	F	M	F	M	F	M	F	M	F	
1938	110	6	147	16	448	61	650	145	1,355	228	1,583
1957	751	9	1,595	40	2,356	102	2,025	201	6,727	352	7,079
1958	1,012	27	2,051	33	2,471	114	1,994	193	7,528	367	7,895
1959	1,201	30	2,323	43	2,942	104	2,270	235	8,736	412	9,148
1960	1,540	43	2,713	49	3,290	131	2,252	241	9,795	464	10,259
1961	1,677	40	2,941	65	3,767	142	2,643	244	11,028	491	11,519
1962	1,744	43	3,199	94	3,800	193	2,646	267	11,389	597	11,986
1963	1,839	57	3,365	98	4,162	199	2,841	271	12,207	625	12,832
1964	1,907	71	3,900	85	4,505	224	3,124	325	13,436	705	14,141
1965	1,888	116	4,387	108	4,969	269	3,430	334	14,674	827	15,501

(b) SEXUAL OFFENCES

	Under 17		17–21		21–30		30 and over		Total		Total
	M	F	M	F	M	F	M	F	M	F	
1938	472	3	351	3	445	33	961	53	2,229	92	2,321
1957	1,183	2	671	5	1,146	23	2,585	24	5,585	54	5,639
1958	1,117	1	794	4	1,117	11	2,353	26	5,381	42	5,423
1959	1,262	5	899	2	1,283	7	2,683	20	6,127	34	6,161
1960	1,214	3	1,018	2	1,276	12	2,407	27	5,915	44	5,959
1961	1,178	2	1,080	10	1,351	14	2,494	21	6,103	47	6,150
1962	1,162	4	1,048	5	1,316	11	2,500	22	6,026	42	6,068
1963	1,019	3	1,027	2	1,400	16	2,636	17	6,082	38	6,120
1964	893	1	978	3	1,329	15	2,338	14	5,538	33	5,571
1965	900	1	960	3	1,224	11	2,365	15	5,449	30	5,479

ITEM 6.3: *Table C*

(c) RECEIVING, FRAUDS AND FALSE PRETENCES

	Under 17		17–21		21–30		30 and over		Total		Total
	M	F	M	F	M	F	M	F	M	F	Total
1938	553	49	366	71	1,235	170	2,399	490	4,553	780	5,333
1957	1,587	121	656	109	1,813	217	3,800	681	7,856	1,128	8,984
1958	1,978	202	802	168	2,091	311	3,981	775	8,852	1,456	10,308
1959	2,206	205	964	159	2,256	259	4,156	726	9,582	1,349	10,931
1960	2,338	214	1,105	175	2,495	297	4,319	653	10,257	1,339	11,596
1961	2,910	297	1,271	229	2,901	350	4,877	754	11,959	1,630	13,589
1962	2,913	391	1,598	211	3,357	397	5,597	846	13,465	1,845	15,310
1963	3,258	384	1,756	229	3,601	409	5,916	850	14,531	1,872	16,403
1964	3,035	388	1,873	269	3,671	414	5,555	740	14,134	1,811	15,945
1965	3,019	430	2,299	335	4,154	405	5,712	805	15,184	1,975	17,159

(d) BREAKING AND ENTERING

	Under 17		17–21		21–30		30 and over		Total		Total
	M	F	M	F	M	F	M	F	M	F	
1938	6,683	110	1,385	11	1,554	38	1,050	22	10,672	181	10,853
1957	11,720	323	3,861	73	4,575	70	2,649	61	22,805	527	23,332
1958	13,908	376	5,396	117	5,803	95	3,082	57	28,189	645	28,834
1959	14,877	486	5,389	85	5,892	84	3,143	58	29,301	713	30,014
1960	16,271	508	5,740	132	6,054	82	2,971	65	31,036	787	31,823
1961	18,310	634	6,564	169	7,015	103	3,384	61	35,273	967	36,240
1962	18,979	613	8,488	197	9,396	133	4,865	89	41,728	1,032	42,760
1963	21,365	627	9,486	217	10,058	152	5,251	93	46,160	1,089	47,249
1964	18,326	572	9,214	234	9,055	162	4,830	95	41,425	1,063	42,488
1965	18,178	547	10,217	231	10,122	138	5,133	80	43,650	996	44,646

ITEM 6.3: *Table C*

(e) LARCENY

	Under 17		17–21		21–30		30 and over		Total		Total
	M	F	M	F	M	F	M	F	M	F	
1938	18,191	1,559	7,688	1,159	10,153	1,666	11,978	3,698	48,010	8,082	56,092
1957	25,254	2,739	9,448	1,693	13,995	1,858	19,628	5,843	68,325	12,133	80,458
1958	28,085	3,412	11,362	2,000	14,747	2,196	19,732	6,432	73,926	14,040	87,966
1959	27,806	3,459	11,747	1,776	16,297	2,193	20,361	6,582	76,211	14,010	90,221
1960	29,136	4,125	13,346	2,173	17,415	2,514	20,458	7,231	80,355	16,043	96,398
1961	32,262	5,078	14,563	2,553	19,080	3,057	21,891	8,751	87,796	19,439	107,235
1962	32,639	5,581	16,073	2,824	21,680	3,670	25,459	11,108	95,851	23,183	119,034
1963	31,963	5,466	17,109	2,806	22,358	3,898	26,006	10,778	97,436	22,948	120,384
1964	29,940	6,104	18,341	3,160	22,291	3,858	24,481	11,091	95,053	24,213	119,266
1965	30,067	6,488	21,376	3,471	24,936	4,165	25,949	12,163	102,328	26,287	128,615

ALL INDICTABLE OFFENCES

	Under 14		14–17		17–21		21–30		30 and over		Total		Total
	M	F	M	F	M	F	M	F	M	F	M	F	
1938	14,724	835	11,645	912	10,131	1,320	14,321	2,071	17,858	4,646	68,679	9,784	78,463
1957	23,697	1,580	18,149	1,681	16,962	2,059	24,964	2,498	32,156	7,174	115,928	14,992	130,920
1958	26,050	2,033	21,628	2,064	21,322	2,461	27,499	2,975	32,835	7,847	129,334	17,380	146,714
1959	25,869	1,968	23,059	2,287	22,342	2,238	30,086	2,933	34,378	8,030	135,734	17,456	153,190
1960	27,622	2,319	24,749	2,670	25,068	2,703	32,144	3,309	34,282	8,616	143,865	19,617	163,482
1961	29,890	2,845	28,244	3,305	27,667	3,193	35,770	3,930	37,146	10,227	158,717	23,500	182,217
1962	28,922	2,967	30,569	3,764	31,864	3,489	41,500	4,716	43,212	12,772	176,067	27,708	203,775
1963	27,477	2,699	33,663	3,945	34,271	3,547	43,719	4,981	44,981	12,435	184,111	27,607	211,718
1964	22,786	2,725	32,796	4,506	35,750	3,910	42,738	4,960	42,405	12,686	176,475	28,787	205,262
1965	22,376	2,697	32,818	4,979	40,486	4,318	47,099	5,275	44,645	13,742	187,424	31,011	218,435

ITEM 6.3:

Table D: Number of Persons Found Guilty of Non-Indictable Offences

MALES

Age group	1938	1963	1964	1965	Percentage variation 1965/64
Under 14*	7,518	8,922	6,695	6,908	+3·2
14 and under 17	17,882	30,634	27,732	26,499	−4·4
17 ,, ,, 21	38,042	49,111	49,476	51,450	+4·0
21 and over	238,770	226,878	204,605	197,134	−3·7
Total	302,212	315,545	288,508	281,991	−2·3

FEMALES

Age group	1938	1963	1964	1965	Percentage variation 1965/64
Under 14*	207	330	253	278	+9·9
14 and under 17	923	1,540	1,473	1,370	−7·0
17 ,, ,, 21	2,545	2,693	2,822	2,903	−2·9
21 and over	34,960	25,940	23,978	24,063	+0·4
Total	38,635	30,503	28,526	28,614	+0·3

* N.B. Age of criminal responsibility was raised from 8 to 10 years by Act of 1963.

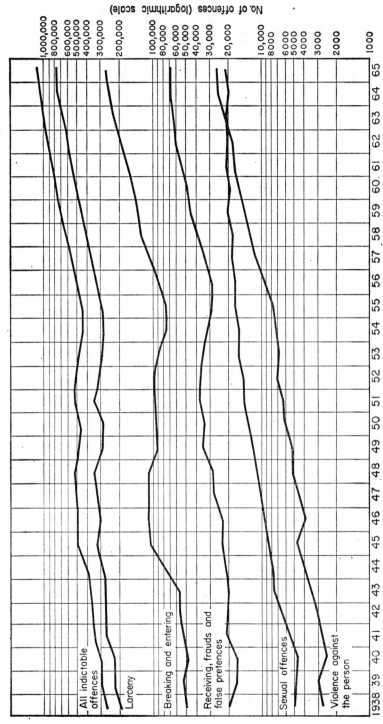

ITEM 6.4: INDICTABLE OFFENCES KNOWN TO THE POLICE 1938 TO 1965

No. of offences (logarithmic scale)

1,000,000
800,000
600,000
500,000
400,000
300,000

200,000

100,000
80,000
60,000
50,000
40,000

30,000

20,000

10,000
8000

6000
5000
4000

3000

2000

1000

1938 39 40 41 42 43 44 45 46 47 48 49 50 51 52 53 54 55 56 57 58 59 60 61 62 63 64 65

All indictable offences

Larceny

Breaking and entering

Receiving, frauds and false pretences

Sexual offences

Violence against the person

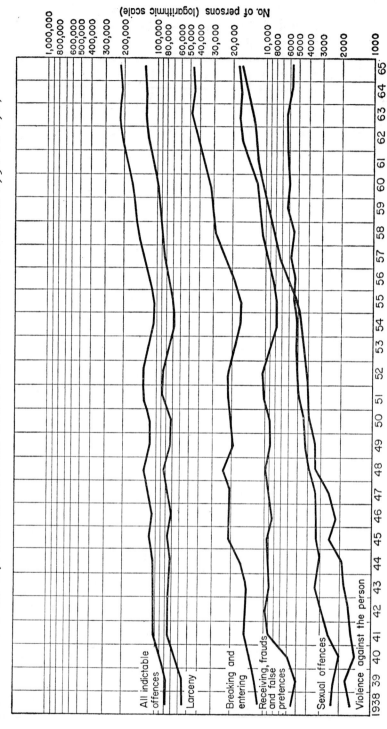

ITEM 6.5: PERSONS FOUND GUILTY OF INDICTABLE OFFENCES 1938 TO 1965

No. of persons (logarithmic scale)

All indictable offences

Larceny

Breaking and entering

Receiving, frauds and false pretences

Sexual offences

Violence against the person

Exercise 7
Criminal Statistics: Types of Offender

Objective

To consider the relative incidence of crime in different age-groups and, in different sexes.

Materials

Criminal Statistics for England and Wales for 1965 (Cmnd 3037), H.M.S.O.

Method

1. Prepare four frequency-polygons showing the frequency of cases of people convicted of *indictable* offences occurring

a. in each of the five age-groups shown in *Criminal Statistics 1965* (pp. xii and xiii para 13) separately for 1938 and 1965, and
b. for males and females. Use Item 7.1.

Alternatively the information in *Criminal Statistics 1965* (Appendix II, p. xlix) may be used to give a fairer comparison which allows for changes in population-composition over the years.

2. Prepare four similar frequency-polygons for *non-indictable* offences in 1938 and 1965 (Item 6.3, Table D). Note that the very large category of motoring offences is omitted from consideration here. Use Item 7.2.

Discussion

Comment on the very different age distributions of indictable and non-indictable offenders and suggest possible reasons.

Discuss possible reasons for the high incidence of indictable female offenders between 1940 and 1945 (shown in the graphs on pp. xiii and xliv of *Criminal Statistics, 1965*).

References

WOOTTON, B., *Social Science and Social Pathology* (Allen & Unwin, London 1959).

ITEM 7.1: TYPES OF OFFENDER, BY AGE-GROUP
AND SEX (INDICTABLE)

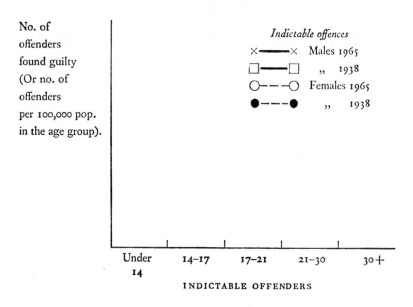

No. of
offenders
found guilty
(Or no. of
offenders
per 100,000 pop.
in the age group).

Indictable offences

×——× Males 1965
□——□ ,, 1938
○– – –○ Females 1965
●– – –● ,, 1938

Under 14   14–17   17–21   21–30   30+

INDICTABLE OFFENDERS

ITEM 7.2: TYPES OF OFFENDER, BY AGE-GROUP
AND SEX (NON-INDICTABLE)

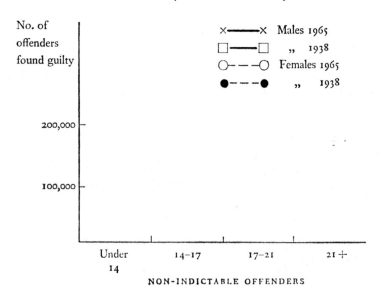

No. of
offenders
found guilty

×——× Males 1965
□——□ ,, 1938
○– – –○ Females 1965
●– – –● ,, 1938

200,000 —

100,000 —

Under 14   14–17   17–21   21+

NON-INDICTABLE OFFENDERS

Exercise 8. Household Expenditure

Introduction

Often data comes in a partly treated form—it may already be grouped or put into categories. This makes it much more manageable but, of course, some of the original data is wasted (the within-group variability) and some refined statistical techniques are not possible. However, if the data is presented clearly and accurately, as it is in most government publications, and used cautiously in the light of its deficiencies, it can be a very useful source of information which would be otherwise unobtainable.

The size and composition of the samples used in many governmental surveys (e.g., Decennial Census) is often very large and highly representative, and quite beyond the capacity of private or commercial research organisations. This means that conclusions drawn from the results of such surveys are likely to be significant and valid. Apart from size and comprehensiveness, government surveys can make use of records and documents not normally available (e.g., income-tax returns) and are also assured of cooperation, in some cases by law.

The use of official statistics to illuminate social conditions is exemplified by Carr-Saunders, Caradog Jones, and Moser in *Social Conditions in England and Wales*. The imaginative use of statistics provides a factual foundation for generalisations about social conditions.

Objective

To use official statistics as a source of information about the spending habits of different income groups.

Materials

Summary Table of Household Expenditure (Item 8.1)

Treatment of data

For the following exercises it is desirable that a desk calculating machine should be available. The transformations are quite simple and straightforward, but the arithmetic may be lengthy. Even a very simple mechanical adding machine would facilitate the speedy and accurate completion of the exercises. A note on the principles of operation of calculating machines is included in Appendix 3.)

1. Calculate the arithmetic mean household income for the total population. This involves selecting a mid point for the income of each group (X mid) (e.g., £20–£30) and multiplying this by the number of households in each group, n, then summing these products $[\Sigma (nX_{mid})]$ and dividing through by total number of families in the sample N.

$$\overline{X} = \frac{\Sigma (nX_{mid})}{N}$$

Use chart provided (Item 8.2).

2. Calculate the standard deviation of household incomes about this mean using the formula

$$\sigma = \sqrt{\frac{\Sigma (nX_1^2)}{N}}$$

where n = no. of households in a group
   X_1 = deviation of that group from the mean X
   X_1^2 = squared deviation from the mean
(see *Glossary*).

3. Using the standard deviation of the sample as a best estimate of the population standard deviation, compute the confidence limits of the mean at the 5% level and the 1% level

$$\sigma_D = \frac{\sigma}{\sqrt{N}}$$

σ_D = standard error of mean
σ = sample standard deviation
N = size of sample

4. Calculate the mean expenditure on *each item* for households with an income of £20 or over and for those with an income below £8 per week, i.e., the top and bottom third of the table. Convert this to percentages to facilitate comparison. This is achieved by multiplying the mean expenditure for an item (say housing) by 100 and dividing by the total mean weekly expenditure of that group. (Chart provided in Item 8.3.)

5. Compare the way the upper and lower income groups dispose of their income graphically—histograms are suggested (superimposed).

Discussion

1. Would it have been more meaningful to use the mean income per *person* rather than per household?

2. Does the spread of incomes roughly conform to a normal distribution? Plot the distribution found using a frequency-polygon (see *Glossary*) and plot a normal distribution based on the mean and standard deviation already calculated, on the same axes.

3. What is the social significance of any differences found between the way the high income groups and low income groups spend their money? In which area were there most differences and what could be the reasons for this? Could this have any importance for advertisers, shopkeepers etc.?

References

Ministry of Labour, *Report of an Enquiry into Household Expenditure in 1953–1954* (H.M.S.O.)

ITEM 8.1: TABLE OF HOUSEHOLD EXPENDITURE
(In Shillings and Pence Per Week)

Weekly income per household	>£50	£30–50	£20–30	£14–20	£10–14	£8–10	£6–8	£3–6	<£3
No. of households	78	271	1,065	2,578	3,425	2,031	1,437	1,279	747
Average no. persons per house	4·21	4·40	4·23	3·75	3·40	3·14	2·72	2·01	1·16
	s. d.	s. d.	s. d.	s. d.	s. d.	s. d.	s. d.	s. d.	s. d.
Housing	65 6	46 3·2	29 8·7	25 3·2	21 11·6	18 4·4	15 5·4	14 10·1	11 7·1
Fuel Light Power	30 4·6	19 0·7	16 0·4	13 7·0	12 2·8	11 8·7	10 10·0	9 9·3	8 1·2
Food	162 9·9	136 11·6	122 7·5	99 10·5	82 11·6	72 5·3	60 11·0	43 4·6	25 5·9
Alcoholic drink	37 8	26 7·6	18 0·9	11 5·5	7 2·5	6 0·7	4 0·6	2 4·6	1 1·3
Tobacco	27 4·6	33 4·2	28 3·1	21 6·1	16 6·8	13 5·5	11 1·4	5 10·3	2 1·1
Clothing	272 6·8*	77 8·0	53 11·9	37 5·4	26 4·8	19 4·8	15 10·1	9 10·0	4 5·6
Household goods	38 1·3	35 0·1	30 1·8	22 3·7	16 10·8	19 9·4	9 9·2	5 7·3	2 9·3
Other goods	52 3·6	37 8·8	28 4·9	21 9·2	16 9·7	14 4·3	17 6·7	7 10·7	4 9·1
Vehicle and Transport	56 0·8	41 7·1	40 7·4	23 8·4	16 3·4	10 10·3	8 3·3	4 0·9	2 0·1
Services	226 11·5	102 4·4	45 3·1	29 10·3	19 2·3	13 11·9	11 4·1	7 9·6	5 3·2
Misc.	5 7·9	3 3·3	2 8·0	2 0·8	1 9·6	1 2·4	0 8·9	0 4·0	0 1·4
Total	975 4·9	559 11·0	415 9·7	308 10·1	237 5·9	195 7·7	159 10·7	111 9·4	67 9·3

Abstracted from *Report of an Enquiry into Household Expenditure in 1953–54*, Ministry of Labour. Published by H.M.S.O. £1 17 6d.

* One member of a household in this group spent £1,903 on one item during the period when records were being kept.

ITEM 8.2: CHART FOR CALCULATION OF MEAN AND STANDARD DEVIATION FROM GROUPED DATA

Household income	X_{mid} to be chosen	n	nX_{mid}	$X_{mid}-\bar{X}$	$(X_1)^2$	$(n.X_1^2)$
>£50						
£30–50						
£20–30						
£14–20						
£10–14						
£8–10						
£6–8						
£3–6						
<£3						
Σ	—		—	—		
$\dfrac{\Sigma}{N}$	—		—	—		

Mean

$$\bar{X} = \frac{\Sigma (nX_{mid})}{N}$$

Standard Deviation

$$\sigma = \sqrt{\sigma^2}$$

$$\sigma^2 = \frac{\Sigma (nX_1^2)}{N}$$

$$\therefore \ \sigma = \sqrt{\frac{\Sigma (nX_1^2)}{N}}$$

ITEM 8.3: CHART FOR CALCULATING MEAN EXPENDITURE
OF TWO GROUPS ON HOUSING (AS AN EXAMPLE)

	Income	*Expenditure*	*No. in group*	1 × 2
		s. d.		
Group 1	>£50	65 6	78	
	£30–50	46 3	271	
	£20–30	29 9	1,065	
	—	Total =	1,414	
		s. d.		
Group 2	£6–8	15 5	1,437	
	£3–6	14 10	1,279	
	<£3	11 7	747	
	—	Total =	3,463	
Column		1	2	3

The mean value for each group is obtained by dividing the total of column 3 by the total of column 2.

This must be repeated for all eleven categories of expenditure.

The value obtained as the mean amount spent by a group on an item is converted to a percentage by multiplying by 100 and dividing by the total expenditure for that group which can be calculated from row 12 of the master table.

A calculating machine would be a great asset.

Exercise 9. Making Predictions from Official Statistics Using Correlation

Introduction

Correlation is the method frequently used for assessing the exact degree of relationship between two variables. The underlying mathematical logic is very simple—it consists of comparing the extent to which the variables fluctuate together with the degree to which they vary independently. If most of the variation in scores is explicable in terms of joint variation in the two variables then a high 'correlation' is obtained. If, on the other hand, most of the variation does not occur in common then a low correlation results.

The biggest danger using the correlation coefficient is in the assumption of causality. The correlation coefficient as a statistic says nothing about the *nature* of the link between the two variables but only about its degree. A high correlation between A and B (which may be statistically significant) does not give any information about the variation in 'A' causing the variation in 'B' or vice versa. The correlation may be completely 'spurious'. An example giving what is probably a 'spurious' relationship is included as Exercise C below.

The correlation coefficient most often used when raw data is available is the Product Moment coefficient devised by Pearson. It is obtained by dividing the covariance of the variables (Σxy) by the product of the two standard deviations multiplied by the number of cases ($N.\sigma_x.\sigma_y$).

A useful computing formula is given by

$$r_{xy} = \frac{\Sigma xy}{\sqrt{(\Sigma x^2)(\Sigma y^2)}}$$

Using this formula means that the standard deviations of the two variables need not be calculated. If these are required for other reasons the formula:

$$r_{xy} = \frac{\Sigma xy}{N.\sigma_x.\sigma_y}$$

can be used.

The Product Moment coefficient varies in two dimensions:

1. The degree or amount of correlation ranges from 0·0 (very low or zero correlation) to 1·0 (which indicates perfect correlation).

2. The direction of the correlation—it can either be positive which means that one variable increases as the other does, e.g., $= + 0·8$; or negative where one variable decreases as the other increases, e.g., $- 0·74$.

Exercises Using Official Statistics
source: *Annual Abstract of Statistics* (H.M.S.O.)

A. Positive Correlation

1. Using Items 9.1 and 9.2, calculate the Product Moment correlation coefficient between expenditure on alcoholic drink and road accident deaths; and between new vehicle registrations and road accident deaths.

Note: It is quite permissible to divide each variable by a constant, e.g., expenditure on alcohol by 1,000 and new registrations by 100. There is no correction necessary.

2. Are these coefficients significant,
      i. statistically (see note below),
      ii. socially?

B. Negative Correlation

1. A negative correlation occurs when two variables fluctuate together but in opposite directions so that an increase in one variable is associated with a decrease in the other. The amount of correlation may range from 0·0 to $-1·0$.

2. Using Item 9.3 calculate the Product Moment coefficient for the two variables 'number of current television receiving licences' and 'admissions to cinemas'.

3. Is it likely there is a causal relationship between these two variables?

C. Spurious Correlation

1. Calculate the correlation between number of births and number of electric blankets produced, using Item 9.4.

2. Is this coefficient statistically significant?

3. Is the relationship completely spurious or could it reflect a common underlying factor, e.g., affluence?

Assessing the Statistical Significance of a Correlation Coefficient

A simple t-test can be applied to a correlation coefficient to determine the degree of confidence with which it can be stated that the coefficient obtained is not a result of sampling error. Generally speaking the higher the coefficient obtained and the larger the sample size (N), the more likely the coefficient is to be significant.

The critical ratio is given by

$$t = \frac{r}{\sigma_r}$$

Where the standard error associated with the *population* correlation coefficient is given by

$$\sigma_r = \frac{1}{\sqrt{(N-1)}}$$

If the critical ratio (t) is larger than 1·96, then the coefficient is said to be significant at the 5 per cent level of confidence, which means that a similar coefficient would only be obtained by chance in 5 cases out of 100, or 1 in 20.

If the t ratio exceeds 2·58 then the coefficient is significant at the 1 per cent level of confidence, in other words, this would only occur in 1 out of 100 cases by chance (sampling error) alone. A coefficient which reaches this level is held to be very significant (statistically), (see *Glossary*).

Tables are available in many statistical texts for checking the level of significance of a correlation coefficient which make it unnecessary to go through the computation outlined above.

Prediction

Correlation coefficients can be used for prediction purposes as well as assessing the degree of relationship between variables. This is practicable as long as the following points are taken into account.

1. The relationship between the two variables must be linear; that is, if they are plotted on a graph one against the other—the result must approximate to a straight line.

2. There must be a fairly high degree of correlation between the variables.

3. It should always be remembered that the predicted value of the one variable when the other is at a certain level will always only be a 'best guess'. Its accuracy will depend on the size of the original correlation coefficient and on the assumption that no new factors will be introduced.

Using the figures in Item 9.1 for Road Deaths, and New Vehicle Registrations, it is possible to obtain a prediction of how many deaths there will be when the number of new registrations reaches, say, two million. Call New Vehicle Registrations (Y) and Road Deaths (X) and substitute in the following equation

$$X^1 = r\, \frac{\sigma_x}{\sigma_y}(Y - \bar{Y}) + \bar{X}$$

[where the predicted value of X (i.e., X^1) is equal to the correlation coefficient of the two variables multiplied by the standard deviation of X (σ_x) divided by the standard deviation of Y (σ_y) multiplied by the given value of Y (in this case two million) from which has been subtracted the mean number of New Vehicle Registrations ($\bar{Y}$); the product of this is then added to the mean number of road deaths ($\bar{X}$).]

If the previous part of this exercise has been completed all the required figures should be available as the by-products of the calculations of the correlation coefficient.

Obtain the predicted number of road deaths for the time when New Vehicle Registrations reach the following level:

 i. 2 million,
 ii. 2·2 million,
 iii. 2·5 million.

Discussion

1. What factors could make the predictions inaccurate and could these be allowed for?

2. Why would this method not be suitable if the relationship between the variables was not linear?

3. Check with any recommended statistical textbook for other methods of predicting and compare them.

ITEM 9.1: VARIABLES IN CONSUMER EXPENDITURE ETC

Variables	1954	1955	1956	1957	1958	1959	1960	1961	1962	1963	1964	
Consumer Expend. on alcoholic drinks in £	794	832	866	906	911	920	954	1,054	1,116	1,177	1,317	million
Road deaths	5,010	5,526	5,367	5,550	5,970	6,520	6,970	6,908	6,709	6,922	7,820	
New vehicle registrations	718·3	906·7	750·8	836·7	981·6	1253·0	1369·4	1259·4	1192·3	1466·0	1711·2	Thousand

ITEM 9.2: TO CALCULATE A PRODUCT MOMENT
CORRELATION COEFFICIENT BETWEEN EXPENDITURE
ON ALCOHOLIC DRINK (X) AND ROAD DEATHS (Y)

Year	X	Y	x	y	x^2	y^2	xy
1954	794	5,010					
1955	832	5,526					
1956	866	5,367					
1957	906	5,550					
1958	911	5,970					
1959	920	6,520					
1960	954	6,970					
1961	1,054	6,908					
1962	1,116	6,709					
1963	1,177	6,922					
1964	1,317	7,820					
Σ							
Means							

$$r_{xy} = \frac{\Sigma xy}{\sqrt{(\Sigma x^2)(\Sigma y^2)}}$$

N = 11. A similar table could be constructed to aid with the
calculation of other coefficients.

ITEM 9.3: VARIABLES IN CURRENT T.V. LICENCES AND CINEMA ATTENDANCES

Variables	1954	1955	1956	1957	1958	1959	1960	1961	1962	1963	1964	
Current T.V. licences	3,249	4,504	5,740	6,966	8,090	9,255	10,470	11,268	11,834	12,443	12,885	thousand
Cinema attendances	1,276	1,182	1,101	915	755	581	501	449	395	357	343	million

ITEM 9.4: VARIABLES IN PRODUCTION OF ELECTRIC BLANKETS AND BIRTHS

Variables	1957	1958	1959	1960	1961	1962	1963	1964	
Production of electric blankets	563	686	1,031	1,400	1,215	1,382	2,199	1,617	thousand
Births	723	741	749	785	811	839	854	876	thousand

Section B

Observation

Introduction (B)

In Section A we were concerned with the analysis of data already available in published form. Social science is not limited to this sort of information however and much useful data can be collected by *observation*. Observation of large or small collections of people may be undertaken by individuals or by teams of investigators working together. Very often the observer may be a member of the group he is observing, i.e., he is a 'participant observer' and his involvement in the group raises some interesting problems of its own.

In *Exercise 10* ('Direct Observation of Behaviour') our main concern is to investigate the effectiveness of direct observation as a method of studying a large number of people who are not linked together into any sort of formal group. An attempt is made to classify observed behaviour and to establish a convenient recording method. In *Exercise 11* an attempt is made to record topics of conversation. *Exercise 12* ('Investigation of a Social Norm') again shows the necessity, in even the simplest forms of observation, to classify and categorise the things observed—in this case the different varieties of behaviour of motorists at 'Halt' signs. In this exercise the results are converted into graphical form in order to allow a conclusion to be drawn as to whether there is a group 'norm' of conduct for motorists. In *Exercise 13* a set of categories is employed to allow the recording of the behaviour of people working together in a small group. As these people discuss a problem which they have to solve, their interaction is quite complex. The category system employed is necessarily a relatively simple one and much of the subtlety of the inter-individual behaviour is lost. In *Exercise 14* observation is made by the individual participants themselves rather than by an outside observer. Reports made by people in the group about their feelings towards other members of the group are systematically analysed and a diagrammatic method is used for showing at a glance the 'preference-structure' of the whole group.

Observation is an important method for the study of individuals as well as groups however and one of the most widely used methods of social observation has always been the *interview*. People are often very ready to discuss themselves and their opinions on a wide variety of issues at great length and skilled interviewers can collect a great *volume* and a great *variety* of information in this way. At first sight the interview would therefore seem to be an excellent method for securing social data. Unfortunately data secured by interviews has a number of serious limitations—not all people are equally articulate in making their views known and what may superficially appear to be differences in attitudes may in fact be simply differences in education or verbal ability. Not all interviewers have equal competence in extracting information—and in a large enquiry involving many interviewers this may be a serious form of error. Furthermore there are often interaction effects between observer and observed—they may not like each other. The interviewer may be (consciously or unconsciously) prejudiced for or against the person he is interviewing—perhaps because of the colour of his skin or his accent. Again the interviewer may be unduly swayed throughout the interview by a favourable or unfavourable first impression. There are in fact many possibilities of error and many precautions which must be taken if information collected at interview is to have any real worth as scientific data. These questions are considered in *Exercise 15*. This exercise investigates the inter-interviewer 'reliability' of the interview, i.e., whether two different interviewers draw the same conclusions when they interview the same person. To overcome some of the difficulties and hazards of interview methods many investigators have collected their questions together in a standard printed form or 'questionnaire'—and this method of enquiry has many advantages in certain types of enquiry. It is a cheap and easy way of collecting much information from large numbers of people and the results are often easy to score. Written questionnaires do however assume that the persons taking them are able to read and are sufficiently interested in the topics dealt with to give them their serious attention before answering 'yes' or 'no', and these assumptions may not always be justified.

The construction of a questionnaire is a matter calling for some care and skill. Some of the important factors in questionnaire design are discussed in *Exercise 17* in Section C which is concerned with 'Measurement'.

Exercise 10
Direct Observation of Behaviour

Introduction

Although theoretically important, direct observation of ordinary everyday behaviour is not often attempted because it is usually too complex to be recorded with any acceptable degree of accuracy. There is, of course, also the purely technical difficulty of observing without affecting the behaviour concerned. If however the observer is prepared to approach the situation with a preformed schema into which observations can be fitted then useful results can sometimes be obtained even though only small parts of the total situation can be studied at any one time.

In this exercise, the behaviour under review is 'time spent drinking coffee' in a common-room or coffee-bar.

Objective

1. To show that careful observation of specified units of everyday behaviour can give interesting and useful information which can be analysed by simple statistical methods.

2. To show how these simple statistical methods allow firm conclusions to be drawn.

Materials

Ordinary wristwatch; time chart such as Item 10.1.

Method

Choose a suitable place in a common-room or coffee-bar from which to make the observations. Note the time at which people enter and the times the same people leave. Also make a note of the subject's sex, size of group and any other details which you consider may be important.

Before observations are begun it is necessary to give consideration to certain factors which may affect the conclusions which may eventually be drawn from the results, e.g.:

1. *Time of day*—it is possible that observations of the average time

taken to drink a cup of coffee may be rendered worthless by large fluctuations caused by variable factors such as queues, having food as well as coffee, etc. The influence of this sort of factor may be reduced by taking observations only at one clearly defined time (say between 10 a.m. to noon), limiting the subjects to those who take a drink only or on the other hand, and if the time is available, comparing results obtained at different times of day.

2. *Size of group*—it may be helpful to define what is meant by 'a group' in this context. Is it to include people who *form* groups or only those who *enter* as groups. It would of course be simpler to limit observations to those who *enter* singly, in pairs, or trios, irrespective of what happens subsequently.

3. If a large number of people are using the room it may be better to choose only third or fifth individuals for inclusion (to make possible a perfectly accurate record). It is imperative that these questions should be decided *before* observations begin in earnest. A short 'pilot' study beforehand usually indicates the decisions to be taken. It is obviously important for the purpose of the observer's presence not to be apparent as this might influence the behaviour under observation. Any subjects whose names are not known must be identified by a brief description and sufficient room should be left on the scoring sheets. Finally, the observer should decide in advance when the period of observation is to end—this may be after a fixed period of time or after a previously decided group size has been reached (e.g. after 15 minutes or after 100 subjects, or the first 50 men and the first 50 women). For statistical reasons it is usually preferable to have the largest possible sample of observations so that generalisations and comparisons can be made with more confidence.

Treatment of Results

1. The raw data should be divided into suitably sized groups, e.g., periods of five minutes so the groups would be 0—4·9 mins.

5—9·9 mins.

10—14·9 mins. etc.

2. Plot the distribution of time taken in minutes against the frequency with which that length of stay was chosen.

3. Calculate the *mean* and *mode* of the scores—the mean being the arithmetical average of the scores and the mode being the value which most frequently appears in the distribution—and the standard deviation of the sample. (See *Glossary*.)

4. How much confidence can you place in your mean? Estimate the reliability of the *sample mean* using the *sample standard deviation* (which is the best available estimate of the whole population's standard deviation) to find the *standard error of the mean*.

5. Divide the total sample into a few sub-groups of your own choice (e.g. males/females or single subjects/groups of subject) and find the respective means and standard deviations of the sub-groups.

6. Test the *significance* of any *differences in the means* by combining the standard deviations of the two samples and obtaining the critical ratio (CR). Use Item 10.2.

(Note: Operations 4 and 6 can only be performed if the sample size is greater than 30.)

Discussion

1. Is the distribution normal or approximately normal, i.e. bell-shaped? If not, how would you explain this?

2. What are the possible reasons for the differences between the mean and the mode (if any)?

3. What conclusions can be drawn from any differences you have found between means of sub-groups?

ITEM 10.1: SUGGESTED RECORDING SHEET

S's name or description	Sex		Time		Length of stay (mins)	Size of group	Food also?
	M	F	Arrive	Depart			

ITEM 10.2: CHART TO HELP WITH THE CALCULATION OF MEANS,
STANDARD DEVIATIONS, AND THE CRITICAL RATIO OF TWO
GROUPS X AND Y (labelled, for example, males and females)

Males	Females	Deviations		Deviations squared	
X	Y	x	y	x^2	y^2
Σ					

Mean $\bar{X} = \dfrac{\Sigma X}{N}$ $\bar{Y} = \dfrac{\Sigma Y}{N}$

Standard Deviation $\sigma_x = \sqrt{\dfrac{\Sigma x^2}{N_x}}$ $\sigma_y = \sqrt{\dfrac{\Sigma y^2}{N_y}}$

Standard Error is found thus: $\sigma_D = \sqrt{\dfrac{\sigma_x^2}{N_x} + \dfrac{\sigma_y^2}{N_y}}$

Critical Ratio $= \dfrac{\bar{X} - \bar{Y}}{\sigma_D.}$

If the critical ratio is equal to or greater than 1·96 then the two means
differ significantly.

Exercise 11. Topics of Conversation

Introduction

The minutiae of social interaction provide a rich source of data for the social scientist and can provide valuable insights into the social motivation of the individuals concerned. When people meet and talk they become aware of each others' facial expressions, raised eyebrows and eye-movements, their gestures and the clothes they wear. All of these have been studied by psychologists and sociologists, either in everyday naturalistic surroundings or in specially constructed laboratory conditions. A much studied question—which does not require specialist equipment—is the subjects chosen in ordinary conversation. The topics chosen have great significance to us because they reflect not only the interests of the individuals concerned but also the 'intellectual currency' of the particular cultural group or sub-group to which the individuals happen to belong.

Objective

To study the choice of topics for conversation.

Method

Observation is not such a straighforward technique as might at first be supposed. Imagine, for example, the suggestion that the behaviour of children in a playground be studied by observation. To draw any useful conclusions from a 30-minute time sample of behaviour it is clear that some system of categories must be employed—such as 'talking', 'sitting', 'playing', 'fighting' for example. It is desirable that some such system be devised before the period of observation so that the observer can be clear about the general classes of behaviour that he is looking for. For this reason it is usually desirable to undertake a 'pilot' study before the main observation session begins. (See *Exercise 13*: 'Analysis of Group Interaction'.)

A selection should be made of those topics of conversation which are considered most likely to arise during normal social intercourse. The categories of behaviour to be observed should be given a summary title or heading and composed into a data sheet containing all the category headings (some suggestions for these are given later). A location should be chosen where conversations can be readily overheard (café, bus, common-room, etc.). The time spent observing should be broken into one-minute intervals and a tick should be marked by the category of conversation which is still being overheard every 60th second. It may, with practice, be possible to record more than one conversation simultaneously. A special mark should be made for any particular aspects of the conversation that have been previously decided as being of interest—for example, 'opening' topics, 'terminal' topics, topics which cause laughter, etc. It may also be useful to distinguish between various sub-groups of the population observed (male/female; child/adult, etc.). Use Item 11.1.

An attempt should be made to use data sheets which are as inconspicuous as possible (an index-card for example). A good collection of such one-minute samples of behaviour should be made—over several lunch-hours or several bus journeys. (The major interest of this exercise will arise out of the comparisons of several distinct types of occasion or sub-groups.)

Treatment of Results

Results should be plotted as histograms and where possible the profiles of the different sub-groups of the population or different occasions for the same sub-group should be compared. Results for the whole class should be combined if possible.

Discussion

1. How adequate were the categories that were chosen and how easy was it to fit conversations into the categories?

2. Were the results in line with expectations?

3. Were there any conspicuous differences between topics chosen by various types of people (or by the same people in different situations)?

4. Did particular topics tend to be used in special ways, e.g., as 'terminal' topics?

5. What changes in the category system now seem appropriate in the light of experience gained during the exercise?

ITEM II.I: EXAMPLE OF A SUGGESTED DATA SHEET

| | One-minute periods | | | | | | | | Total time spent on each topic |
	1st	2nd	3rd	4th	5th	6th	7th	8th	
Weather									
Other People									
T.V.									
Sport									
Politics									
Holidays									
Money									
Past Experiences									

Exercise 12
Investigation of a Social Norm

Introduction

Most societies have rules or 'norms' which prescribe the limits of acceptable behaviour in a given type of situation. There are usually strong pressures towards conformity to these social norms which in fact have considerable social utility since they introduce consistency and predictability into social relationships.

One of the most satisfactory ways of studying social norms is by simple observation of the frequency of occurrence of behaviour of a carefully specified type. It is much more helpful to study drivers' behaviour at 'Halt' signs, for example, by simple observation rather than by interviewing a random sample of drivers on the subject of 'pressures to conform to traffic regulations'. Drivers' behaviour at 'Halt' signs would need to be categorised carefully and quite explicitly, for example into *a.* unchanged speed, *b.* slightly slowed, *c.* slowed, *d.* much slowed, or *e.* stopped.

If, again, a study were to be made of students' arrival for lectures the precise behaviour categories might be: more than 5 minutes before lecture hour, 5, 4, 3, 2, and 1 minutes before and 0 minutes, 1, 2, 3, 4, 5, and more than 5 minutes after lecture hour.

The problem resolves itself into one of recording events quickly and accurately—and unobtrusively (so as not to influence the behaviour observed). Check-lists or blank tables can be constructed to facilitate this task.

Objective

To undertake simple field observations of either

    a. Motorists' behaviour at a 'Halt' sign, or
    b. Students' arrival time at a lecture-room,

and to prepare a summary report of these observations.

Materials

Stop watch or watch with a seconds hand, graph paper (for *a*); hand counter, graph paper (for *b*).

Method

a. At least 50 cars should be observed at each of two 'Halt' signs. The first should be in an area not frequently patrolled by the police; the second in a main street, etc., which is regularly patrolled.

A record form should be constructed beforehand on which ticks can rapidly be made in the appropriate column to record each unit of behaviour as it occurs.

b. A class of at least 25 students which meets frequently in the same lecture-room should be selected for observation.

A suitable record form should be constructed and a record made of arrival times on as many different days as possible.

Treatment of Results

1. Results should be represented graphically by the construction of either a histogram or a frequency-polygon (see *Glossary*) in which the *number of cases* is the ordinate and *category of behaviour* the abscissa. A smoothed curve might be employed if only a few observations were made. A suggested form that these might take is indicated in Items 12.1 and 12.2.

2. An attempt should be made to describe in some numerical way the behaviour of the whole sample of cases observed (i.e., the social norm). Mean, median and mode should each be calculated and considered from the point of view of its usefulness as a summary statement of the group's behaviour.

Discussion

1. What difficulties, if any, were encountered in recording observations and how might these be avoided in future enquiries?

2. What sort of errors may have been introduced?

3. What differences in behaviour were there between the patrolled and unpatrolled situation?

4. Were any qualitative differences in behaviour observed (beyond those described in your categories)? Would it have been possible to record these in the time available?

5. Which parts of your graphs could properly or usefully be considered as showing abnormal or deviant behaviour?

6. Does your smoothed distribution curve show the J-curve form said to be characteristic of 'normative behaviour'?

References

ALLPORT, F. H., 'The J-curve Hypothesis of Conforming Behaviour', *Journ. Soc. Psychol.* 5, pp. 141–83.

FEARING and KRISE, 'Conforming Behaviour and the J-curve Hypothesis', *Journ. Soc. Psychol.* (1941).

ITEM 12.1

a. Total number of cars observed =

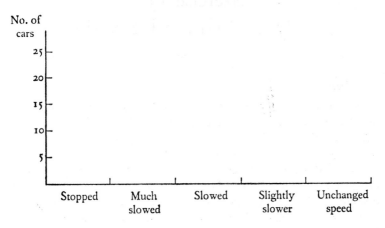

ITEM 12.2

b. Total number of students observed =

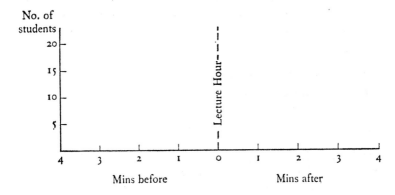

Exercise 13
Analysis of Group Interaction

Introduction

Many attempts have been made to record the behaviour of groups by direct observation. Of these the method of R. F. Bales (*Interaction Process Analysis*) has been one of the most successful and widely used. Bales suggested that the social interactions of small groups could be adequately described and recorded using a twelve category system. The categories he proposed covered such processes as 'agreement', 'showing hostility', 'asking for information'. A set of abbreviations were used to represent these categories and to enable a rapid unobtrusive record to be made during, for example, a committee meeting or a problem-solving session.

Objective

To use the recording scheme of Bales to record interaction in small, problem-solving groups and to try to discover whether it is possible to distinguish leaders from non-leaders on the basis of these records.

Materials

1. Three problems for group discussion. See Item 13.5.
2. Cards numbered 1–5.
3. Recording sheet (Item 13.1).

Method

For this exercise five subjects are required; they should, so far as possible, satisfy the following conditions:

1. They should not know each other or the observers.
2. They should be of the same sex and about the same age.
3. There should be no obvious status differences between them.
4. If possible, they should not be students of the social sciences or mathematics.

When recruited, the subjects should be told that they are needed to take part in an experiment on problem-solving and that they will be

90

required for only half an hour or so. The subjects should be asked to sit around a table at equal intervals with no one person in an obviously dominant position. In front of each a number should be placed which is clearly visible to the observers. One observer (or if possible two) should be instructed to observe one particular subject. Observers should be as far away from the group as is consistent with their having a clear view of the whole group. Three slightly different problems are then provided for each group to solve:

1. An arithmetic problem. Five pieces of information which are essential for the solution are printed on five slips of paper and one is given to each subject. The session stops when the correct solution is found or after 15 minutes.

2. A discussion topic to which there is no right or wrong answer— the group simply having to produce a consensus of opinion as to the best solution. If necessary the discussion should be stopped after 15 minutes.

3. Another arithmetic problem, this time one that cannot be solved with the information available; otherwise it is similar to the first. The subjects must be unaware that a solution is impossible.

The discussion should be stopped after 15 minutes.

Instructions to subjects

Obviously the situation is going to be a little unnatural because of the presence of the observers but an attempt should be made to make the subjects feel at ease. It should be explained that the purpose of the experiment is to see what processes go on in problem-solving, e.g.:

'This is an experiment in problem-solving. It is not a test but an attempt to see what processes go on when groups of people try to solve different kinds of problems. Try not to pay any attention to the rest of us in the room. Just do your best to solve these three problems. In the first one you will each have a card with a piece of information on it and when all this is combined you will have the answer. Please keep your own card in front of you, do not write anything and do not address any remarks to anyone outside the group until you have a generally agreed solution.'

The second problem can be introduced as a case history, e.g.: 'The second problem is different because there is no definite right or wrong answer. Discuss the problem among yourselves and when you have a solution acceptable to the group as a whole let us know.'

And for the third: 'This is another arithmetic problem like the first. Please treat it just as before.'

It is obviously important that there should be no interaction at all between the group and the observers. Ideally the observation would be carried out from behind one-way glass screens but this may not be possible.

The recording categories

The recording system to be used is based on the one devised by Bales (see references). It is somewhat reduced for ease of scoring (nine categories as compared with the twelve used by Bales). Use Item 13.4.

For each 'remark' made by each subject the observer should enter one or more of the abbreviations shown below on the scoring sheet provided (Item 13.1) according to whom the remark is addressed. Each observer has only one subject to record remarks from but these may be addressed to anyone of the other four members of the group or to the group as a whole. If, for example, subject 1 asks a question of subject 2 'inf—' is recorded by subject 1 observer in the space representing subject 2. It is necessary of course to define the 'behavioural unit' which is to be analysed. Probably the most useful unit is the complete sentence (which may in practice range in length from a simple affirmation to a short paragraph). Each unit may be classified under several headings. For example, giving an opinion may in certain circumstances also be an expression of agreement.

After each session observers should be asked to note who they thought had been acting as unofficial leader, and a consensual decision should then be formed by discussion between the observers as to who had been acting as leader for each session (i.e. each problem).

Treatment of Results

1. At the end of the three sessions the scores collected by each observer must be collected together and a matrix (special pattern of scores) formed with responses *from* as one place and responses *to* as the other, the cells being filled with the *number* and *type* of responses. Use Item 13.2.

2. The mean number of responses from and to the leaders should then be calculated (this may be the same individual S three times or three different Ss—one for each problem) and from and to the non-leaders (all three problems being added together).

3. A Chi-squared test should then be made on types of remarks

made *by* leaders and non-leaders using the chart provided (total over 3 problems).

4. The Chi-squared test should be repeated for remarks addressed *to* the leader and non-leaders.

Discussion

1. Are there any consistent differences between those who emerged as leaders and those who remained in the 'rest' of the group?

Note: The rest of the matrix should be examined for differences other than those suggested.

2. Is there any evidence of social 'isolates', i.e., individuals who had significantly fewer remarks addressed to them?

3. Did the 'leaders' address more remarks to the group as a whole?

4. Did different leaders emerge in different types of problem-situation?

5. Were there any differences in the pattern of responses appearing with different problems; e.g., did problem 3 produce more 'withdrawal' responses?

References

BALES, R. F., *Interaction Process Analysis* (Cambridge, Mass. 1950).

BALES, R. F., 'A Set of Categories for the Analysis of Small Group Interaction', *Amer. Soc. Rev.* (1950) 15, pp. 257–63.

KRECH, D., CRUTCHFIELD, R. S., and BALLACHEY, E. L., *Individual in Society* (McGraw Hill, N.Y. 1963), pp. 385–7.

ITEM 13.1

	To 1	To 2	To 3	To 4	To 5	To Group
ARITHMETIC 1						
FROM Fill in here the subject you are recording for						
OPEN ENDED PROBLEM						
FROM						
ARITHMETIC 2						
FROM						

Item 13.1 is to be used in the actual observing situation. Fill in on the extreme left hand column the number assigned to the individual you are observing. Whenever this individual makes a remark enter one of the abbreviations in one of the squares. If, for example, he asks a question of Subject 5 enter (Inf —) in the To 5 box etc.

ITEM 13.2

	To S_1	To S_2	To S_3	To S_4	To S_5	To Group
From S_1						
From S_2						
From S_3						
From S_4						
From S_5						

Item 13.2 is a summary chart in which a matrix representing the whole situation can be recorded. All the remarks made by S_1 to S_2 should be entered into the appropriate box in their abbreviated categories. A separate summary chart is required for each group session.

ITEM 13.3: CHART TO AID CALCULATION OF χ^2 (CHI-SQUARED)

	1. Observed Frequency of Categories of Response = O			2. Expected Frequency = E		3. $(O - E)$		4. $(O - E)^2$		5. $\dfrac{(O - E)^2}{E}$		
Cat	Leader (L)	Non-leader (N L)	Total	L	N–L	L	N–L	L	N–L	L	N–L	Total
1												
2												
3												
4												
5												
6												
7												
8												
9												
Total	b	c	Grand Total D									

Expected frequency (for cell 1) $= a \times \dfrac{b}{D}$ etc.

Notes on the use of Chart to aid calculation of χ^2

Stage 1. Enter the observed frequency ('O' values) of categories of responses for leaders and non-leaders in the extreme left-hand section of the chart.

Stage 2. Calculate the expected frequencies ('E' values) by multiplying the row total (a) by the column total (b) over the grand total (D). Formula: $E = a \times \dfrac{b}{D}$

$\dfrac{b}{D}$ is constant for all nine response categories of leaders and $\dfrac{C}{D}$ constant for non-leaders.

Enter these values in part 2 of the chart.

Stage 3. Enter the differences between the two previous columns in part 3, i.e., $(O - E)$

Stage 4. Square these values, i.e., $(O - E)^2$

Stage 5. Divide the squared differences between observed and expected values by the expected values, i.e., $\dfrac{(O - E)^2}{E}$

Stage 6. Sum these values $\Sigma \dfrac{(O - E)^2}{E}$ and this gives the χ^2 value. A table giving Chi-squared values corresponding to different probabilities (P) will indicate if the divergence between observed and expected values is significant.

The appropriate value for degrees of freedom is found by the following:

$$d.f. = (\text{no. of rows} - 1)(\text{no. of columns} - 1)$$

in this case $d.f. = (9 - 1)(2 - 1) = 8$

The critical Chi-squared values for d.f. = 8 are

P	χ^2
0·05	15·5
0·01	20·1

See any of the statistical texts for a fuller discussion of degrees of freedom and probability. It is sufficient here to say that if the obtained χ^2 value exceeds the critical value for $P = 0·05$ the result is significant. If it exceeds the 0·01 level it is highly significant (i.e., it is very unlikely to have arisen by chance).

ITEM 13.4: BALES CATEGORY SYSTEM (reduced)

Categories	Abbreviations
1. Asks for information	inf −
2. Gives information	inf +
3. Asks for opinion/suggestion	op −
4. Gives opinion/suggestion	op +
5. Agrees	Ag +
6. Disagrees	Ag −
7. Expresses solidarity/tension reduction	Emot +
8. Creates tension/shows hostility	Emot −
9. Expresses withdrawal	with

ITEM 13.5

PROBLEM 1: ARITHMETICAL (SOLUBLE)

The five pieces of information are:
1. John is four inches taller than Robert.
2. Robert is two inches shorter than Derek.
3. Clive's height is exactly between that of John and Derek.
4. Graham is 5 ft 8 inches tall.
5. Graham is halfway between Derek and Clive.

Question

How tall are John, Robert, Derek and Clive?

Answer

John   5 ft 9½ ins   Derek   5 ft 7½ ins
Robert 5 ft 5½ ins   Clive   5 ft 8½ ins

PROBLEM 2: DISCUSSION

Any topic of current interest can be used for discussion.

PROBLEM 3: ARITHMETICAL (INSOLUBLE)

The five pieces of information are:
1. A is four times as far from B as is C.
2. At 30 miles per hour it takes $3\frac{3}{4}$ minutes to get to D from A.
3. C is nearer to B than to D.
4. D is halfway between C and E.
5. E is 2·5 miles from B.

Question

What is the distance between B and D?

Exercise 14. The Sociogram

Introduction

Groups vary in their cohesiveness, and every group has what might be called a 'preference structure', or network of likes, dislikes and indifferences which links its members to one another. Moreno devised a technique which he called 'sociometry' to enable friends, leaders, and social isolates to be detected much more reliably than is possible by direct observation. The essence of the technique is to ask all individuals to indicate those other group members whom they most like or most dislike. A diagram, called a 'sociogram' is then constructed which summarises this information (see Item 14.1). The question asked may be systematically varied (i.e. different 'criteria' may be used) to investigate various aspects of the group's structure.

Objective

To assess the utility of the sociogram.

Method

1. Choose a small group for study—taking into account the following points:

a. The experimenter should be independent of the group he is observing. If the experimenter is a member of the group the other members may be less likely to reveal their true feelings about the rest of the group. If this difficulty cannot be avoided it must be recognised and taken into account.

b. Groups which are maintained on a purely voluntary basis are likely to be less interesting because it is unlikely there will be strong antagonisms (because this would have led to at least one of the opponents leaving the group). It is preferable therefore to take a group which is to some degree *compelled* to remain in being either because of external pressure (e.g. a class or tutorial or work group) or because it is the only way the members can achieve a valued goal (e.g. a sports team or club).

c. The ideal size for these purposes is between 6–10 members. If it is larger than this it becomes difficult to represent in diagrammatic form.

2. The names of the individuals composing the chosen group should now be listed and a copy of the list given to each member of the group.

3. Each member should now be asked to make, privately and without consultation, *two choices*—one of which is positive ('With whom would you most like to work?'—or—'With whom are you most friendly?') and one negative ('With whom would you least like to work?'—or—'With whom are you least friendly?'). These choices should be marked with some appropriate symbol (e.g., + or −) on the list of names which should then be collected by the experimenter.

4. A chart may now be constructed which shows each member of the group as a rectangle containing his name. The collection of lists should be examined, and each declaration of 'positive' relationship should be drawn-in as a continuous line connecting the two rectangles concerned. Each 'negative' relationship should be marked in as a dotted line between the two rectangles concerned. It is usually necessary to experiment a little with the precise placing of the rectangles on the page in order to avoid crossing lines (as much as possible)—and two or three attempts may be needed to produce a satisfactory diagram.

Discussion

1. How useful might this sociogram be? In what kinds of social situation might it be particularly revealing? In what circumstances could this technique *not* be used?

2. How could this sociometric method be used in the planning of teaching or in the planning of residential accommodation for a college?

3. Is it possible to identify leaders or sociometric 'stars' or 'isolates' in your diagram? Would this kind of information be of any use to the group in planning its activities?

4. To what extent were the answers to the simple criterion question asked (e.g. 'With whom are you most friendly?') over-simplifications of real behaviour?

References

MORENO, J. L., *Who Shall Survive* (Beacon House, N.Y. 1953).

PROCTOR, C. H., and LOANIS, C. P., 'Analysis of Sociometric Data' in SELLTIZ, C., JAHODA, M., DEUTSCH, M., and COOK, S. W., (Ed.) *Research Methods in Social Relations* (Holt, Rinehart & Winston, N.Y. 1951).

NORTHWAY, MARY L., *Primer of Sociometry* (University of Toronto Press, 1967).

ITEM 14.1: AN EXAMPLE OF A COMPLETED SOCIOGRAM

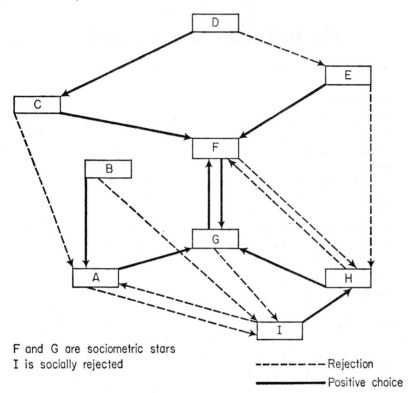

F and G are sociometric stars
I is socially rejected

– – – – – – – Rejection
————— Positive choice

Exercise 15
The Reliability of the Interview

Introduction

The interview is a widely used, and for this reason an important, type of observation. In many assessment and selection procedures, for example, the interview still plays the major part in decision-making.

At first sight the interview would seem to be an ideal method of social observation. Unfortunately data secured by interviews have a number of serious limitations—not all people are equally capable of making their views known and what may superficially appear to be differences in personality or attitudes may in fact simply be differences in verbal ability or education. Not all interviewers have equal competence in extracting information—and in a large enquiry involving many interviewers this may be a serious form of error. Furthermore there are often 'interaction' effects between observer and observed—they may not like each other. The interviewer may be (consciously or unconsciously) prejudiced for or against the person he is interviewing—perhaps because of the colour of his skin or his accent. Again the interviewer may be unduly swayed throughout the interview by a favourable (or unfavourable) first impression. The interview has indeed been criticised on many grounds—as being an inefficient and clumsy way of collecting information—as being too much influenced by subjective factors and other sources of error—as being invalid in the sense that it does not collect the information it purports to collect, and perhaps most seriously as not yielding the same information on two different occasions, or when the information is collected by two different observers. This last issue, inter-interviewer reliability, is the subject of this exercise. Each of the available subjects will be interviewed by two different interviewers to assess the subject's knowledge and opinions of a prose passage he has previously read, and also to assess his personality.

The correlation between the judgements made by the various interviewers about the same subjects will then be computed.

Objective

To test the inter-interviewer reliability of assessments of knowledge, opinions and personality.

Materials

Short document provided at end of exercise. (Item 15.1.)

Method

Each subject should be interviewed at least twice by different interviewers; he should be warned beforehand that this will happen and the object of the exercise explained to him.

The subject should then be asked to read carefully the material provided (Item 15.1) and then interviewed independently by the two interviewers. The interviewers should try to discover the subject's opinion about the material and then quietly put the opposite opinion to him as their own—so that they may have an opportunity to assess, so far as is possible, the characteristics listed below:

1. Knowledge of the material,
2. Opinion–favourable–unfavourable,
3. Determination to stick to own opinions,
4. Intelligence,
5. Stability–instability,
6. Aggression–submission,
7. Extraversion–introversion.

The subject should be rated for each of these on a seven-point rating scale where a score of 7 indicates an extreme positive assessment, i.e., very knowledgeable, favourable opinion, determined, intelligent, stable etc., and a score of 1 indicates extreme lack of knowledge, unfavourable opinion, yielding, unintelligent, unstable, etc. 4 can be regarded as a mid point.

Each interviewer will in this way obtain seven scores for each person interviewed. Use Item 15.2.

Treatment of Results

There are two ways of analysing this data:

1. Agreement between two interviewers when assessing one quality in all subjects can be measured by computing the Product Moment correlation. Thus if two interviewers each conduct say ten interviews on the same ten subjects a correlation coefficient for each of the seven rated variables can be computed. The closer the agreement between the two

interviewers the higher the coefficients will be. A chart for calculating one of the seven coefficients is shown in Item 15.3.

2. For each individual who has been interviewed by two people a double profile can be drawn which will show how similar are the two judges' assessments of the same individual. Use Item 15.4.

Discussion

1. Where was the greatest agreement between interviewers and where the greatest disagreement?

2. Which qualities were easiest to assess?

3. Did differences in verbal skill offset the results? Could they have done so in more varied populations, e.g., with subjects drawn from widely different socio-economic groups?

4. Were some individuals more easy to interview than others? Were they also easier to assess?

5. Were any subjects evidently sensitive to and compliant with what they considered to be your opinions?

6. Do your profiles show any suggestion of a 'halo effect' or of the 'logical error'?

7. What other sources of error may possibly have affected the interviewers' ratings?

8. How could the traditional interviewing method be improved? (See Anastasi, A., *Fields of Applied Psychology*.)

9. What alternatives to interviewing were available to assess the variables used in this exercise?

10. What uses may the interview have other than simply collecting information?

References

GOODE, W. J., and HATT, P. K., *Methods in Social Research* (McGraw Hill, N.Y. 1952) Ch. 13, 'The Interview'.
ANASTASI, A., *Fields of Applied Psychology* (Macmillan, London 1961), Ch. 4, p. 94.
MARX, K., and ENGELS, F., *Manifesto of the Communist Party*.

ITEM 15.1

The bourgeoisie, wherever it has got the upper hand, has put an end to all feudal, patriarchal, idyllic relations. It has pitilessly torn asunder the motley feudal ties that bound man to his 'natural superiors', and has left remaining no other nexus between man and man than naked self-interest, than callous 'cash payment'. It has drowned the most heavenly ecstasies of religious fervour, of chivalrous enthusiasm, of philistine sentimentalism, in the icy water of egotistical calculation. It has resolved personal worth into exchange value, and in place of the numberless indefeasible chartered freedoms, has set up that single unconscionable freedom–Free Trade. In one word, for exploitation, veiled by religious and political illusions, it has substituted naked, shameless, direct, brutal exploitation.

The bourgeoisie has stripped of its halo every occupation hitherto honoured and looked up to with reverent awe. It has converted the physician, the lawyer, the priest, the poet, the man of science, into its paid wage-labourers.

The bourgeoisie has torn away from the family its sentimental veil, and has reduced the family relation to a mere money relation. The history of all hitherto existing society is the history of class struggles.

Freeman and slave, patrician and plebeian, lord and serf, guild-master and journeyman, in a word, oppressor and oppressed, stood in constant opposition to one another, carried on an uninterrupted, now hidden, now open fight, a fight that each time ended, either in a revolutionary re-constitution of society at large, or in the common ruin of the contending classes.

In the earlier epochs of history, we find almost everywhere a complicated arrangement of society into various orders, a manifold gradation of social rank. In ancient Rome we have patricians, knights, plebeians, slaves; in the Middle Ages, feudal lords, vassals, guild-masters, journeymen, apprentices, serfs; in almost all of these classes, again, subordinate gradations.

The modern bourgeois society that has sprouted from the ruins of feudal society has not done away with class antagonisms. It has but established new classes, new conditions of oppression, new forms of struggle in place of the old ones.

Our epoch, the epoch of the bourgeoisie, possesses, however, this distinctive feature: it has simplified the class antagonisms. Society as a whole is more and more splitting up into two great hostile camps, into two great classes directly facing each other: Bourgeoisie and Proletariat. We have seen that the first step in the revolution by the working class, is to raise the proletariat to the position of ruling class, to win the battle of democracy.

The proletariat will use its political supremacy to wrest, by degrees, all capital from the bourgeoisie, to centralise all instruments of production in the hands of the State, i.e., of the proletariat organised as the ruling class; and to increase the total of productive forces as rapidly as possible.

Of course, in the beginning, this cannot be effected except by means of despotic inroads on the rights of property, and on the conditions of bourgeois production; by means of measures, therefore, which appear economically insufficient and untenable, but which, in the course of the movement, outstrip themselves, necessitate further inroads upon the old social order, and are unavoidable as a means of entirely revolutionising the mode of production.

These measures will of course be different in different countries.

Nevertheless in the most advanced countries, the following will be pretty generally applicable.

1. Abolition of property in land and application of all rents of land to public purposes.

2. A heavy progressive or graduated income-tax.

3. Abolition of all right of inheritance.

4. Confiscation of the property of all emigrants and rebels.

5. Centralisation of credit in the hands of the State, by means of a national bank with State capital and an exclusive monopoly.

6. Centralisation of the means of communication and transport in the hands of the State.

7. Extension of factories and instruments of production owned by the State; the bringing in to cultivation of waste-lands, and the improvement of the soil generally in accordance with a common plan.

8. Equal liability of all to labour. Establishment of industrial armies, especially for agriculture.

9. Combination of agriculture with manufacturing industries; gradual abolition of the distinction between town and country, by a more equable distribution of the population over the country.

10. Free education for all children in public schools. Abolition of children's factory labour in its present form. Combination of education with industrial production, etc. etc.

When, in the course of development, class distinctions have disappeared, and all production has been concentrated in the hands of a vast association of the whole nation, the public power will lose its political character. Political power, properly so called, is merely the organised power of one class for oppressing another. If the proletariat during its contest with the bourgeoisie is compelled, by the force of circumstances, to organise itself as a class, if, by means of a revolution, it makes itself the ruling class, and as such, sweeps away by force the old conditions of production, then it will, along with these conditions, have swept away the conditions for the existence of class antagonisms and of classes generally, and will thereby have abolished its own supremacy as a class.

In place of the old bourgeois society, with its classes and class antagonisms, we shall have an association, in which the free development of each is the condition for the free development of all.

ITEM 15.2: ASSESSMENT SHEET FOR INTERVIEW

	1	2	3	4	5	6	7	
No knowledge								knowledge
Unfavourable opinion								favourable opinion
vacillates								determined
unintelligent								intelligent
unstable								stable
aggressive								lacks aggression
extraverted								introverted

Rate the person you have interviewed on each of these characteristics by putting a tick in the spaces numbered from 1–7 on each line, e.g., a tick in space 2 on the first line would mean that the person has very little knowledge of the material he studied.

ITEM 15.3: CHART FOR CALCULATING THE PRODUCT
MOMENT CORRELATION COEFFICIENT BETWEEN TWO
INTERVIEWERS WHO HAVE RATED A NUMBER OF
INDIVIDUALS ON A DEFINED CHARACTERISTIC
(E.G., KNOWLEDGE)

Subjects	Interviewer X	Y	$X - \bar{X}$ x	$Y - \bar{Y}$ y	x^2	y^2	xy
1							
2							
3							
4							
5							
6							
7							
8							
9							
Σ	ΣX	ΣY			Σx^2	Σy^2	Σxy
$\dfrac{\Sigma X(Y)}{N}$	$\bar{X}$	$\bar{Y}$					

$\left.\begin{array}{l}X\\Y\end{array}\right\}$ = raw scores

$\left.\begin{array}{l}x\\y\end{array}\right\}$ = deviations from means

$\left.\begin{array}{l}\bar{X}\\\bar{Y}\end{array}\right\}$ = means of raw scores

r = correlation

$$r_{xy} = \frac{\Sigma xy}{(\Sigma x^2)(\Sigma y^2)}$$

ITEM 15.4: CHART FOR COMPARING INTERVIEW PROFILES

	1	2	3	4	5	6	7
Knowledge							
Opinion							
Determination							
Intelligence							
Stability							
Aggression							
Extraversion							

An individual's profile is obtained by connecting his scores on each of the seven characteristics with straight lines. Compare the two profiles obtained for the same individual by marking the judgements of the two interviewers on the same chart.

Exercise 16. Assessing Prosperity

Introduction

Though direct observation is a powerful tool it can easily become a laborious and unwieldy one if observations are random and undisciplined. Observational studies which are made without any guiding principles and which attempt to record all features of a situation are likely to be wasteful of effort (though they may of course be helpful in the early stages of enquiries into new problems by providing us with new testable hypotheses). In practice it is almost always desirable to conduct a short exploratory 'pilot study' whose main purpose is to discover which aspects of the problem are most likely to repay intensive and detailed further study. If, for example, we wished to construct a short reliable check-list of observable items which would enable an observer to get a good, rapid assessment of the prosperity of any street or area, we could undertake a short pilot study of two 'criterion' areas or streets which we already knew to differ markedly in prosperity. Features of each of these streets might then be recorded quite freely. Next, the two lists of features could be compared and those items which were clearly present in both streets—and which evidently did not distinguish the two—might then be excluded from the main enquiry, and no further attention wasted on them. The pilot study would therefore enable us to select and construct the most parsimonious list which was capable of making a clear separation of the two criterion streets. This list could be used to guide observations of yet further streets. A good check-list would be one which awarded high scores to streets in prosperous areas and lower scores to streets in less prosperous areas.

Objective

To construct a short scoring method to be used for assessing the relative prosperity of houses from their outward appearance.

Method

    1. Assemble a list of at least 20 features which might be considered

on *a priori* grounds to indicate the presence or absence of prosperity in urban housing. Such positive items might be:

   i. Size of house,
  ii. Presence of garage(s),
        and car(s),
 iii. Drive,
  iv. Telephone wires,
   v. New paintwork,
  vi. Size and type of garden,
 vii. 'Name' or 'number'.

Suggested negative items might be:

   i. Multiple dwelling (number of front door bells),
  ii. Washing on line.

Items of doubtful status such as:

   i. T.V. aerial,
  ii. Clean front door step,
 iii. Gates present or absent,
        may of course be included at this pilot stage.

2. Since these features are to be used as items in a check-list they must be carefully considered and a decision taken in each case on how many degrees or categories are to be allowed for a given item. Thus for item (*i*) Size of house—you may decide to use three divisions, e.g., 'large', 'medium', 'small'. Whereas in the case of the T.V. aerial, only present or absent can be recorded.

3. Four identical check-lists should now be constructed preferably on cards (for convenience in handling out of doors), which incorporate your items and the sub-divisions which you have decided upon. (These cards should be arranged to accommodate 10 sets of observations.) It would be a wise precaution to leave extra space on the cards for new variables chosen and added at the time of observation. See Item 16.1.

4. Select 2 criterion areas in your own town which are known locally to be highly contrasted in prosperity.

Visit 2 roads in the 'high prosperity' area and 2 roads in the 'low prosperity' area. Use the check-list cards to record data from 10 houses in each road, i.e., 4 cards should be filled in finally to yield data on 40 houses.

5. Compute the sub-item totals for all cases, i.e., enter in the final

column of each card the total number of entries made for 'Size of house large'. Then the total for 'Size of house medium' etc.

6. Compare the sub-item totals for the 'High' and 'Low' prosperity areas by constructing a table such as that in Item 16.2.

Calculate the appropriate ratio of High-Low totals for each sub-item.

7. Select those items which clearly discriminate between the two. You may choose to reject those items which have a high/low ratio below 2 : 1. Remember that each item could be positive or negative and this must be made clear on the final check-list. For example, it may be found that houses in the low prosperity interior area have washing visible on the line much more frequently than do the high prosperity area. This could then be scored in the negative direction.

8. Draw up the revised version of the check-list and apply it to several streets in different areas. The list can easily be checked for reliability by comparing the ratings made by two observers who visit the area independently.

Discussion

1. Does the final version of the scale show good discrimination between different areas?

2. Is the scale reliable? Is it possible to be quite objective in saying whether a house is, for example, 'small', 'medium', or 'large'?

3. Could the scale have been improved by converting it into a weighted index. See *Exercise 21*.

4. What further work would be required before we could be assured we had produced a scale of general prosperity?

5. What variables other than 'prosperity' have become apparent during your observations?

6. How could the scale be used in research?

7. What other sources of evidence on prosperity could have been obtained? Would it have been more reliable to interview occupants, for example?

ITEM 16.1: PROSPERITY RATING SCALE

Item	*Enter*	*Entries*	*Total for* 10 *houses*
1 House Size	L, M, S*		
2 Garage	+ or −†		
3			
4			
5			
6			
7			
8			
9			
10			
11			

* L, M, S = Large, medium, small
† +, − = present or absent

ITEM 16.2: TABLE FOR COMPARISON OF ROADS IN
TWO CRITERION AREAS

Item	Total Score High Prosperity Road	Total Score Low Prosperity Road	Ratio High/Low
1			
2			
3			
4			
5			
6			
7			
8			
9			
10			
11			

Section C

Measurement Techniques

Introduction (C)

The techniques of social investigation illustrated so far have not used any special tools for extracting data—they have in fact relied upon reports of other people's work or on relatively direct observational methods. None of these techniques could properly be considered, however, as 'measurement' in the scientist's sense.

The methods discussed so far have enabled us to collect a great deal of interesting information—but most of it has been descriptive, qualitative information. The most that we can usually do with such information is to classify it and divide it up into *categories*. This taxonomy is an essential first step in all scientific work, but to progress any further it is necessary to make *quantitative* measurements, and to study closely the way quantitative measurements change in different circumstances. To speak of measurement is to imply that there is a scale of some kind and that it is possible to place an individual (or a piece of information) at some fixed point along that scale—as along a scale of temperature. Many attempts have been made to construct such 'scales' in social science and two types of scale are frequently used. The simplest of these is the *ordinal scale* which is used when it is possible to rank people or events in order—where, for example, we can say that Smith is higher than Brown on our scale, though we may not be able to say *how much* higher he is in strict quantitative terms or indeed how 'high' he is in any absolute sense at all. More rarely we are able to use an *interval scale*. An interval scale, like the scale of a thermometer, is divided clearly into divisions which are an equal distance apart on some known quantitative dimension.

This section begins with some measuring instruments which might be used by the sociologist in surveys. The Questionnaire method is explained in *Exercises 17* and *18*. The Questionnaire is often used in research on political opinion and the field of market research. An Attitude scale (*Exercise 19*) is in some ways more precise and yet it is often more difficult to interpret. An individual is assigned a definite score but it may not always be clear exactly what is the precise meaning of this score.

There are many aspects of individuals which could be selected for measurement. Hair colour, size, weight, or skin colour might be measured. When, however, we restrict our attention to the psychological and social properties of individuals we find that there are two main modes of variation. Individuals vary a good deal, first of all, in their *abilities*. Some are bright, some are dull; some are musically-gifted, others are not. Individuals vary in other ways however—for example, in motives and ambitions, in interests, in values and in *temperament*. Some people are shy, others are not, some are altruistic—others are not. Psychological tests have been developed for measuring each of these two types of variation. Cronbach (*Essentials of Psychological Testing*, Harper, N.Y. 1949) has usefully described tests of the first type, i.e., tests of abilities as 'tests of maximum performance' which are concerned to measure the peak performance of an individual. The second type of test is concerned with qualities of temperament and personality—or as Cronbach calls them 'tests of typical performance'. Here our interest is in the pattern of motives and ambitions, emotions, attitudes, values and preoccupations which go to make up an individual's characteristic personality. Inspection of a handbook of tests (such as the *Mental Measurements Yearbook* by O. K. Buros) will show that a bewildering variety of tests of ability and personality are available. In *Exercises 24* and *25* we consider examples of these two main types of psychological test. In *Exercise 26* we discuss the practical problems which arise in applying them to people, and discuss criteria for evaluating tests and for assessing their merits and demerits for a particular purpose.

There are two very important features which we must be satisfied about before using any psychological test (whether it be an ability or personality test). The first of these is 'validity': does this test actually measure what it purports to measure? If it is an intelligence test, does it really measure intelligence or is it perhaps simply measuring education or even something else? The second major requirement of a test is that it should be 'reliable': does it give substantially the same answer when used a second time on the same individual? Tests which have low reliability or low validity are of little use to us—however superficially attractive or appropriate they may seem to be. Validity and Reliability are discussed in *Exercise 26*.

The measurements or scores yielded by tests make an interesting study in themselves. Some tests have relatively few questions while others may have hundreds. The number of questions answered correctly or in a particular way (usually called the 'raw score') is therefore not a very good guide to the performance of a particular person. What we need to know is how this person's score compares with other people's scores on that particular test. There are several ways of transforming raw scores so that they tell us how the person tested compares with other people. One of these methods is the well-known 'intelligence quotient' or I.Q. There are however several other useful methods of dealing with test scores and these are discussed in *Exercise 27*.

Exercise 17
Construction of a Questionnaire

Introduction

The questionnaire is perhaps the most widely used tool in social science. It is easy to construct, to reproduce and to administer. Its scoring is usually simple and results for large numbers of people can be obtained quite quickly. In common with other measuring instruments it has its pitfalls and limitations. The more serious possibilities of error arise in the construction rather than in the use of questionnaires and it is the purpose of this exercise to consider some of the precautions which should be observed in assembling a reliable questionnaire. As will become evident these precautions, though simple in conception, can be time-consuming. The actual *use* of the questionnaire is therefore postponed until *Exercise 18*.

It is useful to draw a distinction between questionnaires (of which the main concern is to collect information) from attitude scales (which are intended to assess how an individual *feels* about a particular issue). Whereas the results of questionnaire studies usually have relevance and meaning only in relation to particular groups or sub-sections of a specified population, the results of attitude scales do have significance as individual scores. They are measurements of an individual's subjective feelings toward an object or issue. (See *Exercise 19: Attitude Scale Construction.*)

Objective

To design a questionnaire which will give a reliable assessment of a person's knowledge of current political issues and to try and relate this to other variables.

Method

The questionnaire is designed to test knowledge as opposed to attitudes, so the questions must have factual answers which can be either right or wrong as opposed to expressions of agreement or disagreement. A large number of questions should be assembled which refer to the current political scene, e.g.:

'Who is the Minister responsible for Defence?'
'When was the last general election?'
'Who is the local M.P.?'
'Which countries are members of the Common Market?'

Questions should range from the very simple to the extremely difficult so that all levels of knowledge can be sampled. Questions should be rejected which fall into the following categories:

1. Questions *too vague* to permit precise answers, e.g.:
   'What would happen if we went into the Common Market?'
2. *Ambiguous* questions, e.g.:
   'How often should there be an election?'
3. Questions which involve technical or *unfamiliar words*, e.g.:
   'How many members are there of the O.E.E.C.?'
4. Questions relevant to only a proportion of the population and perhaps *meaningless* to many people, e.g.:
   'Who is the Chairman of the local Liberal Party?'
5. Questions which *cannot be scored* as right or wrong because they imply an element of opinion, e.g.:
   'Who is the most skilful orator in Parliament today?'

The remaining questions should be assembled to form the first prototype of the scale. This should be duplicated and administered to pilot samples of at least 40 subjects.

Treatment of Results

The distribution of scores obtained from the pilot sample should be plotted, grouping the data if necessary. If the distribution departs considerably from the normal bell-shaped curve, the reason for this should be investigated. It could mean that: *a*, the population comprising the pilot sample was highly selected in terms of knowledge of politics; or *b*, the scale was failing to discriminate those with a high level of knowledge from those with little knowledge; or *c*, that the scale was truncated, i.e., it was either much too easy (a disproportionate number of scores near the maximum) or too difficult (very many people obtaining very low scores). Ideally, but not necessarily, the middle score on the scale (i.e., half the items answered correctly) would also be the mean and modal scores of the population. (See *Glossary*.)

If the distribution is markedly skewed, then either more items are required, or a new sample with a much wider range of knowledge should be tested. When, however, the scores are distributed roughly normally the next step may be taken. This is to test the discriminating power of each item with a view to reducing the number of items in the final questionnaire to the minimum number required to achieve satisfactory discrimination along the whole scale. This can be done with the 'point-biserial correlation coefficient'.

The point-biserial correlation coefficient gives a measure of the tendency of a single item to provide the same result as yielded by the whole collection of items. It enables us to select 'good' items. A good item is one which is regularly failed by people scoring low on the whole scale and which is regularly passed by people scoring highly on the whole scale. (A 'bad' item on the other hand has no such predictive power—people passing it might fail the whole scale, and people failing the bad item might pass the whole scale.)

The coefficient is worked out (see Lord, F. M.) by taking the mean scores on the total scale of those individuals that passed an item (M_p), subtracting the overall mean of all subjects on all items (M), and dividing the product by the maximum mean for that item (μ_p: i.e., the mean of the top p scores where p = number of individuals passing that item) minus the overall mean (M).

For each item

$$r = \frac{M_p - M}{\mu_p - M}$$

For each item it is necessary to work out two means: the mean scale score of those who passed the item (say 25), and the mean scale score of the top scoring 25 from the whole sample whether or not they passed this item. This will produce a correlation coefficient for each item ranging from 0·0 (which means that this item has no discriminating power) to 1·0 (which indicates perfect discrimination). For each item also it will be known how many people have passed this item (p) which is a measure of the difficulty of the item.

The final questionnaire may now be constructed from carefully selected items which cover the whole difficulty range and which also discriminate well. Some attention should be paid to the order in which the items are assembled and to the precise wording of the instructions at the beginning of the questionnaire. The final questionnaire should be given a title and presented in an attractive way so as to encourage the respondent to devote some of his own time, care and effort in its completion, and it should not be so lengthy as to induce boredom or fatigue.

Discussion

1. What difficulties arose in framing the questions?
2. Discuss the distribution of the pilot sample scores.
3. Are the most discriminating items those which would be expected from initial observation?

References

LORD, F. M., 'Biserial estimates of correlation', *Psychometrika* (1963) 28: pp. 81–5.

CONNOLLY, T. G., and SLUCKIN, W., *Statistics for the Social Sciences* (Cleaver Hume Press, London 1958) p. 138.

Exercise 18. The Use of the Questionnaire

Introduction

This exercise follows on directly from *Exercise 17* and involves the use of the questionnaire constructed in that exercise. To make it possible to generalise from the results it will be necessary to obtain as large a sample of respondents as possible. Reference should be made to *Exercise 20* for more information on methods available for undertaking this sampling.

Objective

To measure political knowledge by means of a questionnaire and to discover whether such knowledge is related to any other variables.

Materials

Copies of the questionnaire constructed in *Exercise 17*.

Method

Copies of the questionnaire should be duplicated together with instructions and questions about other variables such as political affiliation, voting intentions, etc. Enough space should be left for the answers to be written clearly.

This should now be administered to a large sample, either chosen at random, or from a special group (e.g., a college population). In this latter case results will be limited to this group and it will not be possible to generalise with any degree of confidence about the population at large. Record any difficulties or reservations the subjects have. If it is possible to administer this questionnaire to the same subjects as are used in the exercise on attitude scale construction this will add extra interest to the analysis of results.

Suggested set of instructions:

'This is a short list questions about politics. It is not a test but is designed to find out what people are most interested in. Just answer the questions—one or two words are usually sufficient. Thank you for your help.'

Treatment of Results

If the items have been selected correctly then the distribution of scores should still be approximately normal. It may be possible to divide the tested sample into several sub-groups, such as Labour supporters, Liberals, Conservatives, Others, Non-Members, etc. If this is possible the analysis of variance would be an appropriate statistic to apply (see chart in Item 18.1) to discover the relationship, if any, between political knowledge and party affiliation.

If, however, only two means are to be compared, a t-test can be used, employing the standard deviations of each sample to estimate the standard error of the differences between means. (See *Glossary*.)

If it is possible to obtain sets of scores for the same individuals on both the questionnaire and attitude scale, then the scores can be correlated, using the Product Moment Correlation Coefficient and the significance of the correlation may be tested.

Discussion

   1. Were any difficulties met in administering the questionnaire?
   2. Were there any significant differences between party supporters on amount of political information?
   3. Were *members* of parties better informed than supporters?
   4. Were men better informed than women? If so, what could be a possible explanation?

ITEM 18.1

DISTRIBUTION OF RAW SCORES IN 5 GROUPS

Labour	*Liberal*	*Cons*	*Other*	*None*
X_1	X_2	X_3	X_4	X_5
$\Sigma X_1 =$	$\Sigma X_2 =$	$\Sigma X_3 =$	$\Sigma X_4 =$	$\Sigma X_5 =$
$n_1 =$	$n_2 =$	$n_3 =$	$n_4 =$	$n_5 =$

$$\Sigma X = \Sigma X_1 + \Sigma X_2 + \Sigma X_3 + \Sigma X_4 + \Sigma X_5$$
$$N = n_1 + n_2 + n_3 + n_4 + n_5$$

1. Total S.S. $= \Sigma X^2 - \dfrac{(\Sigma X)^2}{N}$

2. Sum of squares between groups $= \dfrac{(\Sigma X_1)^2}{n_1} + \dfrac{(\Sigma X_2)^2}{n_2} + \dfrac{(\Sigma X_3)^2}{n_3} + \dfrac{(\Sigma X_4)^2}{n_4} + \dfrac{(\Sigma X_5)^2}{n_5} - \dfrac{(\Sigma X)^2}{N}$

3. S.S. within groups $= 1) - 2)$

SQUARE OF RAW SCORES

X_1^2	X_2^2	X_3^2	X_4^2	X_5^2
ΣX_1^2	ΣX_2^2	ΣX_3^2	ΣX_4^2	ΣX_5^2

$$\Sigma X^2 = \Sigma X_1^2 + \Sigma X_2^2 + \Sigma X_3^2 + \Sigma X_4^2 + \Sigma X_5^2$$

ITEM 18.2: ANALYSIS OF VARIANCE SUMMARY TABLE

Source of variation	Sum of squares	Degrees of freedom	Mean square
Between groups			
Within groups			
Total			

$$\text{Degrees of freedom} = N - 1$$
$$\text{Mean square} = \frac{\text{S.S.}}{\text{D.F.}}$$
$$F = \frac{\text{Mean square between groups}}{\text{Mean square within groups}}$$

Exercise 19. Attitude Scale Construction

Introduction

An Attitude Scale is a very convenient method of getting a quick measure of a large number of individuals' attitudes to an object, institution, person or idea. Each individual is assigned a score on the basis of his agreement or disagreement with a set of statements. There are three main types of attitude scale: 'Differential Scales' (such as the *Thurstone Scale*), 'Summated Rating Scales' (such as the *Likert Scale*), and 'Cumulative Scales' (such as the *Bogardus* and *Guttman Scales*).

In the *Thurstone Scale* (which is used in this exercise) the individual is asked to indicate whether he agrees or disagrees with a series of statements which are of gently graded strength. A score is computed by inspection of the items with which the individual agreed.

In the Likert Scale the individual is not asked to make an 'all or nothing' response (as in the Thurstone method), but simply to indicate whether he strongly agrees, agrees, is indifferent, disagrees, or strongly disagrees, with a series of varied, contrasting, and fairly strongly-worded statements. Some of the statements are favourable and some unfavourable to the issue in question. A score is computed by summing scores for all the items answered. If the individual strongly agrees with all the items we know to be favourable (and strongly disagrees with all the items we know to be unfavourable) then he scores highly on the whole test. If, by contrast, he strongly agrees with the unfavourable (and disagrees with the favourable) then he scores low on the test. Any departure from strongly agreeing with items, *reduces* the total score to an intermediate value.

The advantages of Likert scales are that they are relatively simple to construct and give high reliability for a given number of items. They also allow subtle shades of agreement to be distinguished—and they can yield useful information from individual item response analysis. Likert scales suffer from the disadvantage that they are ordinal (rather than interval) scales and are therefore of little use in measuring *changes* in individual response. Furthermore a given score on the Likert scale can be achieved by any number of combinations of individual item responses, so that a score has little meaning. Scores can only be interpreted in terms of norms, i.e., in relation to the scores of other people. Though it is easy enough to interpret very high or very low scores—the status of intermediate scores cannot be understood without comparison with norms.

In Cumulative Scales such as the Guttman 'Scalogram' technique, the items are carefully pre-tested and arranged in a special sequence. The items are of graded strength and extend from early items, 1 and 2, which only very tentatively express a certain point of view, to items 6 and 7 which are forthright expressions of that particular sentiment. If a person agrees with statement number 3 we can be sure (from the pre-testing) that he will also agree with the weaker statements numbers 2 and 1. Similarly, we can be sure that if he says 'disagree' to number 4 he will also say 'disagree' to the stronger numbers 5, 6, 7, etc. Ideally an individual with a higher total score on the scale is just as high or higher on every item than an individual with a lower total score. When this occurs the scale is said to be unidimensional. The total score of an individual in fact enables a perfect prediction or reproduction to be made of his whole pattern of responses. Perfect 'reproducibility' is in practice never attained. It is possible, however, by a technique described by Guttmann to calculate a coefficient of reproducibility (i.e., the accuracy with which the pattern of scores can be reproduced from the total score). Guttmann has not described how to select items but Edwards has proposed a combination of Thurstone and Likert methods to help in item-selection. Interest in these cumulative scales grew out of the work of Bogardus (1925) on 'social-distance scales' which assessed individuals' attitudes to people of different nationalities. Here questions of progressively-graded strength were used for the first time. An early question might be: 'Would you allow Negroes into this country?' A later question would be: 'Would you accept a Negro lodger in your house?' and finally: 'Would you allow a Negro to marry your daughter?' The 'valence' of an individual's attitude was taken to be the highest degree of intimacy he would accept with the race or nationality in question.

The great advantage of attitude scales generally is that they often show high validity (when measured against real behaviour). They also have high reliability. The reasons for this high validity and reliability may well be that they measure rather stable concepts of self and that they have a fairly large number of items so that variations in the validity of individual items in different contexts do not matter greatly. Further advantages are that they do not suggest their own answers and they do not depend critically on answers to single questions about a particular attitude (both of which questionnaires tend to do). According to Thurstone some attitude scales have the advantage of being 'interval' scales—but this has been questioned by other workers. Again attitude scales give well-differentiated measurements among populations, i.e., they spread people well out along an attitude dimension. Among their disadvantages are their tendency to set up an unnatural frame of reference for the respondent because of their rigid forced-choice alternative questions. Furthermore they may sometimes seem trivial or even foolish to educated respondents.

As in the case of other instruments purporting to measure human mental processes it is necessary to reassure oneself about the reliability and validity of the scores from attitude scales. We must discover whether the individual score is reliable, i.e., whether it really reflects a stable pattern of beliefs and feelings—or whether the score is simply an artefact of the scale. Reliability may be assessed by the 'split-half' method, or alternatively the 'test-retest' method may be used. Validity is important too: does the attitude scale really measure what it is supposed to be measuring, i.e., does it distinguish criterion groups known to differ on this dimension? It is often very difficult of course to obtain such criterion groups (e.g., when studying attitudes to drug addiction or homosexuality). Concurrent validity (i.e., high correlation with other accepted measures) can often be assessed. A third aspect of an attitude scale which must be assessed is its unidimensionality, i.e., is the scale measuring one thing and one thing only? Item analysis and the point-biserial correlation coefficient can be used here. The correlation between scores on each item and scores on the total scale should be high. If we employ only such items which have high correlation then the scale will be unidimensional.

Objective

To construct, test, and administer a modified Thurstone type of attitude scale and analyse the results in terms of 'population norms'.

Method

1. Create a large pool of statements (not questions) about socialism (or any other topic) consisting of at least 50–60 items covering the whole range of opinion about the topic, e.g.:

a. 'In my opinion socialism is the greatest evil threatening mankind today.'

b. 'Socialism is the only hope the world has of ever attaining peace and prosperity.'

c. 'Socialism is not basically different from many other political beliefs.'

2. Number each individual item and duplicate on to slips of paper (as many copies as there are to be judges).

3. Assemble a panel of judges (e.g., the whole class) each having a copy of each item on a separate slip of paper. Arrange a set of marker cards on a table numbered from 1–7. Each of the judges should then put each individual slip on to whichever pile he considers most suitable. Pile 1 indicates that 'the statement is extremely unfavourable to the topic under consideration' (e.g., statement *a*, above), and Pile 7 indicates 'a very favourable statement' (e.g., *b*, above), while the central pile (no 4) indicates neutrality. The judges should try to do this objectively, not allowing their own personal attitudes to influence their judgements. Everyone, whether personally for or against socialism, could agree that statement *a*, is unfavourable to socialism.

There has been considerable argument as to whether the attitudes of judges do influence their ranking, but here we must assume that it does not. It is clearly an advantage to have as many judges as possible. Judges should receive the slips of paper with the items on in random order so that they are not all judging the same item together. There should be no discussion between judges.

4. On each slip the number of the pile it was sorted into should be marked, and the slips should be rearranged into piles so that all 'statement no. 5' are together etc.

5. The mean ranking of each item and the standard deviation should then be computed.

6. A set of between 10 and 20 items should then be selected on the following criteria:

a. that they cover the whole range of scale scores as far as possible in equal steps (e.g. about 0·3 scale points interval),

b. that the items have the lowest possible standard deviations (because these are the items about which there was least disagreement between the judges).

7. The items should then be written out or printed in random order together with questions covering other information you consider relevant (e.g., age, sex, education, party affiliations, occupation etc.)

as well. After each statement the words AGREE and DISAGREE should be printed. Respondents should be asked to draw a circle around the response they chose .It is useful to have a standard set of instructions at the head of the form, e.g.:

'This is a short list of questions to find out what people think of (socialism). It is not a test and there are no right or wrong answers. Please put a circle around AGREE or DISAGREE for each sentence. Thank you.'

8. A separate record should be kept of the scale values for each item. The questionnaire should be administered to a chosen population (e.g., college and non-college males and females), getting the largest possible sample (say 20–30 respondents from *each* member of the class).

9. Each respondent's score should be calculated by adding together the scale values of the items with which he *agreed*, and dividing by the number of agreements. The items with which he disagreed should be ignored.

Treatment of Results

1. Plot the distribution of scores, grouping the data if necessary.

2. Divide the sample into sub-groups according to any other information you have collected (e.g., sex, party affiliation etc.). Where the means differ, a test of significance with a t-test should be made.

3. Work out population norms in terms of percentile ranks, e.g., 10 per cent of the population had a score of above x; 20 per cent of the population had a score of above y etc.

4. If the time is available a measure of the 'reliability' of the scale can be obtained by the test-retest method. As its name implies this means testing a group of subjects on two occasions. The time interval is not crucial but two points need to be taken into consideration.

a. The interval must not be so short as to allow the subjects to remember their previous responses.
b. On the other hand, the interval should not be too long otherwise a genuine change in the underlying attitude of some of the subjects might well have occurred.

An interval of between a week and a month would be reasonable. The actual measure of reliability is the Product Moment Correlation Coefficient between the two sets of scores.

Discussion

1. Were there any difficulties in scoring or administration? Were there difficulties with ambiguous or two part questions? How could these be overcome?

2. Was the distribution of scores normal? If not, why not?

3. If information about party affiliation was gathered did this information validate the scale, i.e., did socialists have a more favourable attitude towards socialism?

4. Compare the Thurstone scale used in this exercise with the other main types of attitude scale.

References

EYSENCK, H. J., *Psychology of Politics* (Methuen, London 1954).

Exercise 20. Sampling Public Opinion

Introduction

In many branches of science it has been shown that single observations are likely to be misleading. Physical scientists try to take as large a number of observations as possible so that chance errors of observation can be cancelled out by taking an average. This is even more necessary in social science where the variation between examples of a phenomenon tends to be greater. There is the further problem that we may select for observation (and averaging) cases which are misleading because they happen to be unusual. It is important to ensure that we choose a group or 'sample' of cases to observe, which has a good chance of containing the right proportion of all the major types of case likely (so far as we know) to occur in the large group or 'population' that we are trying to study. A number of different methods have been developed to help us to select for observation from the total population a relatively small number of cases which are really representative of the whole population. These sampling methods are discussed in this exercise in which we study the political opinions of a population.

Conclusions about a large population which are based on observations made on small samples are bound to be imperfect—however carefully we have selected samples, and statisticians have devoted much attention to the study of just how imperfect, for example, an average drawn from a sample is likely to be. Let us assume, for example, that we wish to find the average I.Q. of all the patients in a large hospital with 2,000 patients, but that we have time to test only 50 of them. And let us suppose that after testing this small sample of 50 we find what appears to be an average I.Q. of 82. What the statisticians' methods enable us to do is to state with a certain level of confidence that the true average for the whole hospital of 2,000 'lies somewhere between 80 and 84'. If we have been very lucky it might even be 82. The statisticians will tell us that we can state even more confidently that the correct answer lies between 78 and 86. But unless we are prepared to measure all of the 2000 patients in the hospital we can never say with 100 per cent confidence that we have found the real average. Since we have measured only 50 cases we shall have to be satisfied with (for example) a 95 per cent level of confidence in our average. We shall have 95 chances out of 100 of being right.

Objective

To compare estimates of *political persuasion* of the people of Townward obtained by *i.* quota, *ii.* random, *iii.* stratified sampling, and *iv.* systematic sampling methods.

Materials

The People of Townward (Item 20.1).
Table of Random Numbers (Item 20.2).

Method

In each case a final sample of 50 should be aimed at.

1. QUOTA SAMPLING

As shown in Item 20.1, the people of Townward vary in a great number of ways.

i. Decide which four of the variables listed are likely to be most relevant to the fair assessment of the whole town's political colouring. Let these be A, B, C, and D.

ii. Decide the proportions in which A, B, C and D must occur in your final sample (e.g., if A is 'sex' then you may decide to use 50 per cent M and 50 per cent F).

iii. Construct a blank table to accommodate your decisions in *ii* above which indicate the numbers to be collected.

iv. Search unsystematically through the pages of Item 20.1, until you have collected 50 individuals with satisfactory values of A, B, C and D. As you locate each satisfactory individual enter his political affiliation in the table.

2. RANDOM SAMPLING

i. Consult Item 20.2 (Table of Random Numbers) and beginning at any point in the table, select the first 50 random numbers below 501. If numbers larger than 500 appear in the random number table they should be passed over.

ii. Consult Item 20.1 (The People of Townward), and enter in a specially constructed table the political affiliation of the 50 selected people.

iii. Total for each political party.

3. STRATIFIED SAMPLING

i. Consider the ways in which the whole population varies and decide on the aspects which will be most relevant to a fair sampling for political opinion. You will then be in a position to define each of your 'strata' in terms of 1 (or more) of the known variables.

ii. Mark with a distinctive sign on Item 20.1 all members of your Stratum 1. Use a different mark for all members of Stratum 2.

iii. Number sequentially from 1 (to n) in the list all the Stratum 1 members then from 1 (to n₂) all the Stratum 2 members.

iv. Using the table of random numbers select a random sample from your Stratum 1. Then select a random sample from Stratum 2 and so on. You must decide whether the proportion of the whole stratum (sampling fraction) you take from Stratum 1 is the same as that from Stratum 2. This depends entirely on your beliefs about the structure of the total population of Townward. It may be that you will decide to have more of Stratum 2 represented than Stratum 1.

v. Totals should then be computed for each of the political persuasions.

4. SYSTEMATIC SAMPLING

i. Decide how large your final sample is to be.

ii. On the basis of *i*, choose a value for n such that taking every nth member of the list will yield the desirable sample size.

iii. Starting at a point in the Townward list decided for you by the random number table, record the political affiliation of every nth person.

iv. Compute a total for each of the parties.

v. Using whichever type of sample you consider to be most appropriate, investigate some of the interrelationships between the nine variables listed for each individual in item 20.1, e.g.,

a. Is car ownership related to political opinion?
b. What is the breakdown of party support by age and sex?
c. How does education affect voting behaviour?

Treatment of Results

1. Compare percentages of each party obtained by the four different methods. Investigate and describe any large discrepancies.

2. Given the information that 5 years ago the percentage affiliations of each party were as follows:

Lib. 17 per cent; Cons. 32 per cent; Lab. 45 per cent;

compute from your *random sample data* whether the change your figures suggest is greater than that to be expected by chance errors in the sampling. Has there been a real shift of party allegiance or is the apparent difference suggested by your figures due to the difference between your sample and the whole electorate? Use χ^2.

If χ^2 is large, then the recent sampling observations come from a different total population, i.e., there *has* been a change.

Discussion

1. Which is the least and which the most laborious sampling method for material of this kind?

2. What may be the cause of the difference between the various estimates?

3. What are the dangers inherent in each method?

4. Which method do you think gave the best estimates?

ITEM 20.1: THE POPULATION OF TOWNWARD

The population given below is the whole of the voting population of one small ward. Each individual is numbered and information on nine characteristics is given.

KEY

Column 1   Number

Column 2   Car ownership   Y = yes
    N = no

Column 3   Age groups   1 = 21 years
2 = 21–30 years
3 = 31–45 years
4 = 46–65 years
5 = > 65 years

Column 4   Sex   M = male
F = female

Column 5   Marital status   M = married
N = unmarried

Column 6   Occupational group   1 = professional and higher managerial
2 = managerial and business (incldg. self-employed)
3 = skilled manual
4 = semi-skilled manual
5 = unskilled manual
HW = housewife
Rtd = retired

Column 7	Education	S = secondary
		G = grammar
		H = higher
Column 8	Income	1 = < £10 per week
		2 = £10–£15 ,,
		3 = £16–£20 ,,
		4 = £21–£30 ,,
		5 = > £30 ,,
Column 9	Voting	Lab. = Labour
		Lib. = Liberal
		Cons. = Conservative
		D.K. = Don't know
		Other = All others
Column 10	Religion	E = Church of England
		R = Roman Catholic
		N = Non-conformist
		Other = All other (including none)

1	2	3	4	5	6	7	8	9	10	
No.	Car	Age	Sex	Mar. Stat.	Occ.	Educ.	Inc.	Voting	Religion	Notes
1	N	5	F	M	HW	S	—	Lib.	N	
2	Y	2	F	M	2	H	3	Lab.	R	
3	Y	2	F	M	2	H	4	Lib.	Other	
4	Y	2	M	M	2	S	4	Con.	E	
5	Y	3	F	M	1	H	4	Con.	E	
6	Y	4	M	M	4	S	2	D.K.	N	
7	N	4	M	M	3	S	2	Lab.	E	
8	Y	4	F	M	HW	G	—	D.K.	Other	
9	N	3	M	M	3	S	2	Other	E	
10	N	3	F	M	3	S	2	D.K.	E	
11	N	3	M	M	4	S	2	Lab.	E	
12	Y	2	M	M	3	G	4	Lab.	Other	
13	Y	3	F	M	3	S	2	Lab.	E	
14	N	4	M	M	5	S	2	Lab.	N	
15	Y	4	F	M	2	G	4	D.K.	E	
16	Y	2	F	M	1	G	5	Con.	E	
17	Y	3	M	M	3	S	3	Lab.	N	
18	Y	3	F	M	2	S	4	Con.	E	
19	Y	2	M	M	3	S	3	Con.	R	
20	Y	3	M	M	3	S	3	Lab.	E	

1	2	3	4	5	6	7	8	9	10	
No.	Car	Age	Sex	Mar. Stat.	Occ.	Educ.	Inc.	Voting	Religion	Notes
21	Y	3	F	M	3	S	2	Lab.	E	
22	Y	3	M	M	3	S	3	Con.	R	
23	N	2	F	M	5	S	2	Lab.	E	
24	Y	4	F	M	3	S	2	Lab.	E	
25	N	4	M	N	5	S	2	Lab.	E	
26	N	2	F	M	3	G	2	Lab.	N	
27	N	2	F	M	4	S	2	Lab.	E	
28	Y	5	F	N	3	G	3	D.K.	N	
29	N	5	F	N	HW	S	—	Lab.	E	
30	Y	2	F	M	3	G	3	Con.	Other	
31	Y	3	M	M	3	S	3	Lab.	E	
32	Y	3	M	M	3	H	2	Lab.	N	
33	Y	2	F	M	1	G	4	Con.	N	
34	N	3	M	M	2	G	2	Lab.	E	
35	N	3	M	N	3	S	3	Lab.	R	
36	Y	3	F	M	1	G	4	D.K.	N	
37	Y	5	F	M	Rtd	S	2	Con.	E	
38	Y	3	M	M	3	G	3	D.K.	N	
39	N	2	F	M	3	S	2	Lab.	N	
40	Y	3	M	M	3	S	2	Con.	E	
41	Y	3	M	M	2	G	5	D.K.	E	
42	Y	3	M	M	3	S	2	Lab.	E	
43	N	3	M	M	4	S	3	Lab.	E	
44	Y	3	M	M	3	S	2	Lab.	N	
45	Y	2	M	M	3	G	4	Con.	E	
46	N	2	M	M	2	H	3	Lab.	N	
47	N	3	M	M	4	S	1	Lab.	E	
48	N	5	F	N	HW	S	—	Lab.	E	
49	Y	3	M	M	3	S	2	Lib.	Other	
50	Y	5	F	N	HW	S	—·	Lab.	E	
51	Y	2	M	M	2	S	4	Con.	E	
52	Y	3	F	M	1	G	4	D.K.	N	
53	Y	3	F	M	3	S	2	Lab.	E	
54	N	5	F	N	HW	S	—	Lab.	N	
55	Y	3	M	N	3	S	2	Lib.	Other	
56	N	3	M	M	4	S	1	Lab.	E	
57	N	2	F	M	3	G	2	Lab.	N	
58	Y	3	M	M	3	S	3	Lab.	E	
59	Y	2	M	M	3	G	4	Con.	E	
60	Y	2	F	M	2	H	3	Lab.	R	
61	Y	3	M	M	3	H	2	Lab.	N	
62	N	4	M	N	5	S	2	Lab.	E	

1	2	3	4	5	6	7	8	9	10	
No.	Car	Age	Sex	Mar. Stat.	Occ.	Educ.	Inc.	Voting	Religion	Notes
63	N	3	F	M	3	S	2	D.K.	E	
64	Y	2	F	M	3	G	3	Con.	Other	
65	Y	5	F	N	3	G	3	D.K.	N	
66	Y	3	M	M	3	G	3	D.K.	N	
67	N	3	M	M	4	S	3	Lab.	E	
68	N	3	M	N	3	S	3	Lab.	R	
69	Y	3	F	M	2	S	4	Con.	E	
70	N	4	M	M	3	S	2	Lab.	E	
71	Y	5	F	M	Rtd	S	2	Con.	E	
72	Y	2	M	M	3	S	3	Con.	R	
73	Y	2	F	M	1	G	5	Con.	E	
74	N	2	F	M	3	S	2	Lab.	N	
75	Y	3	F	M	1	H	4	Con.	E	
76	Y	3	M	M	3	S	3	Lab.	E	
77	N	3	M	M	2	G	2	Lab.	E	
78	Y	3	M	M	2	G	5	D.K.	E	
79	N	2	F	M	4	S	2	Lab.	E	
80	N	4	M	M	5	S	2	Lab.	N	
81	Y	2	M	M	3	G	4	Lab.	Other	
82	Y	3	F	M	3	S	2	Lab.	E	
83	Y	4	F	M	3	S	2	Lab.	E	
84	Y	2	F	M	2	H	4	Lib.	Other	
85	Y	3	M	M	3	S	3	Con.	R	
86	N	3	M	M	4	S	2	Lab.	E	
87	Y	4	M	M	4	S	2	D.K.	N	
88	Y	4	F	M	2	G	4	D.K.	E	
89	Y	4	F	M	HW	G	—	D.K.	Other	
90	Y	3	M	M	3	S	2	Lab.	N	
91	Y	3	M	M	3	S	2	Con.	E	
92	N	2	F	M	5	S	2	Lab.	E	
93	Y	3	M	M	3	S	2	Lab.	E	
94	N	2	M	M	2	H	3	Lab.	N	
95	N	3	M	M	3	S	2	Other	E	
96	Y	2	F	M	1	G	4	Con.	N	
97	Y	5	F	N	HW	S	—	Lab.	E	
98	N	5	F	N	HW	S	—	Lab.	E	
99	Y	3	M	M	3	S	3	Lab.	N	
100	N	5	F	N	HW	S	—	Lab.	E	
101	Y	2	M	M	3	S	3	Con.	R	
102	N	2	F	M	3	G	2	Lab.	N	
103	N	4	M	N	5	S	2	Lab.	E	
104	Y	5	F	N	3	G	3	D.K.	N	

1	2	3	4	5	6	7	8	9	10	
No.	Car	Age	Sex	Mar. Stat.	Occ.	Educ.	Inc.	Voting	Religion	Notes
105	N	3	M	M	2	G	2	Lab.	E	
106	Y	3	M	M	3	H	2	Lab.	N	
107	Y	3	M	M	3	S	3	Lab.	E	
108	Y	3	F	M	3	S	2	Lab.	E	
109	N	2	F	M	4	S	2	Lab.	E	
110	N	3	M	N	3	S	3	Lab.	R	
111	Y	3	F	M	2	S	4	Con.	E	
112	Y	3	M	M	3	S	3	Lab.	E	
113	Y	3	M	M	3	G	3	D.K.	N	
114	N	4	M	M	5	S	2	Lab.	N	
115	Y	2	F	M	2	H	3	Lab.	R	
116	N	4	M	M	3	S	2	Lab.	E	
117	Y	4	F	M	2	G	4	D.K.	E	
118	Y	2	F	M	1	G	5	Con.	E	
119	Y	3	F	M	1	H	4	Con.	E	
120	Y	3	F	M	3	S	2	Lab.	E	
121	Y	3	M	M	3	S	3	Con.	R	
122	N	3	F	M	3	S	2	D.K.	E	
123	Y	4	F	M	3	S	2	Lab.	E	
124	N	5	F	N	HW	S	—	Lab.	E	
125	Y	2	F	M	3	G	3	Con.	Other	
126	Y	5	F	M	Rtd	S	2	Con.	E	
127	N	3	M	M	4	S	3	Lab.	E	
128	N	2	F	M	5	S	2	Lab.	E	
129	Y	3	M	M	3	S	2	Lab.	N	
130	Y	3	M	M	3	S	2	Lab.	E	
131	N	5	F	N	HW	S	—	Lab.	E	
132	Y	2	M	M	3	G	4	Lab.	Other	
133	N	2	M	M	2	H	3	Lab.	N	
134	N	3	M	M	3	S	2	Other	E	
135	Y	3	F	M	1	G	4	D.K.	N	
136	N	2	F	M	3	S	2	Lab.	N	
137	Y	4	F	M	HW	G	—	D.K.	Other	
138	N	3	M	M	4	S	2	Lab.	E	
139	Y	3	M	M	3	S	3	Lab.	N	
140	Y	3	M	M	3	S	2	Lib.	Other	
141	Y	5	F	N	HW	S	—	Lab.	E	
142	Y	2	F	M	2	H	4	Lib.	Other	
143	N	3	M	M	4	S	1	Lab.	E	
144	Y	3	M	M	3	S	2	Con.	E	
145	Y	2	F	M	1	G	4	Con.	N	
146	N	5	F	N	HW	S	—	Lab.	N	

1	2	3	4	5	6	7	8	9	10	
No.	Car	Age	Sex	Mar. Stat.	Occ.	Educ.	Inc.	Voting	Religion	Notes
147	Y	2	M	M	2	S	4	Con.	E	
148	Y	4	M	M	4	S	2	D.K.	N	
149	Y	2	M	M	3	G	4	Con.	E	
150	Y	3	M	M	2	G	5	D.K.	E	
151	N	3	F	M	3	S	2	Lab.	E	
152	Y	3	M	M	3	S	2	D.K.	E	
153	N	5	F	M	HW	S	—	Lab.	E	
154	N	4	F	M	HW	S	—	D.K.	E	
155	Y	4	F	M	4	S	2	Con.	E	
156	N	2	M	N	5	S	2	Lab.	N	
157	Y	2	F	M	HW	G	—	Con.	R	
158	N	5	F	N	HW	S	—	Lab.	N	
159	N	2	M	N	2	G	3	D.K.	Other	
160	N	5	M	N	Rtd	S	2	D.K.	E	
161	N	4	M	M	5	S	2	Lab.	R	
162	N	3	F	M	3	S	2	Lab.	E	
163	Y	3	M	M	3	S	2	Con.	E	
164	N	4	F	N	2	G	4	Con.	E	
165	N	3	F	M	3	S	1	Lab.	E	
166	Y	4	F	M	2	G	5	Con.	N	
167	N	3	M	M	4	S	2	Lab.	E	
168	N	4	F	M	4	S	2	Con.	E	
169	N	4	F	M	4	S	2	Con.	E	
170	Y	5	M	M	3	S	2	Con.	E	
171	N	3	F	M	5	S	1	Lab.	E	
172	N	3	F	M	3	S	2	Lab.	E	
173	N	5	F	M	HW	S	—	Con.	E	
174	N	2	M	N	4	S	2	Other	R	
175	N	3	F	M	3	S	2	Lab.	N	
176	Y	3	M	M	3	S	2	Lab.	E	
177	Y	5	M	M	Rtd	G	5	Con.	E	
178	N	3	M	M	5	S	2	Con.	E	
179	Y	4	F	M	HW	G	—	D.K.	Other	
180	N	3	M	M	4	S	2	Lab.	E	
181	N	3	F	M	3	S	2	Lab.	N	
182	N	3	M	M	3	S	2	Other	E	
183	Y	5	M	M	1	H	4	Lib.	R	
184	N	5	M	N	Rtd	S	1	Lib.	Other	
185	Y	2	M	M	2	G	3	Lab.	N	
186	N	3	F	M	4	S	2	Lab.	E	
187	Y	3	M	M	1	H	5	Lib.	Other	
188	Y	2	M	N	1	H	4	Lab.	E	

1	2	3	4	5	6	7	8	9	10	
No.	*Car*	*Age*	*Sex*	*Mar. Stat.*	*Occ.*	*Educ.*	*Inc.*	*Voting*	*Religion*	*Notes*
189	N	4	F	M	HW	S	—	D.K.	E	
190	N	3	F	M	4	S	2	Lab.	E	
191	Y	5	M	M	3	S	3	Other	Other	
192	N	4	M	M	4	S	3	Lab.	R	
193	N	5	F	N	HW	S	—	Lab.	N	
194	Y	5	F	M	HW	S	—	D.K.	E	
195	Y	2	M	N	2	H	3	Other	Other	
196	N	4	M	M	3	S	2	Lab.	E	
197	Y	4	M	M	4	S	3	Con.	R	
198	N	2	M	N	3	G	3	Con.	N	
199	N	2	M	M	5	S	2	Lab.	Other	
200	Y	4	F	M	3	S	4	D.K.	E	
201	N	2	M	N	4	S	2	Other	R	
202	N	3	M	M	4	S	2	Lab.	E	
203	Y	2	M	M	2	G	3	Lab.	N	
204	N	3	M	M	3	S	2	Other	E	
205	N	2	M	N	2	G	3	D.K.	Other	
206	N	5	M	N	Rtd	S	2	D.K.	E	
207	Y	2	M	N	1	H	4	Lab.	E	
208	N	4	F	N	2	G	4	Con.	E	
209	Y	5	F	M	HW	S	—	D.K.	E	
210	N	4	M	M	4	S	3	Lab.	R	
211	Y	4	F	M	HW	G	—	D.K.	Other	
212	N	2	M	N	5	S	2	Lab.	N	
213	N	3	F	M	3	S	2	Lab.	E	
214	N	4	F	M	HW	S	—	D.K.	E	
215	Y	3	M	M	3	S	2	Con.	E	
216	Y	5	M	M	3	S	2	Con.	E	
217	N	5	F	N	HW	S	—	Lab.	N	
218	N	5	F	N	HW	S	—	Lab.	N	
219	Y	3	M	M	3	S	2	Lab.	E	
220	Y	3	M	M	3	S	2	D.K.	E	
221	N	5	F	M	HW	S	—	Lab.	E	
222	N	3	F	M	5	S	1	Lab.	E	
223	Y	5	M	M	3	S	3	Other	Other	
224	N	2	M	M	5	S	2	Lab.	Other	
225	Y	2	M	N	2	H	3	Other	Other	
226	Y	5	M	M	1	H	4	Lib.	R	
227	N	3	M	M	5	S	2	Con.	E	
228	N	3	F	M	3	S	1	Lab.	E	
229	Y	5	M	M	Rtd	S	5	Con.	E	
230	Y	3	M	M	4	S	2	Lab.	E	

1	2	3	4	5	6	7	8	9	10	
No.	*Car*	*Age*	*Sex*	*Mar. Stat.*	*Occ.*	*Educ.*	*Inc.*	*Voting*	*Religion*	*Notes*
231	N	3	F	M	3	S	2	Lab.	E	
232	N	4	F	M	4	S	2	Con.	E	
233	Y	3	M	M	1	S	5	Lib.	Other	
234	N	3	F	M	3	S	2	Lab.	N	
235	Y	4	N	M	4	S	3	Con.	R	
236	N	5	F	M	HW	S	—	Con.	E	
237	N	2	M	N	3	G	3	Con.	N	
238	N	4	M	M	3	S	2	Lab.	E	
239	Y	2	F	M	HW	G	—	Con.	R	
240	N	3	M	M	4	S	2	Lab.	E	
241	Y	4	F	M	2	G	5	Con.	N	
242	N	4	F	M	HW	S	—	D.K.	E	
243	Y	4	F	M	3	S	4	D.K.	E	
244	N	3	F	M	3	S	2	Lab.	E	
245	N	3	F	M	3	S	2	Lab.	N	
246	N	4	M	M	5	S	2	Lab.	R	
247	N	3	F	M	4	S	2	Lab.	E	
248	N	4	F	M	4	S	2	Con.	E	
249	N	5	M	N	Rtd	S	1	Lib.	Other	
250	Y	4	F	M	4	S	2	Con.	E	
251	N	3	F	M	3	S	2	Lab.	N	
252	N	5	F	N	HW	S	—	Lab.	N	
253	N	3	F	M	4	S	2	Lab.	E	
254	N	5	M	N	Rtd	S	1	Lib.	Other	
255	N	3	F	M	3	S	2	Lab.	E	
256	N	3	M	M	5	S	2	Con.	E	
257	Y	5	M	M	1	H	4	Lib.	R	
258	N	4	F	M	HW	S	—	D.K.	E	
259	N	5	F	N	HW	S	—	Lab.	N	
260	Y	3	M	M	3	S	2	Con.	E	
261	N	4	M	M	5	S	2	Lab.	R	
262	Y	4	F	M	HW	G	—	D.K.	Other	
263	N	4	F	M	4	S	2	Con.	E	
264	N	3	M	M	3	S	2	Other	E	
265	N	5	F	M	HW	S	—	Con.	E	
266	Y	5	M	M	3	S	3	Other	Other	
267	Y	4	F	M	3	S	4	D.K.	E	
268	Y	2	M	N	1	H	4	Lab.	E	
269	N	4	M	M	3	S	2	Lab.	E	
270	N	3	M	M	4	S	2	Lab.	E	
271	N	5	F	M	HW	S	—	Lab.	E	
272	Y	5	F	M	HW	S	—	D.K.	E	

1	2	3	4	5	6	7	8	9	10	
No.	Car	Age	Sex	Mar. Stat.	Occ.	Educ.	Inc.	Voting	Religion	Notes
273	N	2	M	N	3	G	3	Con.	N	
274	N	3	M	M	4	S	2	Lab.	E	
275	Y	3	M	M	3	S	2	D.K.	E	
276	Y	3	M	M	3	S	2	Lab.	E	
277	N	3	F	M	3	S	1	Lab.	E	
278	N	2	M	N	5	S	2	Lab.	N	
279	N	4	F	N	2	G	4	Con.	E	
280	N	3	F	M	3	S	2	Lab.	E	
281	Y	5	M	M	Rtd	G	5	Con.	E	
282	Y	2	F	M	HW	G	—	Con.	R	
283	N	5	M	N	Rtd	S	2	D.K.	E	
284	N	3	F	M	4	S	2	Lab.	E	
285	Y	2	M	M	2	G	3	Lab.	N	
286	Y	3	M	M	1	H	5	Lib.	Other	
287	Y	5	M	M	3	S	2	Con.	E	
288	N	3	F	M	3	S	2	Lab.	E	
289	N	3	F	M	3	S	2	Lab.	N	
290	N	4	F	M	HW	S	—	D.K.	E	
291	N	2	M	M	5	S	2	Lab.	Other	
292	N	4	F	M	4	S	2	Con.	E	
293	N	4	M	M	4	S	3	Lab.	R	
294	Y	4	F	M	4	S	2	Con.	E	
295	Y	2	M	N	2	H	3	Other	Other	
296	Y	4	F	M	2	G	5	Con.	N	
297	N	3	F	M	5	S	1	Lab.	E	
298	N	2	M	N	4	S	2	Other	R	
299	Y	4	M	M	4	S	3	Con.	R	
300	N	2	M	N	2	G	3	D.K.	Other	
301	Y	4	F	M	4	S	2	Con.	E	
302	Y	2	M	M	2	G	3	Lab.	N	
303	N	3	F	M	5	S	1	Lab.	E	
304	N	2	M	N	2	G	3	D.K.	Other	
305	Y	4	F	M	2	G	5	Con.	N	
306	N	4	M	M	3	S	2	Lab.	E	
307	N	5	M	N	Rtd	S	2	D.K.	E	
308	Y	5	M	M	Rtd	G	5	Con.	E	
309	N	3	F	M	3	S	2	Lab.	E	
310	N	3	M	M	5	S	2	Con.	E	
311	N	4	F	M	HW	S	—	D.K.	E	
312	N	4	F	M	4	S	2	Con.	E	
313	N	5	M	N	Rtd	S	1	Lib.	Other	
314	N	3	F	M	3	S	1	Lab.	E	

1	2	3	4	5	6	7	8	9	10	
No.	Car	Age	Sex	Mar. Stat.	Occ.	Educ.	Inc.	Voting	Religion	Notes
315	N	2	M	M	5	S	2	Lab.	Other	
316	N	4	M	M	5	S	2	Lab.	R	
317	N	3	F	M	4	S	2	Lab.	E	
318	Y	2	F	M	HW	G	—	Con.	R	
319	N	2	M	N	5	S	2	Lab.	N	
320	N	5	F	N	HW	S	—	Lab.	N	
321	N	5	F	M	HW	S	—	Lab.	E	
322	Y	5	M	M	3	S	2	Con.	E	
323	Y	5	M	M	3	S	3	Other	Other	
324	Y	5	M	M	1	H	4	Lib.	R	
325	N	2	M	N	4	S	2	Other	R	
326	N	4	F	N	2	G	4	Con.	E	
327	N	4	M	M	4	S	3	Lab.	R	
328	N	3	F	M	3	S	2	Lab.	E	
329	N	5	F	N	HW	S	—	Lab.	N	
330	Y	2	M	N	2	H	3	Other	Other	
331	N	3	F	M	4	S	2	Lab.	E	
332	Y	3	M	M	3	S	2	Lab.	E	
333	N	3	F	M	3	S	2	Lab.	N	
334	Y	4	M	M	4	S	3	Con.	R	
335	N	3	M	M	3	S	2	Other	E	
336	Y	3	M	M	3	S	2	D.K.	E	
337	Y	N	F	M	HW	G	—	D.K.	Other	
338	Y	5	F	M	HW	S	—	D.K.	E	
339	Y	4	F	M	3	S	4	D.K.	E	
340	N	4	F	M	HW	S	—	D.K.	E	
341	N	4	F	M	4	S	2	Con.	E	
342	Y	3	M	M	1	H	5	Lib.	Other	
343	N	5	F	M	HW	S	—	Con.	E	
344	Y	3	M	M	3	S	2	Con.	E	
345	Y	2	M	N	1	H	4	Lab.	E	
346	N	3	M	M	4	S	2	Lab.	E	
347	N	3	M	M	4	S	2	Lab.	E	
348	N	2	M	N	3	G	3	Con.	N	
349	N	3	F	M	3	S	2	Lab.	E	
350	N	3	F	M	3	S	2	Lab.	N	
351	Y	2	F	M	1	G	4	Con.	N	
352	Y	3	M	M	3	G	3	D.K.	N	
353	Y	2	F	N	2	H	4	Lib.	Other	
354	N	2	F	M	4	S	2	Lab.	E	
355	N	4	M	M	3	S	2	Lab.	E	
356	Y	3	M	M	3	S	3	Con.	R	

1	2	3	4	5	6	7	8	9	10	
No.	Car	Age	Sex	Mar. Stat.	Occ.	Educ.	Inc.	Voting	Religion	Notes
357	Y	4	M	M	4	S	2	D.K.	N	
358	N	5	F	N	HW	S	—	Lab.	E	
359	N	5	F	N	HW	S	—	Lab.	E	
360	N	3	M	M	2	G	2	Lab.	E	
361	Y	3	M	M	3	S	3	Lab.	E	
362	Y	3	M	M	3	S	3	Lab.	N	
363	Y	4	M	M	4	S	3	Con.	R	
364	N	2	F	M	5	S	2	Lab.	E	
365	Y	3	F	M	1	H	4	Con.	E	
366	Y	2	M	N	2	H	3	Other	Other	
367	Y	2	M	M	2	S	4	Con.	E	
368	Y	5	M	M	Rtd	G	5	Con.	E	
369	N	4	M	N	5	S	2	Lab.	E	
370	N	3	F	M	3	S	1	Lab.	E	
371	Y	3	F	M	1	G	4	D.K.	N	
372	Y	2	M	M	3	S	3	Con.	R	
373	Y	3	M	M	3	S	2	Lib.	Other	
374	N	3	M	M	4	S	2	Lab.	E	
375	N	3	F	M	4	S	2	Lab.	E	
376	Y	3	M	M	4	S	3	Lab.	E	
377	N	5	F	M	HW	S	—	Lab.	E	
378	N	5	F	N	HW	S	—	Lab.	N	
379	Y	2	M	N	1	H	4	Lab.	E	
380	N	3	M	N	3	S	3	Lab.	R	
381	Y	2	F	M	2	H	3	Lab.	R	
382	N	5	M	N	Rtd	S	2	D.K.	E	
383	Y	5	F	M	Rtd	S	2	Con.	E	
384	N	4	M	M	3	S	2	Lab.	E	
385	Y	2	M	M	3	G	4	Lab.	Other	
386	N	3	M	M	4	S	1	Lab.	E	
387	N	3	F	M	3	S	2	Lab.	E	
388	N	2	F	M	3	G	2	Lab.	N	
389	Y	4	F	M	4	S	2	Con.	E	
390	N	2	F	M	3	S	2	Lab.	N	
391	Y	3	F	M	3	S	2	Lab.	E	
392	N	3	M	M	4	S	3	Lab.	E	
393	Y	3	M	M	3	H	2	Lab.	N	
394	Y	3	F	M	3	S	2	D.K.	E	
395	N	4	M	M	5	S	2	Lab.	N	
396	Y	2	F	M	3	G	3	Con.	Other	
397	Y	3	M	M	2	G	5	D.K.	E	
398	Y	4	F	M	3	S	2	Lab.	E	

1	2	3	4	5	6	7	8	9	10	
No.	Car	Age	Sex	Mar. Stat.	Occ.	Educ.	Inc.	Voting	Religion	Notes
399	Y	3	F	M	3	S	2	Lab.	E	
400	Y	2	M	M	3	G	4	Con.	E	
401	Y	5	F	M	Rtd	S	2	Con.	E	
402	Y	3	F	M	1	G	4	D.K.	N	
403	N	4	M	N	5	S	2	Lab.	E	
404	N	4	M	M	3	S	2	Lab.	E	
405	N	3	F	M	3	S	1	Lab.	E	
406	Y	3	M	M	3	S	2	Lib.	Other	
407	N	2	F	M	4	S	2	Lab.	E	
408	Y	4	F	M	4	S	2	Con.	E	
409	Y	3	M	M	4	S	3	Lab.	E	
410	Y	3	F	M	3	S	2	D.K.	E	
411	N	3	M	M	4	S	1	Lab.	E	
412	Y	4	F	M	3	S	2	Lab.	E	
413	N	2	F	M	3	S	2	Lab.	N	
414	Y	3	F	M	1	H	4	Con.	E	
415	N	2	F	M	3	G	2	Lab.	N	
416	N	3	M	M	2	G	2	Lab.	E	
417	Y	2	M	M	1	H	4	Lab.	E	
418	Y	3	F	M	3	S	2	Lab.	E	
419	Y	2	M	M	3	S	3	Con.	R	
420	Y	2	F	M	1	G	4	Con.	N	
421	Y	5	M	M	Rtd	G	5	Con.	E	
422	Y	3	M	M	2	G	5	D.K.	E	
423	N	5	F	N	HW	S	—	Lab.	N	
424	Y	2	M	M	3	G	4	Con.	E	
425	N	5	F	M	HW	S	—	Lab.	E	
426	N	3	M	N	3	S	3	Lab.	R	
427	N	3	F	M	3	S	2	Lab.	E	
428	N	5	F	N	HW	S	—	Lab.	E	
429	N	3	F	M	4	S	2	Lab.	E	
430	N	3	M	M	4	S	3	Lab.	E	
431	Y	3	M	M	3	G	3	D.K.	N	
432	Y	2	F	M	3	G	3	Con.	Other	
433	N	4	M	M	5	S	2	Lab.	N	
434	N	4	M	M	3	S	2	Lab.	E	
435	Y	2	F	M	HW	S	3	Lab.	R	
436	Y	2	M	N	2	H	3	Other	Other	
437	N	5	F	N	HW	S	—	Lab.	E	
438	Y	3	N	M	3	S	3	Con.	R	
439	Y	4	N	M	4	S	4	D.K.	N	
440	N	5	M	N	Rtd	S	2	D.K.	E	

1	2	3	4	5	6	7	8	9	10	
No.	Car	Age	Sex	Mar. Stat.	Occ.	Educ.	Inc.	Voting	Religion	Notes
441	Y	3	M	M	3	H	2	Lab.	N	
442	Y	2	F	M	2	H	4	Lib.	Other	
443	N	2	F	M	5	S	2	Lab.	E	
444	Y	4	M	M	4	S	3	Con.	R	
445	Y	3	M	M	3	S	3	Lab.	N	
446	N	3	M	M	4	S	2	Lab.	E	
447	Y	3	F	M	3	S	2	Lab.	E	
448	Y	2	M	M	3	G	4	Lab.	Other	
449	Y	3	M	M	3	S	3	Lab.	E	
450	Y	2	M	M	2	S	4	Con.	E	
451	N	4	M	M	3	S	2	Lab.	E	
452	Y	3	M	M	3	S	2	Lib.	Other	
453	Y	3	F	M	3	S	2	Lab.	E	
454	N	3	M	M	4	S	3	Lab.	E	
455	Y	2	F	M	1	G	4	Con.	N	
456	N	4	M	M	5	S	2	Lab.	N	
457	Y	2	M	M	3	G	4	Lab.	Other	
458	N	5	F	N	HW	S	—	Lab.	E	
459	Y	3	M	M	2	G	5	D.K.	E	
460	N	5	F	N	HW	S	—	Lab.	E	
461	N	2	F	M	5	S	2	Lab.	E	
462	Y	3	F	M	3	S	2	Lab.	E	
463	Y	3	F	M	1	G	4	D.K.	N	
464	N	3	M	M	4	S	2	Lab.	E	
465	Y	2	M	M	3	G	4	Con.	E	
466	Y	3	F	M	1	H	4	Con.	E	
467	N	2	F	M	3	S	2	Lab.	N	
468	Y	3	M	M	3	S	3	Lab.	N	
469	Y	5	M	M	Rtd	G	5	Con.	E	
470	Y	3	M	M	3	S	3	Lab.	E	
471	N	4	M	M	3	S	2	Lab.	E	
472	N	2	F	M	3	G	2	Lab.	N	
473	N	3	F	M	4	S	2	Lab.	E	
474	Y	3	M	M	3	S	3	Con.	R	
475	Y	2	F	M	2	H	4	Lib.	Other	
476	Y	5	F	M	Rtd	S	2	Con.	E	
477	Y	2	M	N	2	H	3	Other	Other	
478	Y	3	M	M	3	G	3	D.K.	N	
479	N	3	F	M	3	S	1	Lab.	E	
480	Y	2	M	M	2	S	4	Con.	E	
481	Y	2	F	M	3	G	3	Con.	Other	
482	N	4	M	N	5	S	2	Lab.	E	

1	2	3	4	5	6	7	8	9	10	
No.	Car	Age	Sex	Mar. Stat.	Occ.	Educ.	Inc.	Voting	Religion	Notes
483	Y	4	F	M	3	S	2	Lab.	E	
484	Y	3	M	M	3	H	2	Lab.	N	
485	Y	4	M	M	4	S	2	D.K.	N	
486	Y	2	M	N	1	H	4	Lab.	E	
487	Y	3	M	M	4	S	3	Lab.	E	
488	Y	4	M	M	4	S	3	Con.	R	
489	Y	2	F	M	2	H	3	Lab.	R	
490	N	3	M	N	3	S	3	Lab.	R	
491	N	2	F	M	4	S	2	Lab.	E	
492	N	5	M	N	Rtd	S	2	D.K.	E	
493	N	3	M	M	4	S	1	Lab.	E	
494	N	3	F	M	3	S	2	Lab.	E	
495	N	3	M	M	2	G	2	Lab.	E	
496	Y	2	M	M	3	S	3	Con.	R	
497	Y	4	F	M	4	S	2	Con.	E	
498	Y	3	M	M	4	S	3	Lab.	E	
499	N	5	F	M	HW	S	—	Lab.	E	
500	N	5	F	N	HW	S	—	Lab.	N	

ITEM 20.2: TABLE OF RANDOM NUMBERS *(See Glossary.)*

23	47	43	73	86	36	96	47	36	61	46	98	63	71	62
97	74	24	67	62	42	81	14	57	20	42	53	32	37	32
26	76	62	27	66	56	50	26	71	07	32	90	79	78	53
12	56	88	99	26	96	96	68	27	14	03	03	72	93	15
55	59	56	35	64	38	54	82	26	22	31	62	43	09	90
16	12	77	94	39	49	54	43	54	82	17	37	93	23	78
84	42	17	53	31	57	24	55	06	88	77	04	74	47	67
63	11	53	78	59	16	95	55	67	19	98	10	50	71	75
33	21	12	34	29	78	64	56	07	82	52	42	07	44	38
57	60	86	32	44	09	47	27	96	54	49	27	46	09	62
18	18	07	92	46	44	17	16	58	09	79	83	86	19	62
26	62	38	97	75	84	16	07	44	99	83	11	46	32	24
23	42	40	64	74	82	97	77	77	81	07	45	32	14	08
52	36	28	19	95	50	92	26	11	97	00	56	76	31	38
37	85	94	35	12	83	39	50	08	30	42	34	07	96	88
76	29	17	12	13	40	33	20	38	26	12	89	51	03	74
56	62	18	37	35	96	83	50	87	75	97	12	25	93	47
99	49	57	22	77	88	42	95	45	72	16	64	36	16	00
16	08	15	04	72	33	27	14	34	09	45	59	34	68	49
31	16	93	32	43	50	27	89	87	19	20	15	37	00	49
68	54	30	13	70	55	74	30	77	40	44	22	78	84	26
74	57	25	65	76	59	29	97	68	60	71	91	38	67	54
27	42	37	86	53	48	55	90	65	72	96	57	69	36	10
00	39	68	29	61	66	37	32	20	30	77	84	57	03	29
29	94	98	94	24	68	49	69	10	82	53	75	91	93	30
16	90	82	66	59	83	62	64	11	12	67	19	00	71	74
11	27	94	75	06	06	09	19	74	66	02	94	37	34	02
33	24	10	16	20	33	32	51	26	38	79	78	45	04	91
38	23	16	86	38	42	38	97	01	50	87	75	66	81	41
31	96	25	91	47	96	44	33	49	13	34	86	82	53	92
66	67	40	67	14	64	05	71	95	86	11	05	65	09	68
14	90	84	45	11	75	73	88	05	90	52	27	41	14	86
68	05	51	18	00	33	96	02	75	19	07	60	62	93	55
20	46	78	73	90	97	51	40	14	02	04	02	33	31	08
64	19	38	97	79	15	06	15	93	20	01	90	10	75	06
05	26	93	70	60	22	35	85	15	13	92	03	51	59	77
07	97	10	88	23	09	98	42	99	64	61	71	62	99	15
68	71	86	85	85	54	87	66	47	54	73	32	08	11	12
26	99	61	65	53	58	37	78	80	70	42	10	50	67	42
14	65	52	68	75	87	59	36	22	41	26	78	63	06	55
17	53	77	58	71	71	41	61	50	72	12	41	94	96	26
90	26	59	21	19	23	52	23	33	12	96	93	02	18	39
41	23	52	55	99	31	04	49	69	96	10	47	48	45	88
60	20	50	81	69	31	99	73	68	68	35	81	33	03	76
91	25	38	05	90	94	58	28	41	36	45	37	59	03	09

Starting anywhere in the table take groups of three digits, e.g., 034, 343, 238

Exercise 21. An Index of Social Need

Introduction

Index numbers are used to reduce several qualitatively different characteristics into a common quantitative variable. They provide a technique for standardising different elements so that they can all be expressed in the same units. Perhaps the most familiar indexes are price indexes and the cost of living index.

A price index uses the concept of 'base year' and the price of the commodity in that year is made equal to 100. Subsequent fluctuations in the price of the goods or services under consideration are expressed as percentage changes from this base. For example, using 1962 as the base index of 100 the retail price of fresh and tinned fruit in October 1966 stood at 96. With the same base (1962 = 100) the index of the price of alcoholic drink stood at 125·6 (H.M.S.O.: *Monthly Digest of Statistics*, November 1966). Therefore it is possible to make a direct comparison of the relative changes in the price of fruit and drink even though one was originally reckoned in pence per pound and the other in shillings per bottle.

The cost of living index, or the Index of Retail Prices, is an example of the second major type of index, which is constructed from many individual price indexes, which are differentially weighted and combined to reflect the cost of living to an average family. From the knowledge gained in surveys of family expenditure a selection of the most important items in the standard family's budget is obtained (see *Studies in Official Statistics No. 6*, 'Method of Construction and Calculation of the Index of Retail Prices', H.M.S.O.). These items are then weighted in terms of the *proportion* of the average family's income which is spent on them. The proportion of the family's income which is spent on meat is several times greater than the proportion spent on butter, so the price of meat will have a much greater weighting in the final index. (In fact, in 1966, meat and bacon was assigned a weighting of 76; butter, margarine, lard and cooking fat 15; the total of all the weightings being 1,000.) If the cost of meat were to rise by 10 per cent this would have a more significant influence on the Retail Price Index than would a comparable rise in the price of butter. The official base year now in use is 1962 = 100. The index stood at 117·4 in October 1966. Index numbers of these two types make many interesting comparisons possible because they reduce several qualitatively different characteristics into a common quantitative variable—the index number. Compare, for example, the indexes of production and weekly wage rates in 1967.

Industrial Production	132·0
Wages	140·0

(Economist, 9th September 1967)

1958 = 100

Wages have obviously been rising more rapidly than industrial production has been increasing and this is one of the causes of inflation.

The third type of scale, which is illustrated in this exercise, is designed to enable the user to compare different individuals who possess a selection of a pool of attributes of varying importance but all relevant to the referent of the index. Local authorities have to decide whether to accept or reject applications for municipal housing. Usually the problem will be one of priorities since there are normally more needy applicants than houses available. One simple way of deciding which family shall have the next available house could be based on the time spent on the waiting list, but this would be to ignore other factors which the Authority might feel are important as, for example, the number of children, family income, present accommodation. Most Authorities would consider it unfair for a childless couple earning £2,000 p.a. to be given a house even if they had been on the waiting list longer than a much poorer family with several children. The function of the index here, then, is to combine all the indicators of social need which are considered relevant so that two or more families can be compared and ranked in overall magnitude of need. The various factors will not all be given equal importance in coming to a final decision, so a weighting system must be employed. This can take the form of a 'points' system. For example, five points may be awarded for each child, ten points for an income of less than £200 per head per year, etc. Once the rules have been laid down for awarding the points it is possible to score application forms in routine fashion without having to refer each case separately to the Housing Committee.

Objective

To select variables together with appropriate weights which might be used in the allocation of low-cost local authority housing and to assemble these into a workable check-list yielding an 'Index of Housing Need'.

Method

1. Compile a list of variables which you feel might well be taken into account by housing managers when allocating local authority houses. Use any or all of the variables listed in Item 21.1 together with any others you feel may be relevant.

2. Consider each of the variables in turn, entering them into Column 1 of the table provided (Item 21.2). In Column 2 enter the measurable aspects of this variable in terms of sub-categories (e.g., income may be divided into categories below £400, £400–£600, £600–£800, etc.).

3. Assign weights to each of the variables selected on the basis of the sub-categories chosen, and enter in Column three (e.g., income below £400, 8 points; £400–£600, 6 points; £600–£800, 3 points).

4. If possible obtain a copy of the rules followed by a local authority from the Housing Manager and compare the local system with the system you have devised.

Treatment of Results

Assess the index scores of the following families and rank them in order of need:

1. Widower with three children: 14, 16, 17. Income of £700 plus pension of £250. At present living in two rooms without hot water and sharing a bathroom. Works in district but has only lived there for seven months. No service with the Armed Forces. One of the children educationally sub-normal.

2. Family of two parents, three children and invalid grandmother. Family income £900 plus £200 from mother's part-time employment. At present paying £6 per week for a terraced cottage with no bathroom and an outside toilet. Resident in district for nine years and on council waiting list for three and a half years. Father works outside district. Grandmother needs minimum medical attention once a week.

3. Caravan dwellers, father with minor leg injury from Second World War (Navy). At present unemployed but seeking job. Two children with another expected, the eldest aged 11 now showing

excellent academic aptitude. Four years' residence. One year on waiting list.

4. Immigrant family (no marriage or birth certificates available). Father, bus driver on £14 per week. Five children at present in care, as family has no home following default on mortgage partially due to excessive interest charges. Mother being treated for mild tuberculosis. Previously occupied council flat in another district with no serious offences but often late with rent payments. Lived in district 18 months. On waiting list for same period.

5. Retired couple with unmarried son. Total income of family £860 p.a. Living in one large room in old house but with fairly adequate facilities. Some doubt about future employment of 37-year-old son because of increasing frequency of epileptic fits. Parents lived in district for over 40 years, on council waiting list for 11 years. Father has three past convictions for theft and fraud but no evident misconduct for past nine years.

6. Young family, father council workman with good war record but low income. Mother a part-time midwife (many patients on the council estate). Total income of family, £900 p.a. Two children of their own plus one adopted locally. Both parents had lived in the district from childhood until they had to move four years ago becuse of shortage of suitable accommodation. Both work in district. At present living with wife's parents 13 miles away. Eldest child goes to school near home.

Also, try to consider as examples, families with which you are personally acquainted, and develop a waiting list, placing them in order of need.

Discussion

1. Which variables were easiest to assess for relevance, and which were the most difficult?

2. Do you think a points' index is a 'fair' way of assessing a social need?

3. If you were a housing manager how would you collect the information required for your index? Would you undertake any further investigations, e.g., by interview? And what would be the specific objectives of your interviews?

4. Do you *intuitively* agree with the ranking on the waiting list as assessed by the index?

5. Is it right to allow the points' index to be used by an official of the

authority without having to bring each case before the Housing Committee?

Marital status of applicant
Single persons, old persons
Separated, divorced persons
Size of family
Number of dependants
Number of children
Number of old persons in household
Nature of present accommodation, overcrowding, water supply, washing facilities, drainage, reports from Health Inspectors
Caravan dwelling
Proximity of schools
Income earned, unearned, Income bar?
Nature of occupation, day work, shift work
Farm work
Distance from work
Special disabilities, illnesses in household, needs for special medical services
Duration of residence in the district
Service with Armed Forces. Years of service abroad
Present or previous house or property ownership
Time since original application

ITEM 21.2: TABLE FOR CALCULATING RELATIVE HOUSING NEEDS OF SEVERAL FAMILIES

Item	Sub-categories	Points	Points Awarded							
			Family 1	Family 2	Family 3	Family 4	Family 5	Family 6	Family 7	Family 8
Totals										

Exercise 22. The Measurement of Meaning

Introduction

Osgood and Suci (1955) tried to analyse the personal meaning of words or concepts by asking individuals to consider in turn each of several adjectives and to decide to what extent these adjectives truly described the concept in question. In fact, Osgood used not single adjectives but bipolar *pairs* of adjectives (such as good-bad, clean-dirty, large-small), and asked his subjects to imagine a seven-point scale with 'good' at one end and 'bad 'at the other; the individual was to decide just where the concept lay along this seven-point scale. By factor-analytic techniques applied to ratings given for many different words on such bipolar scales, Osgood was able to show that there are three general factors underlying meaning: *1.* an 'evaluative' factor, *2.* a 'potency' factor, and *3.* an 'activity' factor. Of these the evaluative factor was the most prominent. By studying an individual's scores on the adjective-scales corresponding to the evaluative factor we could make a useful assessment of the strength of his attitudes to the concept being studied.

Objective

To use Osgood's Semantic Differential Scale to assess the personal emotional content of the meaning of a number of different concepts.

Method

Decide on the words to be used to define the concepts you wish to study. Interesting comparisons can often be obtained by asking different groups to rate the same word (e.g., ask Labour and Conservative supporters to rate 'socialism'), or by comparing the profiles of different words (e.g., Hitler and Gandhi) given by the same person.

Print the word or concept at the head of the duplicated sheet (Item 22.1) and ask your subjects to complete the rankings. Interesting examples:

1. Ask male and female respondents to assess the concept of 'sex'.
2. Compare profiles for 'mother' and 'father'.
3. Obtain the profile for the concept 'me'.

Treatment of Results

For each individual assessment of a concept a profile is produced simply by linking the crosses. These can be summed by assigning a value to each step and averaging for the whole class. The combined profile can then be plotted and compared visually with other classes' profiles of the same concept or the same class's profile of other concepts.

Discussion

1. Discuss any differences found in profiles of different concepts and differences between groups both in terms of total profiles and by breaking down into sections (evaluative, potency, activity).

2. Is the semantic differential a good measure of meaning? What advantages does it show over other methods for the study of meaning?

References

Osgood, C. E., and Suci, G. J., 'Factor Analysis or Meaning', *Journ. Exp. Psychol.* 1955, 50: pp. 325–38.

Krech, D., Crutchfield, R. S., and Ballachey, E. L., *Individual in Society* (McGraw-Hill, N.Y. 1963).

ITEM 22.1

Name: Concept:
Age: Sex: Polit: etc.
                                         etc.

Bad	...	...	...	...	...	Good
Worthless	...	...	...	...	...	Valuable
Dirty	...	...	...	...	...	Clean
Insincere	...	...	...	...	...	Sincere
Foolish	...	...	...	...	...	Wise
Ignorant	...	...	...	...	...	Intelligent
Dangerous	...	...	...	...	...	Safe
Sad	...	...	...	...	...	Happy
Poor	...	...	...	...	...	Rich
Unpredictable	...	...	...	...	...	Predictable
Tense	...	...	...	...	...	Relaxed
Sick	...	...	...	...	...	Healthy
Weak	...	...	...	...	...	Strong
Delicate	...	...	...	...	...	Rugged
Passive	...	...	...	...	...	Active
Slow	...	...	...	...	...	Fast
Cold	...	...	...	...	...	Warm

Exercise 23. Comparison of Four Measures of Introversion

Introduction

C. G. Jung's suggestion that individuals may be classified in terms of 'introverted' or 'extraverted' attitudes has attracted much attention from personality theorists. Freyd (1924) gathered together, from Jung's writings, and from elsewhere, many descriptions of introversion and produced the following summary definition:

'An introvert is an individual in whom exists an exaggeration of the thought processes in relation to directly observable social behaviour with an accompanying tendency to withdraw from social contacts.'

This specific personality quality of introversion might be assessed in a number of different ways. We could *interview* our subject, and form an impression on the basis of his discussion of such topics as interests, likes and dislikes, holidays, friends, etc.

Alternatively we might formalise and systematise this question-and-answer approach by assembling a list of questions relating to introversion to make up a questionnaire. This might ask just the same questions as did the interviewer.

A further method might be to ask our subject to *rate himself* on a 5 point scale for introversion—where 1 is low and 5 high on introversion. Some explanation of the nature of introversion would be needed here —but this could take a standard form—perhaps as printed instructions.

A fourth method of assessing a person's introversion would be to ask the *opinion of his friends* and associates. They may have known him for some time and have seen him in many different types of situation.

It is interesting to reflect on the relative merit of these four 'measures' of introversion. The interview is flexible but time-consuming, is not at all standard, and is open to serious error (see *Exercise 15*). The questionnaire is cold, impersonal and somewhat artificial—but it does present exactly the same stimulus material to all subjects. (They may not all, of course, understand it equally well.) The rating-scale, like the questionnaire, demands a certain conceptual ability (and this may be unfair) though it does have the merit of being a standard instrument.

The judgement of many different people—or the combination of these into a single, consensual judgement would seem to reduce the chances of error. Yet not all personality qualities are public. The observers just may not have had sufficiently close experience of a significant aspect of an individual's personality. Again when judgements are being combined the more forceful judges may carry more than their fair weight in the final consensual judgement. In the exercise which follows, a comparison is made of these four different approaches. It will be difficult to assess which of the four is the best or most accurate estimate since we have no absolute or universally agreed definition (let alone measure) of introversion with which to compare the various estimates.

What we need is an agreed 'operational definition' of introversion. An operational definition is a definition which contains a set of instructions for the observer. Operational definitions are not concerned with possible explanations or underlying processes; they are concerned simply with external observable events. Hence many different observers can agree on exactly what it is they are observing even though they may hold highly divergent views on the cause or explanation or significance of whatever it is they are observing. If now we are prepared to accept, say, the *questionnaire score* on introversion as our operational definition of introversion, we can then proceed to assess the relative efficiency of the other three methods by comparing their score with the 'true' score.

Objective

To compare measures of introversion obtained by:
a. questionnaire, *b.* self-rating, *c.* brief interview, *d.* consensual judgement.

Materials

Heidbreder's Introversion Questionnaire (1926) based on Freyd's definitions of introversion and extraversion (Item 23.1).

Method

The four methods of assessment can be attempted in any order, in fact it may be preferable for different people to vary the order.

A. THE QUESTIONNAIRE

Fill in the questionnaire included at the end of this exercise (Item 23.1). Try to respond fairly quickly to the questions without considering at this stage their individual implications. Mark 'Yes' where the statement applies to you, '?' where unsure, and 'No' where the statement does not apply.

There is no time limit but 10 minutes should suffice.

Record personal impressions, introspections, comments, immediately after completing the questionnaire.

B. SELF-RATING

On the basis of Freyd's definition of an introvert quoted in the introduction attempt a self-rating for introversion/extraversion on the 10-point scale at the end of the exercise (Item 23.2). A 10-point scale is used to reduce the number of tied judgements.

C. INTERVIEW

Divide into groups of ten. Everyone in the group should undertake a brief interview (3 to 5 minutes) of one other member of the group on which to base a 10-point rating scale. Avoid a vice-versa arrangement where the same pair interview each other. Give each member of the group a number and work on the following pattern:

| INTERVIEWER | 1 | 2 | 3 | 4 | 5 | 6 | 7 | 8 | 9 | 10 |
| INTERVIEWEE | 2 | 3 | 4 | 5 | 6 | 7 | 8 | 9 | 10 | 1 |

A rating scale is included at the end of the exercise (Item 23.2). Discuss topics such as interests, hobbies, holidays, reading, close friends, etc.

D. CONSENSUAL JUDGEMENT

Each member of the group must rate each other member on the 10-point scale included at the end of the exercise (Item 23.2).

Treatment of Results

1. Compile group results for the questionnaire scores of each member of your group. The questionnaire score is the number of items answered 'Yes' minus the number of items answered 'No'. Rank the members of the group from 1–10 on the basis of their results, 1 being the highest introversion rank and 10 being the lowest. Some scores may be negative.

2. For the consensual judgement of the group for each individual take the mean of all the judgements, e.g., if there are 10 members of

your group then each individual will have nine ratings—say 4,3,4,2,1,5, 4,4,3. The mean will therefore be 3·3 and these values should again be ranked in order 1–10.

3. Convert the self-rating and interview ratings into rankings in the same way with 1 being the most introverted and 10 being the least (i.e., the most extraverted).

4. Fill in the chart included at the end of this exercise (Item 23.3), listing the rankings of the ten individuals on the four different measures of introversion.

5. Calculate the rank order correlation coefficient (ρ) for each of the pairs of rankings, i.e., six coefficients in all. A chart to help with the calculation of one of the coefficients is included (Item 23.4).

6. In assigning the rankings two scores may be the same and therefore the ranking will be 'tied'. Solve this problem by assigning to each score the mean ranking of the two places they would have occupied. If for example two scores are equal after the first four rankings have been made (i.e., they should occupy positions 5 and 6) each should be assigned a ranking of 5·5.

7. The computed values of ρ may have arisen entirely by chance and their significance must be assessed (i.e., the probability that they did not arise purely by chance). From tables it can be found that with $N = 10$, for a 5 in 100 probability ρ must be at least 0·56. If ρ is much above this we can be fairly confident that we have discovered a real relationship and that chance has not produced an illusory relationship.

If the number of individuals in your group is not ten, consult statistical tables to discover the minimum value of ρ required for statistical confidence.

Discussion

1. Which measure of your own introversion do you feel inclined to accept: self-rating, consensual rating, or test? Why?

2. Is it possible to consider *any* of the scores as an objective measure of introversion?

3. Can you account for the discrepancy, if any, between self, consensual and test scores?

4. Can the test questions be criticised on grounds of social acceptability?

5. On what other grounds would you criticise the questionnaire?

6. How similar would you expect your answers to the questionnaire to be if you were to be retested in, say, one month's time. (From such

retesting the *reliability* of the test might be assessed; if this is possible it should be done.)

7. How were test scores of the class distributed? From the point of view of test *utility* what sort of distribution would have been desirable?

8. Would there be any benefit from using a longer rating scale (say 50 point scale)?

References

ANASTASI, A., *Psychological Testing* Part 4 (Collier-Macmillan, N.Y. 1954).

SYMONDS, P. M., *Diagnosing Personality and Conduct* (Appleton-Century, N.Y. 1931), p. 195.

HEIDBREDER, E., in *Journ. Abnorm. Soc. Psychol.* (1926) 21: pp. 120–34.

ITEM 23.1: A PERSONALITY TEST

(Modified from M. Freyd (*Psychol. Rev.* [1924] 33: pp. 74–87) and E. Heidbreder (*Journ. Abnorm. and Soc. Psychol.* [1926] 21: pp. 120–134).

Below is a list of 50 personal traits. Put a + before each trait that characterises you; place a — before each trait that represents the opposite of your trait; and place a ? before each trait which is doubtful.

1. I limit my acquaintances to a select few.
2. I feel hurt readily, and am sensitive about remarks or actions which have reference to me.
3. I am suspicious of the motives of others.
4. I worry over possible misfortunes.
5. I indulge in self-pity when things go wrong.
6. I get rattled easily, losing my head in excitement or moments of stress.
7. I keep in the background on social occasions, avoiding leadership at social affairs.
8. I am critical of others.
9. I prefer to work alone rather than with people.
10. I have ups and downs in mood *without* apparent cause.
11. I am meticulous; that is, I am extremely careful about my dress and painstaking about my personal property.
12. I blush frequently.
13. I pay serious attention to rumours.
14. I express myself better in writing than in speech.

15. I resist discipline and orders.
16. I limit my acquaintances to members of my own sex.
17. I avoid all occasions for talking before crowds, since I find it difficult to express myself.
18. I am a radical; that is, I want to change the world instead of adjusting myself to it.
19. I am outspoken, saying what I consider the truth, regardless of how others may take it.
20. I introspect; that is, I turn my attention inward toward myself.
21. I prefer participation in competitive intellectual amusements to athletic games.
22. I am strongly motivated by praise.
23. I daydream.
24. I am selfish.
25. I dislike and avoid any process of selling or persuading anyone to adopt a certain point of view (except in the religious field).
26. I am sentimental.
27. I prefer to read about a thing rather than experience it.
28. I am extremely careful about the friends I make: that is, I must know a person pretty thoroughly before I call him a friend.
29. I shrink from actions which demand initiative and nerve.
30. I prefer to work things out on my own hook; that is, I hesitate to accept aid.
31. I talk to myself.
32. I derive enjoyment from writing about myself.
33. I keep a diary.
34. I shrink when facing a crisis.
35. If I unburden at all, I do so only to close personal friends and relatives.
36. I am reticent and retiring; that is, I do not talk spontaneously.
37. I have new and sometimes eccentric ideas.
38. I work in fits and starts.
39. I am a poor loser; that is, I become considerably upset and indisposed after the loss of a competitive game.
40. I depreciate my own abilities, but assume an outward air of conceit.
41. I am absentminded.
42. I hesitate in making decisions on ordinary questions in the course of the day.
43. I accept an idealistic philosophy.

44. I have ups and downs in mood *with* apparent cause.
45. I rewrite my social letters before mailing them.
46. I move slowly.
47. I am governed by reason rather than by impulse or emotion; that is, I can give good reasons for my actions.
48. I admire perfection of form in literature.
49. I make mistakes in judging the character and ability of others.
50. I am thrifty and careful about making loans.

ITEM 23.2: INTROVERSION RATING SCALES

Ratings of other Group Members you have not interviewed

Self

After Interview

Group No. 1 2 3 4 5 6 7 8 9 10

10 Strongly extraverted

9 distinctly extraverted

8 moderately extraverted

7 slightly extraverted

6
5 intermediate

4 slightly introverted

3 moderately introverted

2 distinctly introverted

1 strongly introverted

1 2 3 4 5 6 7 8 9 10

Put a X in the rating position that you consider best characterises person under consideration, e.g, if you consider him to be moderately introverted put a X in space 3.

ITEM 23·3: CHART FOR THE COMPILATION OF RAW SCORES AND RANKINGS OF INDIVIDUALS ON FOUR MEASURES OF INTROVERSION

Raw Scores

Individual	Questionnaire	Self Rating	Interview	Consensual Judgement
1				
2				
3				
4				
5				
6				
7				
8				
9				
10				

Final Rankings

Questionnaire	Self Rating	Interview	Consensual Judgement

ESS—M

ITEM 23.4: CHART FOR CALCULATING RANK ORDER CORRELATION COEFFICIENT (ρ)

Individual	1	2	3	4	5	6	7	8	9	10	Total
Rank by Method A											
Rank by Method B											
Difference in Rank (d)											
(d²)											

$$\rho = 1 - \frac{6\Sigma\ (d^2)}{N^3 - N}$$

d = difference in rank
N = Number of items per ranking

Exercise 24. Measures of Personality

Introduction

Human personality can be studied in many ways. The individual's special characteristics can be studied, for example, by direct informal observation during an interview. The observer can judge what he sees in the light of his own experience and his own beliefs about human nature. He can go further and describe the individual in words—and such verbal descriptions can often be sensitive, apt and highly colourful, especially (as is the case with many biographers) where the observer is verbally gifted. Though such descriptions clearly add to our understanding they can never carry much conviction as scientific evidence— the essence of which is an agreed system of description and classification of the things observed. Though some early attempts were made to describe a few major categories or types of personality and to allocate individuals to one or other of these, it has been increasingly realised that a quite complex descriptive system is necessary which allows for the considerable subtlety of variation between people. Some modern psychologists prefer to describe individuals in terms of their possession of a large number of distinct traits; others to describe an individual by noting his position along a continuum or dimension of personality—or along several such dimensions simultaneously. The existence and specification of such dimensions and traits is still a matter of active research and universal agreement has by no means been achieved. Nevertheless a large number of more or less objective tests have been produced which purport to describe an individual's possession of traits—or his position along one or more dimensions. Though not universally accepted some of these tests merit attention as a genuine attempt to introduce objectivity into the description and measurement of personality. These tests occur in such profusion and variety that it is necessary at this stage to classify them in some way.

A useful first classification of tests is in terms of *traits measured*. There are a number of tests which attempt to measure psychiatric vulnerability (such as the Bell Adjustment Inventory). Quite different tests are concerned with social characteristics (such as Allport's Ascendance/Submission Test). Still others are concerned with basic human needs and motives (such as Murray's Thematic Apperception Test)—and others again with orientation to life or 'values' (e.g., Allport–Vernon–Lindzay Study of Values). There are many tests whose prime concern is with interests (such as the Strong Vocational Interest Blank) and there are a large number of attitude scales (such as those discussed in *Exercise* 19).

A second classification of personality tests could be made in terms of the *techniques* they employ. The first group and the most straightforward is the direct question-and-answer inventories such as the Strong or Bell tests mentioned above. Here the questions are quite unambiguous and the answers permitted are highly limited—often being restricted simply to 'yes' or 'no'. Highly-structured tests such as these can be easily and quickly scored and their results are not usually affected by the linguistic skill of the subject.

The second group consists of quite different and less straightforward techniques—the so-called 'projective tests' where the stimulus material is quite deliberately vague, ambiguous or indistinct. The effect of using such relatively 'unstructured' stimulus material is to increase the range and variety of possible responses, and so the tests are sometimes able to reflect subtle or unusual aspects of the subject's personality (which would be lost in, for example, the rigid, highly-structured questionnaire). Unfortunately this gain in sensitivity is often paid for by a loss in rigour and results tend to be influenced by the verbal skills of the subject. The Murray Thematic Apperception Test (T.A.T.), the Rorschach Ink-Blot Test, the Pictures and the 'Faces' test used in this Exercise are examples of such relatively unstructured tests.

In the third group of techniques come those tests which permit a wide variety of responses from the subject but which present quite unambiguous stimuli. With tests of this sort both the stimulus and the response may be non-verbal in character. These are the so-called performance tests of personality, and range from studies of gestures and expressive movement to studies of brain-wave (E.E.G.) activity and measures of changes in skin resistance (the psychogalvanic reflex or P.G.R.). These tests are highly objective in the sense that they do not depend on the idiosyncrasies of the observer. They do, however, require highly sophisticated equipment and are often difficult to arrange.

Before *any* of these tests may be used, however, it is absolutely necessary that we should be satisfied about their reliability (i.e., does this test give the same result on two different occasions when applied to the same person?), and their validity (does this test really measure what it purports to measure?). (These questions are discussed further in *Exercise 26.*) Standard methods are available for assessing the *reliability* of personality tests (such as split-half and test-retest methods) but how can we test the *validity* of such tests of personality?

To discover whether a test is valid we shall need to compare what the test declares about the person tested with the truth about this person.

Unfortunately in the absence of a universally-agreed system of personality description it is difficult to validate personality tests convincingly, since we can never be sure what is the *true* personality description of the individual tested. We cannot therefore compare test results with the true personality. What we shall attempt to do in this exercise is the next best thing—namely to assess the extent to which results from different personality measures lead us to the same conclusion about the person we are dealing with, i.e., we shall be concerned with 'concurrent validity'. (There are other ways of assessing test validity and these are discussed in Anastasi's *Psychological Testing.*)

One widely used measure of personality is the interview and we could therefore compare test results with interview results. In this exercise we shall consider the question: 'Given personality test data and interview data from several individuals, how well can we match the two together correctly?'

Objective

The objective of this exercise is to assess the extent to which the use of a 'projective' personality test (similar to Murray's T.A.T.) on several individuals can lead to the selection of the correct personality description from several possible alternatives. Can we successfully match projective test analyses to personality sketches derived from interviews?

Materials

Five stimulus pictures (Items 24.1, 24.2, 24.3, 24.4, and 24.5).
List of 'Needs and Press' (H. A. Murray) (Item 24.6).

Method

1. Each member of the class should first of all write a brief (5 or 6 line) account of what he believes to be happening in each of the

stimulus pictures 24.1, 24.2, 24.3, 24.4, 24.5, on the item attached (Item 24.7).

An attempt should be made in the case of each picture to indicate 'what each of the main characters is doing, what they are feeling and thinking, and what the outcome is'.

2. Each member of the class should write a brief (5 or 6 line) personality sketch of his partner on Item 24.8 (naming the partner in the space provided). An attempt should then be made to 'score' the content of the 5 stories in 1 above using H. A. Murray's list of 'needs' and 'press' (Item 24.6). Where any of the participants in the stories is seen to be reacting to an environmental pressure of any sort this part of the story should be underlined and the appropriate symbol from Item 24.6 marked alongside. Similarly where any *need* is expressed or inferred from the content of the stories this also should be marked alongside.

3. Forms for five individuals will then be selected by the tutor who will allocate alphabetical labels A B C D and E to the five chosen character sketches, and F G H I J to the five chosen protocols (the order of these will be randomised so that F does not correspond to A or G to B etc.).

4. The five character sketches and the five protocols each with a separate alphabetical label should now be duplicated for distribution to the whole class (or they may be dictated by the tutor and recorded individually).

5. The character sketches and test responses should now be scrutinised carefully and an attempt made by each member of the class separately to match the five corresponding items.

Thus sketch B may be considered by one student to correspond with Protocol J.

6. A contingency table should now be constructed by the tutor which summarises the results obtained by the whole class after they have tried to match the character sketches with the test responses. (use Item 24.9). The 'correct' matches are of course known only to the tutor and he should construct the blank or draw on the blackboard the contingency table accordingly. Let us assume that character sketch A corresponds in reliability to test responses H and B to G, C to F, D to I and E to J.

If all (let us say ten) members of the class had correctly matched all items it would be possible to put ten ticks in the top left hand cell (AH) of the contingency table and so on diagonally across the table until we had ten ticks also in the (EJ) cell. In practice of course the ticks will be more or less unevenly scattered over all 25 cells of the table—and not just in the five correct cells. The question now arises: 'Do the ticks *tend* to concentrate themselves in the five correct cells or are they spread over the whole table in nothing better than a random way?' A special statistic known as Chi-squared is available to answer just this kind of question. (See Connolly and Sluckin.)

The value of Chi-squared should be computed for the class results. If Chi-squared has a sufficiently high value then we may draw the conclusion that the results obtained for the class as a whole depart significantly from chance, i.e., that the class is in part able to draw some useful guidance about the personalities of their five chosen colleagues from their responses to a projective test. (We are assuming, of course, as seems reasonable, that the character sketches themselves have some meaning.) If however Chi-squared is too low, then we may conclude that these projective test responses were worthless as a guide to personality.

7. If time permits, a supplementary exercise may be undertaken using the Liggett S.V.T. Faces test, four faces of which are reproduced in Item 24.10. Each subject taking part in the exercise (not necessarily simultaneously) should be allotted an identifying number and should examine the faces carefully and write down (using the form shown in Item 24.11) the answers to the following questions in respect of each separate face:

a. 'What would you expect him to be like as a person?'
b. 'If he was an actor what part could he play?'
c. 'If he had had some trouble what might it have been?'

A classification of types of response should then be attempted by groups of 2, 3 or 4 subjects working together. This should be done for *a*, *b*, and *c* separately. The categories for *a* may include terms such as 'reference to the criminality', 'reference to gentle, kind features', 'reference to age', 'reference to occupation' and many more. The categories for *b* may be more colourful, less inhibited variants of those in *a* and the categories in *c* might relate to such factors as financial troubles, police troubles, health troubles (physical), health troubles (psychological) or indeed many others.

The carefully numbered protocols (bearing no name) should then be circulated around the whole class and each member should attempt to judge which other member of the class produced each protocol.

His judgement of each separate protocol should be recorded on a personal contingency table he constructs for himself (such as that shown in Item 24.12). When all subjects have seen all protocols a combined contingency table should be assembled for the whole class by the instructor or by an assistant who asks for an indication, perhaps by a show of hands, of the number of cases in each cell of the table.

The value of χ^2 should then be computed for the combined results, as in the earlier part of this exercise. If χ^2 is sufficiently high then it may be concluded that the null hypothesis (that there is no association between judgements and reality) has been disproved at a particular level of probability. This would suggest that this very abbreviated verbal form of the test was in some way indicating individual differences in personality.

Discussion of Supplementary Exercise

1. Was there general agreement among members of the small groups who attempted to evolve a scoring system for the verbal responses?

2. What difficulties arose in the attempt to classify responses?

3. If introversion scores from *Exercise 23* are available for the group, compare the frequency and categories of verbal response given by the five most and the five least introverted members of the class.

Does any difference appear between response-category types or frequencies?

Discussion of Main Exercise

1. Were the few test responses available for each subject sufficient to permit matching? Would more responses per person have eased the task?

2. Did the attempt to score the responses in terms of Murray's list help in the matching? What could such scoring contribute in larger scale enquiries? What other analytical categories would you use?

3. Were some individuals easier to match than others?

4. How similar were different persons' responses to the same stimuli? How might the variety of responses evoked be increased? What other sorts of stimuli might have been useful?

5. How far is it possible to rank the five participants for the single quality *introversion* on the basis of: *a.* character sketches, and *b.* test responses? If introversion scores are available for these individuals from *Exercise 23*, they might be compared.

6. Is it possible to assess anything other than *concurrent* validity for projective tests of this kind? (See Anastasi and *Exercise 26* on kinds of validity.)

7. What do you consider to be the potential strengths and weaknesses of projective tests? To what extent are some of these overcome by the simultaneous use of *pairs* of stimuli as suggested by Liggett (1959)?

References

ANASTASI, A., *Psychological Testing* (Collier-Macmillan, N.Y. 1954), Ch. 20.

VERNON, P. E., *Personality Assessment* (Methuen, London 1964).

LIGGETT, J., 'The paired use of projective stimuli', *Brit. Journ. Psychol.*, 1959, 50, 269–75.

LIGGETT, J., *The S.V.T. Faces Test* (J. and P. Bealls, Newcastle 1957) from which Item 24.10 is taken.

ITEM 24.1

ITEM 24.2

ITEM 24.3

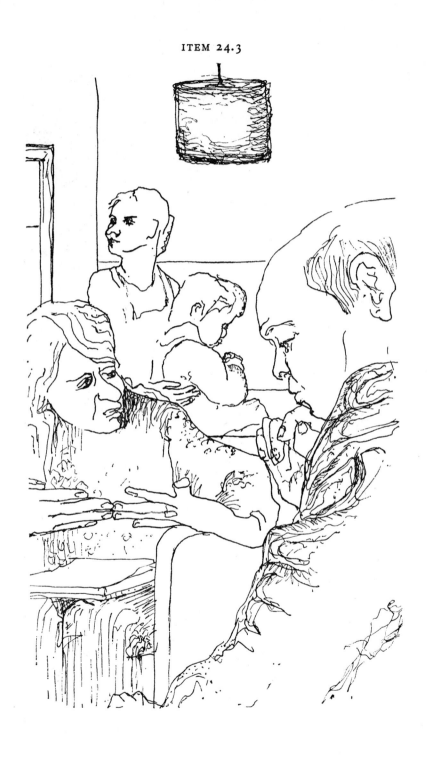

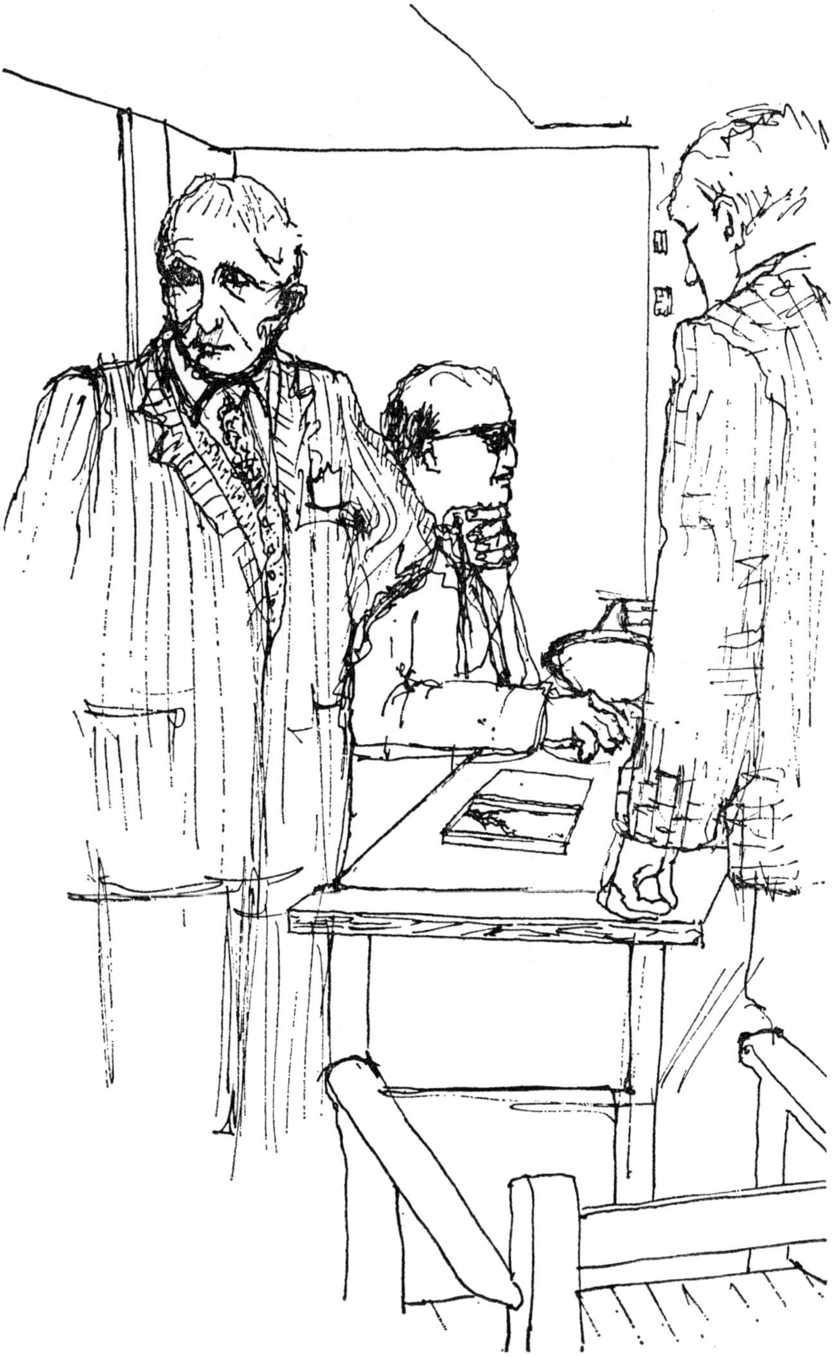

ITEM 24.6: A LIST OF MURRAY'S NEEDS AND PRESS

The following is a very brief list of Murray's Needs and Press as introduced in Murray, H. A. *et al.*, *Explorations in Personality* (Oxford University Press, N.Y. 1938).

A *'need'* represents determinants of behaviour from within the individual.

A *'press'* is a determinant of behaviour from the environment.

NEEDS

1. Abasement (submission)
2. Achievement
3. Affiliation (co-operation)
4. Aggression
5. Autonomy (independence)
6. Counteraction (to overcome a failure)
7. Deference
8. Dependence
9. Dominance
10. Exhibition
11. Harmavoidance
12. Infravoidance (avoiding humiliation)
13. Nurturance (to give sympathy)
14. Order
15. Play (fun)
16. Rejection
17. Sentience (sensuous enjoyment)
18. Sex
19. Succourance (to be supported)
20. Understanding

PRESS

1. Affiliation, friendships
2. Aggression
3. Birth of sibling
4. Danger or misfortune
5. Deception or betrayal
6. Deference, praise, recognition
7. Dominance, coercion and prohibition
8. Family Insupport
9. Inferiority, physical, social intellectual
10. Lack or loss
11. Nurturance, indulgence
12. Rejection, unconcern, scorn
13. Retention, withholding objects
14. Rival, competing, contemporary
15. Sex
16. Succourance, demands for tenderness

ITEM 24.7

Name of person tested: _____

What is happening in the pictures?
What is each character doing, feeling and thinking?
What is the outcome?

Space for Scoring

Picture 1

Picture 2

Picture 3

Picture 4

Picture 5

ITEM 24.8

Name of person described below: _____

5 or 6 line personality sketch:

ITEM 24.9: CONTINGENCY TABLE FOR MATCHING PROTOCOLS
AND CHARACTER SKETCHES

		\multicolumn{5}{c}{*Character Sketches*}
		A	B	C	D	E
Protocols	F					
	G					
	H					
	I					
	J					

ITEM 24.10: PART OF THE LIGGETT SELF-VALUATION TEST

ITEM 24.11

Identification Number of Subject completing this form. . . . . . .
(No name to be written on form).

	Person	*Role*	*Trouble*
Face 1			
Face 2			
Face 3			
Face 4			

ITEM 24.12: PERSONAL CONTINGENCY TABLE TO RECORD ONE INDIVIDUAL'S JUDGEMENT OF RELATION BETWEEN PROTOCOLS AND PERSONS

	Names of persons tested					
1						
2						
3						
4						
5						
6						
7						

Identification number of circulated forms

(A contingency table for the whole class will be produced later by simple combination of several of these individual records.)

Exercise 25. Measures of Ability

Introduction

'Ability' like many other psychological variables is often poorly defined. The word is used in very different senses—sometimes as a single all-pervading faculty which some possess and others do not; sometimes, as for Binet, a collection of separate faculties such as judgement, practical sense or initiative; sometimes as the capacity to solve abstract problems rapidly; sometimes again as the capacity to profit from experience, and in many other ways. Possible definitions are of course limitless and consequently an operational behaviouristic approach is needed: 'What are the operations whereby this quality is to be measured?' But there are innumerable possible measures available. The question is—do any of these measures cover common ground. If they do then we can usefully begin to talk about 'ability' and define it in terms of the test procedures assessing it. Many investigators have correlated sets of scores from different tests to see if there is a common or general component underlying performances in them all. This analysis of correlations is called *factor analysis* and it is the purpose of this exercise to consider some broad features of this special method.

It has been found that there is indeed a great deal of common ground between different tests. This is shown by the fact that the people who do well on one sort of test tend to do well on others. The common element has been described in terms of a 'general factor' or 'g' (a mathematical construct which efficiently describes many test performances). Several investigators have shown however that there is more similarity between the test scores on *some* tests than can be accounted for simply by a general factor alone, and it has been realised that certain groups of tasks have something further in common which is absent from other tasks. To account for this similarity between more limited groups of tests it has been found useful to speak of 'group factors'. Examples of such group factors are 'v : ed' (a mathematical construct which satisfactorily explains correlations which are observed to occur between different tests of verbal and educational skills), and 'k : m' (which describes spatial, manipulative and motor skills). These general and group factors do not entirely account for test scores however. There is in addition a so-called 'specific' factor which arises because of the peculiar features of each individual test.

Analyses of many different sets of test data have repeatedly shown the utility of a three-fold analysis: into a general factor (g), group factors (v : ed, and k : m) and specific factors (S_1 S_2 S_3 etc.).

Some tests are more efficient than others in measuring these factors and the mathematical method called factor analysis enables a practical decision to be made as to which tests should be retained for further use—and which should be discarded because their 'factor saturation' is small. There are several ways of undertaking factor analyses and different ways of expressing the results. (Thurstone's system, for example, does not take the 'hierarchical' form reported above—but speaks of several distinct factors of similar importance). But the aim of all methods of factor analysis is the same—to achieve an accurate and complete mathematical description of the behaviour of many people on a series of tests. Factors are categories for classifying performances. Quite incidentally they may also encourage us to theorise, if we wish, about the psychological nature of intelligence (or personality, since factor analysis has also been used very successfully to analyse personality test scores).

Materials

5 tests
Test A Vocabulary, Item 25.1
    B Similarities, Item 25.2
    C Coding,   Item 25.3
    D Digit span, Item 25.4
    E Maze,   Item 25.5

Method

1. Ten subjects should be numbered S_1 S_2 S_3 .... (not named). All subjects should answer all five tests which should be scored by some other person.

2. All Raw Scores should then be entered in a summary table (Item 25.6).

3. We need to know how each test, A, etc., correlates with every other test B, C, D, E, etc., i.e., we need the correlations AB, AC, AD, AE, BC, BD etc.

The work of computing product-moment correlation coefficients

	A	B	C	D	E	
A		S_1	S_2	S_3	S_4	
B			S_5	S_6	S_7	
C				S_8	S_9	
D					S_{10}	
E						

(Diagram showing how work of computing correlations
is shared between ten subjects)

should be shared among the ten subjects as shown in the diagram. Thus S_1 computes the correlation between all persons scores in Test A with all persons scores in Test B. A sheet for computing correlation coefficients is provided (Item 25.7). A summary table (Item 25.8) should now be prepared showing all the intercorrelations between the scores on the five tests.

4. The next problem is to decide *which test is correlating most* with all the other tests. This is found by inspecting the vertical column totals of Item 25.8. It might be found, for example, that the D column total is the highest, that A comes next, then E, C and B in descending order.

5. Item 25.8 should now be rearranged by inspection of the column totals so that the highest totals appear at the left of a new rearranged matrix.

6. The later stages of the factor analysis are beyond the scope of this book and will not be attempted here, but it may be useful now to note some of the broad features of the later processes in such an analysis. Inspection of this rearranged matrix may show a high correlation between two particular tests (D and A in our example). At the same time, the correlation between D and B might be found to be low. There may in fact be a cluster of high correlations in the top left and another in the bottom right of the diagram. (Inspection of the content of the different tests might suggest why.) At the same time however it might be seen that the other correlations in the diagram (i.e., top right and bottom left) were not negligible. This would suggest that

all the tests were measuring something which they share in common, i.e., a general factor. The next stage in the factor analysis would be to try to remove from the table of intercorrelations the contribution of this general factor. It would be most interesting to see what would be left behind in the table after this had been done. Different tests will no doubt contain this general factor to a different degree. Techniques are available, which are not discussed here, to determine the extent or proportion or 'loading' on this factor for each separate test. The loading might be found to be high (e.g., ·8) or low (e.g., ·4). Let us assume, for the purposes of this exercise, that Test D has been found to have a general factor loading (henceforth described as 'g-loading') of ·8 and Test B a g-loading of ·4, with the other tests having intermediate values, namely, ·7 for A, ·6 for E, and ·5 for C.

A new table could then be constructed which showed the result of multiplying each test's g-loading with every other test's g-loading. Each of the products in this new table could then be considered as indicating the contribution made by the general factor to one particular correlation coefficient in the re-arranged correlation matrix. Thus, ·8 × ·7, i.e., ·56, is g's contribution to the original correlation (which might have been, say, ·75) between Tests D and A. We could now *subtract* each of these calculated g contributions from each of the actual correlations in the rearranged matrix. We would be left with a residue (·19 in the case of D and A) which is that part of each intercorrelation which is *not* due to g.

Inspection of this new table of 'residuals' might then show some interesting features. For example we may find that the residual of the correlation between D and A is very much larger than the residual of the correlation between D and B. The new table might suggest in fact that the early tests (D and A) have something in common. Similarly the later Tests C and B may also appear to have something in common. The top right-hand and the bottom left-hand corner residuals may be quite negligible, however, suggesting that the early tests have little in common with the late tests. The relatively large residuals in the early tests could then perhaps be explained in terms of a group factor shared by a number of tests of similar content. Inspection of the early tests may show that they do indeed have something in common. They may, for example, all contain *verbal* problems. The relatively large residuals from the intercorrelations of the late tests with themselves might similarly be found to result from their having, for example, a largely *practical* or *spatial* or motor content and very little verbal

content. Thus we might conclude that there was a group factor underlying the verbal tests and a different group factor underlying the
spatial tests.

It is possible to press this kind of analysis further. The next step
would be to subtract from the residual correlations the contributions
respectively of these group factors. If this were done we should be left
with a table of very low correlations indeed. It would be reasonable to
attribute the final residuals to the operation of highly specific factors,
due to the individual characteristics of particular tests. Each test on this
view would have its own unshared specific factor to contribute.
Factor analysts who have undertaken this type of analysis have concluded that each test evidently has three separate factorial components:
first, a general factor component (g); secondly, a group-factor component (e.g., v or k); and thirdly, a highly specific factor component
(s). The relative proportions in which these were represented in any
given test might vary widely. A vocabulary test might, for example, be
represented by

64 per cent g, 25 per cent v and 11 per cent s.

Discussion

1. By consulting Ch. 1 of Vernon's *The Structure of Human Abilities*,
find the meaning of the following terms and explain them with
examples:

    i. Saturation,

    ii. Communality,

    iii. Variance of factors.

2. Granted that factors have been established mathematically—
how can they then be labelled and identified? Should they and can they
be described in words?

3. Is it possible to envisage a measure of pure intelligence or 'g',
and would it be useful if this were possible?

References

VERNON, P. E., *The Structure of Human Abilities* (Methuen, London 1950).
WECHSLER, D., *WAIS Manual* (Psychological Corporation, N.Y. 1955).

Notes on the Tests

Five small tests follow. These are of the same type as those most commonly used in assessing intelligence. They are not however parts of actual tests but have been constructed specially for this exercise. Consequently they have not been validated and no norms are available (see *Exercises 26* and *27*). Therefore the scores have no absolute meaning in terms of I.Q. They can be used for comparing individuals used as subjects and for correlating their scores on the different tests. The examples have been made deliberately more difficult than on a standard test because the subjects which will probably be used in this exercise are likely to be of more than average ability. Obviously any familiarity with the tests will make the results meaningless. It is strongly recommended that naïve subjects be used if possible. The total testing time per subject should not exceed 15 minutes.

Be very strict in the scoring. Never allow individuals to score their own tests.

ITEM 25.1

Test 'A' —Vocabulary

Define the following words. Check the definitions with a dictionary and score 2 for completely correct, 1 for partially correct and 0 for wrong. Be very strict in the scoring.

Maximum score = 50

1. Patency
2. Duplex
3. Fuscous
4. Stearin
5. Pied
6. Retrench
7. Acolyte
8. Chitterling
9. Protagonist
10. Fallacious
11. Achromatic
12. Rhombus
13. Harpy
14. Rue
15. Incubus
16. Tantamount
17. Jamb
18. Kleptomania
19. Counterpoise
20. Firkin
21. Towy
22. Marly
23. Indemnify
24. Knoll
25. Sloven

ITEM 25.2

Test 'B' Similarities

In what way are the following pairs of things alike. Obtain a consensual opinion on the correct answers. Score 2 for a fully correct answer, 1 for an answer that indicates the correct line of thought and 0 for a wrong answer or if the subject mentions differences. Scoring should be strict. Maximum score 24.

1. Bread — Paper
2. Excitement — Boredom
3. Tube — Tunnel
4. Feet — Wheels
5. Pencil — Chisel
6. Aqueduct — Bridge
7. Top — Side
8. Necklace — Painting
9. Cane — Zebra
10. Wind — Current
11. Praise — Punishment
12. Oxygen — Iron

ITEM 25.3

Test 'C'—Coding

The first row of digits below is paired with a symbol. The task is to go through the test putting the appropriate symbol beneath each digit. You have one minute to do as many as you can.

Time limit one minute.   Maximum score = 48

1	2	3	4	5	6	7	8	9
o	L	∧	⊐	=	×	⊓	⊙	÷

6	5	4	9	6	4	3	2	1	8	3	6

1	9	4	6	8	5	7	2	3	7	4	9

6	5	2	9	1	6	7	8	2	7	8	4

2	9	4	3	8	6	8	6	4	5	9	7

8	3	4	9	5	2	3	1	4	8	6	2

ITEM 25.4

Test 'D'—Digit Span

Repeat the lists of digits to the subject and ask them to repeat them immediately afterwards—carry on through the list and stop when two consecutive failures occur.

Then administer List two in exactly the same way except that the subject has to repeat the list backwards.

Try to say the digit at roughly equal intervals. The score is given by the number alongside the last list repeated correctly in each series. Maximum score = 23.

Series 1.	Forwards												Score
1.	3	4	9										1
2.	8	5	2	6									2
3.	9	2	8	5	1								3
4.	2	9	8	2	7	5							4
5.	9	6	4	1	2	8	5	6					5
6.	3	8	2	9	5	6	3	8	1				6
7.	7	4	8	5	2	6	1	8	4	9			7
8.	8	9	2	1	5	7	3	4	8	2	6		8
9.	6	4	9	3	7	4	6	2	9	1	3	7	9
10.	2	4	7	1	5	9	2	8	3	7	6	2 5	10

Series 2.	Backwards									
1.	3	7								5
2.	1	3	7							6
3.	9	2	5	8						7
4.	3	6	9	4						8
5.	7	1	9	3	5					9
6.	6	3	7	5	7	4				10
7.	7	8	3	4	9	1	9			11
8.	9	6	4	7	9	6	8	2		12
9.	7	4	9	2	8	1	6	5	9	13

ITEM 25.5

Test 'E'—The Maze

Draw a path through the maze beginning from 'START'. The pencil must be kept moving and do not touch the lines of the maze. Time limit two minutes.

Score ½ for every second saved on two minutes. Deduct from this 5 points for a turn around and two points for touching one of the lines.

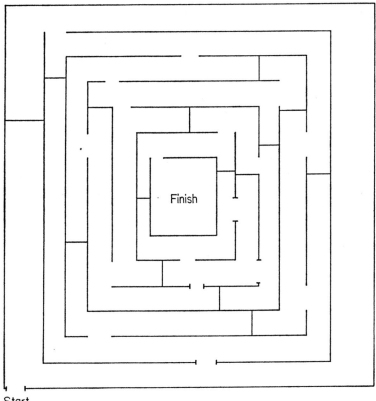

Finish

Start

ITEM 25.6: TABLE FOR ENTERING THE RAW SCORES OF
10 SUBJECTS ON 5 TESTS OF ABILITY

Subject	Score A	Score B	Score C	Score D	Score E
1					
2					
3					
4					
5					
6					
7					
8					
9					
10					

ITEM 25.7: CHART FOR CALCULATING PRODUCT MOMENT CORRELATION (r)

Raw Scores						
Test A X	Test B Y	x	y	x^2	y^2	xy
Σ						
Means						

$$r_{xy} = \frac{\Sigma xy}{\sqrt{(\Sigma x^2)(\Sigma y^2)}}$$

ITEM 25.8: SUMMARY TABLE SHOWING VALUES OF r BETWEEN
PAIRS OF TESTS

	A	B	C	D	E
A					
B					
C					
D					
E					
Column totals					

Note: All cells in both halves of the table should be filled in. Vertical column totals should then be made and entered at the bottom of the table.

Exercise 26
Evaluation of Psychological Tests

Introduction

Psychological tests are often attractively produced and printed. Their novel designs and illustrations and their general format are frequently of great intrinsic interest, and all too often this interest is transformed into unquestioning respect, with the result that tests are treated less cautiously and critically than they should be. Nevertheless, some well-constructed tests, wisely and carefully used, have great utility and enable us to make practical human decisions or to design research enquiries with much greater assurance and precision. The *potential* usefulness of psychological tests is no longer a matter of controversy. Tests of maximum performance (ability tests) play an extremely useful part in education and tests of typical performance (personality tests) are widely used and accepted in clinical, counselling and educational work.

Before any test is employed for any purpose, however, it is essential that the user makes a thorough enquiry to discover whether the test has been adequately constructed, whether it has been administered already to a sufficiently large number of people to allow satisfactory norms to be made available—and whether it has been demonstrated to possess those two most important attributes—reliability and validity. In addition the user must enquire about the designer's declared purpose in constructing the test and must satisfy himself that this test is the best choice for his particular local and immediate requirements.

A. RELIABILITY

As applied to psychological tests 'reliability' has a special meaning. It does not refer to 'quality', goodness or worthwhileness for any special purpose, but rather to the regularity or consistency with which the test will give the same score on different occasions when applied to the same person. Numerous chance factors operate when a test is being taken and what the test interpreter needs to know is the probable inaccuracy in the test score due to such chance factors. The reliability of a test could be expressed as a correlation coefficient between sets of scores given by the same group of people on two different occasions. If two such sets of scores were identical the correlation coefficient would be $+ 1\cdot0$ and the consistency would be perfect.

Unfortunately a correlation coefficient is not an entirely satisfactory way of describing test reliability because the size of a computed correlation coefficient happens to depend on the *range* of scores in the particular group of people used to compute the correlation. The greater the range of scores happens to be, the greater is the computed correlation. Consequently a reliability coefficient of this kind computed from a large, heterogeneous population (e.g., in the Services) may be quite misleading when the test is to be used on a small, selected (e.g., student) population, having a relatively small range of ability. It is often more satisfactory therefore to use the *standard error* of scores as a guide to the reliability of a test. This tells us in effect what we might expect to happen if a person were to take the same test over and over again (assuming for the moment no improvement due to learning). The standard Error here indicates the range of variations we could expect in that person's score, i.e., the zone of inaccuracy which surrounds an obtained score.

Given that John Smith's score is 138 on Test A and that the S.E. of measurement of Test A is $3\cdot4$ we can say that the chances are high that his true score (unadulterated by random influences) lies between 138 plus $3\cdot4$ and 138 minus $3\cdot4$. How high are the chances? (See Connolly & Sluckin.)

B. VALIDITY

The second indispensable property of a test is that it should be *valid*, i.e., that it should measure what it pretends to measure, e.g., intelligence (and not something quite different, such as education). There are several ways of checking a test's validity.

1. *'Concurrent'* validity can be assessed by finding out whether the test gives the same answer as another independent source of information, for example, does a new intelligence test give the same I.Q. for John Smith as an old well-established intelligence test such as the Binet Scale? As a second example, does a so-called 'neuroticism' test give the same estimate of John Smith's neuroticism as that given by a psychiatrist who knows him well?

2. *'Predictive'* validity is assessed by finding out how far the test successfully *predicts* a particular outcome, for example, does a so-called

'Recidivism Prediction Test' really indicate the likelihood of future court appearances of the person tested? Is there in fact a high correlation between test scores and the number of future appearances in court? Both concurrent and predictive validities are commonly reported as correlation coefficients (Rank difference or Product Moment).

3. *'Content' validity* can be assessed by careful inspection of the test items to see that they are composed of material which is truly relevant for present purposes, for example if it were wished to test children's general knowledge of world geography a 'Geographical Knowledge Test' whose items were restricted to the physical geography of Africa would be useless and misleading. The study of content validity is particularly important in achievement testing.

4. *'Construct validity'* is more difficult to assess. It concerns the degree to which, for example, a test said to be measuring 'introversion' or 'anxiety' or some other hypothetical construct is sensitive to real changes in these. Thus a test purporting to measure anxiety whose scores convincingly rose when the persons being tested were exposed to the threat of electric shock would have a certain construct validity.

It is important to note however that published validity coefficients can give no more than a hint of the relevance of a test to a particular local use. Validity must almost always be established locally before a test is used in a serious enquiry. Furthermore, the significance of a particular magnitude of a validity coefficient requires some consideration and depends on the conditions of use. Thus, for example, if a test is to be used for 'creaming off' the best 10 per cent of a class of schoolchildren for specialised education, the validity coefficient must be very much higher (for a given expectation of error) than if the test is to be used to 'cream off' the best 50 per cent. (See Cronbach's *Essentials of Psychological Testing*, 1960, ... on 'Selection Ratio'.)

Objective

To compare two tests for *a.* reliability, *b.* validity, and *c.* adequacy of construction and presentation with particular reference to their use for a specified purpose, namely, selection for higher education.

Materials

Two complete sets of test materials.
Suggested tests are A: Wechsler Adult Intelligence Scale (WAIS), and   B: Stanford-Binet Scale

Method

1. Examine both sets of materials. Determine how much information is presented on reliability and validity in the test manuals.

2. Try to find references to examples of the use of these tests in selection for higher education, for example with 10, 11 and 12 year old children—both from the manuals and from the reviews in
Buros, O. K., *Mental Measurements Yearbook*, and texts such as
Cronbach, L. J., *Essentials of Psychological Testing*, or
Anastasi, A., *Psychological Testing*.

3. Read some opinions of reviewers of the two tests in the *Mental Measurements Yearbook*, and the criticisms of the tests given by Anastasi or Cronbach.

4. Make a brief summary of the normative information presented in the test manuals, with a careful note of the populations to which they refer.

5. Complete the table in Item 26.1 by reference to the test manuals and the above texts.

Treatment of Results

Prepare a summary statement (about 200 words) which comments upon the particular strengths and weaknesses of each test and which justifies the selection of one test rather than the other for your stated purpose.

Discussion

1. To what further uses (other than selection for higher education) could these tests be applied? What further headings would be needed in the comparative table in order to assess the relative suitability of A and B for such purposes?

2. What further issues (beyond the purely technical ones described in this exercise) should be considered before deciding to use psychological tests? What considerations may affect the desirability (as distinct from the possibility) of using tests? What may determine the acceptability of tests to the persons tested?

References

WECHSLER, D., *The Measurement and Appraisal of Adult Intelligence* (Williams & Wilkins, Baltimore 1958).

BUROS, O. K., *5th* or *6th Mental Measurements Yearbook* (Gryphon Press, New Jersey 1959).
ANASTASI, A., *Psychological Testing* (Collier-Macmillan, N.Y. 1954).
CRONBACH, L. J., *Essentials of Psychological Testing* (Harper, N.Y. 1960).

ITEM 26.1: COMPARISON OF 2 TESTS

	A	B
Title		
Author		
Publisher		
Date of publication		
Latest date of manual available		
Groups for which intended		
Cost		
Time required for administration		
Stated purpose of test		
General description of test items		
Scoring method		
General comments on adequacy of manual		
Information on validity *a.* concurrent validity *b.* predictive validity *c.* content validity *d.* construct validity		

ITEM 26.1 (continued)

	A	B
Information on validity for your stated purpose, e.g., for selection for higher education		
Information on stability (reliability)		
Adequacy of reliability for your stated purpose		
Norms presented Nature: Number of cases:		
Specific inadequacies:		

Exercise 27. Raw and Standard Scores

Introduction

Psychological tests are valuable because they apply standard stimulus conditions to everyone tested; hence they are fair. Furthermore they provide rules for the objective scoring of responses, i.e., they are not affected by the subjective standards of the observer. They yield test scores which enable meaningful comparisons to be made between different people. Even the raw scores (such as the number of correct answers) from an ability test may be useful in telling us which is the best applicant for a job. A single raw score could be useful in selecting staff if we knew from past experience that a certain minimum score was needed to do a certain job satisfactorily. Generally speaking however, raw test scores are only useful to us if we know how well a large number of *other* people have done in this test, so that we can compare our individual's score with the mean score of the general population. We therefore need 'norms' (which should always be available in the test-manual; if they are not the test should be discarded).

Raw scores are further limited, however, because they do not allow us to make useful comparisons between performances on different tests. If Jones gets 22 correct on an English test and 14 correct on an arithmetic test is he better at English or Arithmetic? If we have norms, i.e., we know the mean score of a large number of other comparable people on each test, we *may* be able to say that Jones is better than average at English but poorer than average at Arithmetic, but we are quite unable to say *how much* better. We cannot compare three English items with eight Arithmetic items. To do this we need a system of scoring using universal units which are comparable whatever the test we happen to be using. There are, in fact, several such scoring systems available to us and these will be examined in this exercise. Though such 'standard score' systems differ in small details, they are all based on the same notion—that of expressing the individual's score as a *deviation* from the mean score of the population with which he is compared. The unit of deviation used is the standard deviation (σ), and the raw score is transformed into a standard score by dividing the difference between the raw score and the raw score mean by the standard deviation.

$$\text{Thus standard score} = \frac{\text{Raw score—Mean of population's raw score}}{\text{Standard deviation}}$$

There are only minor differences between the various standard score systems, and these have been introduced simply for reasons of convenience (e.g., to avoid negative signs and decimals).

The simplest system is the *Z-score system* where the mean is taken as zero, and the standard deviation is 1·0. Person A, who for example has scored 2 S.D. units above the mean, is said to have a Z-score of + 2. Person B, scoring 3 S.D. units below the mean, has a Z-score of − 3.

Now consider a further example in terms of raw scores. Let us say that Person C has a raw score of 56 on a test whose population mean raw score is known from the manual to be 61 and whose S.D. is known to be 8. This person's score is

$$\frac{56 - 61}{8} = 0\cdot625 \text{ S.D. units below the mean, i.e., his Z-score is} -0\cdot625.$$

Another system, the *T-score system*, avoids this use of negative signs and the need for decimals by taking the mean as 50. One standard deviation unit is equal to 10 on this scale. Person A (2 S.D. above) has a T-score of 70 and Person B (3 S.D. below) has a T-score of 20.

Modern intelligence tests use a system known as the *Deviation I.Q.* This standard score transformation is used in the Wechsler Adult Intelligence Scale, for example, where the mean is set at 100 and the S.D. is 15. Person A (2 S.D. above) would have a Deviation I.Q. of 130, and Person B (3 S.D. below) would have a Deviation I.Q. of 55 (i.e., 100 minus 3 × 15).

The great advantage of standard scores is that they allow comparisons to be made between performances on different tests. We can use the standard scores which we have so far described for comparison however, only when both distributions of test raw scores are of equal form, e.g., when both distributions are *normal*. If the raw scores of the general population do not follow the normal distribution curve, e.g., if they are 'skewed', then a special procedure to produce 'normalised' standard scores must be undertaken before comparing the test performances with one another. A further advantage of standard scores is that differences between standard scores are proportional to differences between raw scores, and that they can be used to compute averages and correlations. The disadvantage of standard scores is that untrained people cannot interpret them—their meaning is by no means as obvious to administrators and others interested in test results as other types of transformed score (such as percentiles).

Objective

To compare the varieties of standard score available and to investigate these in relation to a specific test of ability.

Materials

WECHSLER, D., *The Measurement and Appraisal of Adult Intelligence* (Williams & Wilkins, Baltimore 1958).
ANASTASI, A., *Psychological Testing* (Collier-Macmillan, N.Y. 1954).

Method

Complete Item 27.1 in the following way:
  1. Mark on Item 27.1 intervals of 1, 2, and 3 S.D. above and below the mean.
  2. Mark in the Z-scores corresponding to these intervals.
  3. Mark in the T-scores corresponding to these intervals.
  4. Mark in Wechsler's 'scaled score' system. (This is based as a matter of convenience for the Wechsler test on a mean 'scaled score' of 10 and an S.D. equal to 3 'scaled score' units.)
  5. Mark in values of 'Deviation I.Q.s' on the diagram (neglecting for the moment that it would be quite improper to base an I.Q. assessment on the results of a single sub-test).
  6. Compute the Z-score of Person C who has a raw score of 72 on a test whose mean score is stated in a test-manual as 62 and S.D. to be 4.
  7. Compute the T-score of the same person and mark his position on your diagram.
  8. Select one sub-test from any intelligence scale and briefly describe what normative results are available in the manual for this sub-test. To whom do the norms relate?

ITEM 27.1

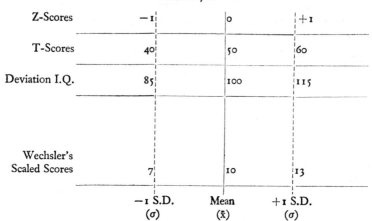

Z-Scores	−1	0	+1
T-Scores	40	50	60
Deviation I.Q.	85	100	115
Wechsler's Scaled Scores	7	10	13
	−1 S.D. (σ)	Mean (x̄)	+1 S.D. (σ)

Section D

Design of Investigations

Introduction (D)

It often falls to the social scientist to test specific hypotheses which may, if eventually found to be true, attain the status of empirical generalisations or laws. The hypotheses may arise from a wide range of sources. Observation of motorists' behaviour at pedestrian crossings might give rise to the hypothesis that frustration produces aggression. The same hypothesis might equally well arise from speculative theorising (such as that of psychoanalytic writers). Sometimes hypotheses arise directly from previous research, and sometimes again they arise during the course of quite practical investigations as, for example, into the legibility of aircraft dials in difficult flight conditions. The method which the social scientist brings to his task of *testing hypotheses* is the subject of the fourth section of this book.

It is important to understand the meaning and significance of several basic concepts in experimental design and to examine projected experiments (and even those reported in journals) for weaknesses in design. The object in conducting an experiment is to observe what happens to one variable when another systematically alters or is systematically altered; this enables us to say whether one variable is, in some way, related to the other.

Sometimes the social scientist tests a hypothesis by a carefully designed survey of existing events, processes or behaviour. On the other hand, it may sometimes be more economical of time and effort deliberately to alter the situation which gives rise to the events, processes or behaviour, i.e., to perform an experiment.

It has sometimes been objected that this deliberate intervention by the experimenter can have a restrictive effect and can make enquiries artificial and trivial. On the other hand as John Madge (1953) has pointed out, precise, limited investigation of this kind is surely much more useful than those impressionistic, broad, sweeping enquiries which are 'realistic, large, important, woolly and totally inconclusive'. The experimental method has in fact been conspicuously successful in a wide variety of social enquiries—particularly in investigations of small group processes. It has been less successful in studies of large groups, communities and organisations. In these areas, progress has certainly been made, but usually by the use of methods which Argyle (1957) describes as 'valid non-experimental methods', whose underlying assumptions and precautions are similar to those of the best experimental methods, but where there is no actual *manipulation* of conditions by the observer. It is important to remember that such well-designed, non-experimental enquiries need have no less rigour than experiments in the more conventional sense, whose methodology they share; their conclusions need carry no less conviction.

The variable that is under the control of the experimenter and manipulated by him is known technically as the *independent variable*. The variable which is expected to fluctuate as a result of changes which the experimenter makes in the independent variable is known as the *dependent variable*. It is measurement of the dependent variable which produces results. A simple illustration is contained in the following example. A psychologist studied the effect of lighting level on performance of a simple task (speed of assembling a jig-saw puzzle). The independent variable was the light level which he could increase or diminish, and the dependent variable was the speed with which the task was performed.

This is the simplest possible type of experimental design and has been called the simple successive conditions design. The same people are exposed first to one value of the independent variable (poor lighting) and then to a second value of the independent variable (good lighting), and the change in the dependent variable (speed of working) is then measured. It is obviously important that only a single independent variable (in this case the light) should fluctuate. If others are present it is impossible to say what is producing the observed change in the dependent variable. In the famous Hawthorn Studies the investigators were studying the effect of different working conditions on rate of production in a factory. In one study they found (as might be expected) that as illumination increased so output improved; but they also found that when the light in certain other workshops was decreased production still improved! This was because level of illumination was not the only, or even the most important, independent variable operating. The subjects of this experiment were also being affected by the social pressures of being separated from their usual working situation and being made aware that their level of output was being checked.

Because it may be difficult to say with certainty just what factors *are* operating in a situation a *control group* is used in some kinds of experimental design. This means simply that the experiment is repeated on two groups in only one of which the independent variable (e.g., the lighting) is deliberately changed. This is the experimental group. The other, control group is treated in exactly the same way, except that the independent variable is not introduced or not changed (e.g., the lighting is kept constant). The experimenter usually tries to ensure before the experiment starts that the two groups are nearly equal on other variables which might affect the results (such as intelligence, skill, social class, etc.). That is, the two groups are *matched*. It would now be known that the two groups are initially similar and that their experience is identical apart from the carefully defined differences in the independent variable (only one has better lighting), so it is possible to regard any observed differences in the dependent variable (change in speed of working) as being directly related to the independent variable (illumination). To design a new study, therefore, of the effects of illumination on output, two groups would be needed who were similar in their experience of the job, speed of working and perhaps intelligence, i.e., they would be *matched*. The groups would be put in different experimental rooms. In the *control group* the level of illumination (the independent variable) would be *low*. In the *experimental group*, by contrast, the level of illumination would be *high*. The output of the two groups (dependent variable) would then be measured and compared. This design has been called the 'after only' design because the people taking part are measured only once (and not twice—before and after—as in our first example of the 'successive conditions' design). The advantage of this 'after only' method over the previous successive method is that it does not give the people involved opportunity to improve through practice. In the successive conditions method they might have improved quite considerably from first to second testing simply by becoming acquainted with the task—and not because of the lighting improvement. The trouble with this method, however, is that it assumes that the experimental group and the control group are equivalent in all respects (i.e., that they have been perfectly matched), and it is never possible to be certain about this.

It is sometimes possible and advantageous to combine these two designs. In this case there would be an experimental group and an equivalent control group. The control group would have a consistently low illumination throughout. The experimental group, however, would have a low illumination at first and then later a high illumination. Both groups would be measured twice for speed of working—both early and late in the experiment. It would then be possible to compare the output of the experimental group under increased illumination both with its own prior performance and with the performance of the control group who had been treated identically in all ways except lighting.

Sometimes our main interest may be not so much the effect of different conditions but the effect upon *different types of people* of the *same* conditions. Here the independent variable to be altered is the type of person (white or black? bright or dull? male or female?). The dependent variable to be studied might be speed of working. The conditions of work would be constant for everyone. This is sometimes called an 'Individual Differences' design. If a numerical measure were available for the independent variable (such as I.Q. scores), then different speeds of working could be correlated with different individual I.Q.s. Unfortunately however, the independent variable is not always continuously variable (as it is with intelligence) but can only be dichotomised (as for example into male/female).

There are a number of more complex and interesting designs available, however, which allow *several* independent variables to be studied simultaneously—and these use more advanced statistical methods (such as analysis of variance) rather than the correlational methods of the individual differences design, or the measure of differences between means of the 'after-only' and 'successive conditions' designs. With the more complex designs it is possible to break down the total variation observed in the results into component parts which can be safely attributed to each separate variable—and this represents a wonderful economy in time and effort. Not only do such methods show the relative importance of the different variables in relation to each other (i.e., the differences *between* whole groups), but they can also tell us a good deal about the variations *within* the separate groups of people taking part. Thus one group might be shown to be highly heterogeneous from the point of view of intelligence, and yet another might turn out to be composed entirely of people within a few I.Q. points of one another. The 'Latin Square' design is an example of a design of this more complex type.

According to Townsend, there are two main classes of design:

1. The 'factorial' designs, in which the main concern is to discover *what factors* are involved in a process;

2. The 'functional' designs, in which the main concern is to find *the size of the relationship* between the factors in a relationship which

is already *known* to exist. These are the two basic paradigms for the design of experiments and in all their different possible variations they provide adequate facility for most of the experimental problems arising in the social sciences.

In a *factorial design* two matched groups are used. In the experimental group the independent variable is introduced, whereas in the control group it is not. The dependent variable is measured for both groups and compared. This kind of design is used to determine what factors *do* influence the dependent variable, and, although it can do this perfectly satisfactorily, it is a relatively insensitive design because it provides no indication of the degree or type of relationship between the independent and dependent variables. Thus the hypothesis that alcohol impairs driving ability could be tested by the following simple factorial design. The members of the experimental group could each be given a drink of alcohol (independent variable). The control group would be given a drink of water. Both groups would then be asked to drive and the mean number of errors for the two groups compared (dependent variable). But how does the *degree* of impairment of driving skill depend upon the amount of alcohol consumed? To answer this question a functional design is needed. Groups matched for driving ability would be used and a different value of the independent variable (alcohol) applied to each group and the dependent variable (driving) recorded for each. The results of such an experiment could be analysed either by comparing average driving ability at several different specified alcohol levels or alternatively by correlating the fluctuations in the independent variable (alcohol) with those in the dependent variable (driving skill). A good functional design could yield quite precise information about this relationship.

The experiment on alcohol outlined above might yield a relationship shown in the graph (see Item D1).

This would enable precise predictions to be made about the amount of impairment which could be expected to follow the consumption of a given quantity of alcohol. If the relationship is a consistent one, it may also be possible to extrapolate to previously untried situations—for example to give a good estimate of impairment at an alcohol level not previously tested (see Item D2).

Closer analysis will show that these designs vary in two ways; firstly, in the way in which they achieve the matching of the groups and, secondly, in the nature of the independent variable.

Groups should always be matched to make them equal, or at least very similar with respect to all the variables considered relevant. This can be achieved in a number of ways.

1. *The same individuals can be used to form both the experimental and control groups* (or in the case of a functional design all of the experimental groups). This does ensure perfect matching on such elements as pretest ability, motivation and experience, but unfortunately new problems are introduced when the same individuals are tested repeatedly. If, for example, we were trying to test the hypothesis that a special form of training increases intelligence we might be tempted to test all our subjects to assess the individual (and so subsequently the group mean) intelligence, then to administer the special training and then measure them all again. The trouble with this design is that it neglects the fact that intelligence test scores might well increase simply because of the experience of being tested previously. Again, and in the opposite direction, fatigue might affect test scores and this might disguise other changes because it was more pronounced at the end of the experiment than at the beginning. In a functional experiment it may also be important to take careful note of the *order* in which different values of the independent variable have been applied. A special design, known as the 'Latin square design', has been created to overcome this difficulty.

2. A second way of matching groups is by carefully selecting two individuals who are known to be similar on the human variables considered to be important—and then *assigning one of the pair to the experimental group and the other to the control group*. Unfortunately it is sometimes difficult to find individuals who are truly equivalent on the many different variables one might wish to match. In an experiment on the effectiveness of propaganda in producing attitude change it would be highly desirable to match for variables such as party-affiliation, sex, age, education and many others besides. This kind of matching is technically ideal but practically impossible. All too often it is necessary to waste many an otherwise useful subject simply because a matching person, similar on all important criteria, cannot be found. In enquiries where measurement or testing is necessary a large amount of time can be wasted finding information about subjects who are subsequently going to be excluded anyway for lack of a suitable match.

3. *Group parameters may be matched.* That is to say the groups are so selected as to be made equal with regard to average possession of each important variable. For example, members of each group may have had an average of six years of secondary education and an average intelligence quotient of 110. The range or extent to which the variable is

distributed within each group should also be carefully matched. It could obviously lead to error if one group were relatively homogeneous and another group showed considerable individual variability.

4. In the fourth method of matching the experimenter *randomises the way in which individuals are allocated to groups*. This is usually adopted in situations where precise matching would be a long and difficult operation or where all the important variables are not known or cannot be measured. In many experiments previous experience of the situation might well be relevant and this could be very difficult to determine. Again the genetic background of the subjects might be important. However could this be assessed? The way out of this difficulty is to allocate individuals to groups at random by taking their names from an alphabetical list in a sequence dictated by a table of random numbers. It is known from mathematical sampling theory that it is only with very large groups of people that it is possible to be confident that two groups drawn at random from a population will in fact be similar on the variables distributed in that population. The randomised group technique therefore can only be used in studies where it is possible to investigate large numbers of cases.

The second important way in which functional and factorial designs differ is in their treatment of the independent variable. In a factorial design the independent variable is always dichotomised. In the functional design, however, the independent variable can be continuously variable, or alternatively it can be grouped, or yet again it can be dichotomised. A functional design to study the way neuroticism is related to frustration tolerance might, for example, use the score on a neuroticism test as the independent variable. The scores of different individuals could either be dichotomised at a certain crucial level, and the two ensuing groups compared, or the scores could be grouped into three or more groups, or alternatively the scores could be used as they stand and correlated with some derived measure of frustration tolerance.

It is a useful exercise to attempt to construct a brief outline of a design to enquire into each of the following problems. In some cases it will be found that several alternative designs are possible, in which case the method most economical in time and expenditure should be chosen.

Design experiments to investigate the following questions:

1. Are class background and educational achievement associated in some way?

2. Do personality factors affect the assessment of a person's intelligence in an interview situation?

3. What is the relationship between speed limits and actual driving speed?

4. Are students who excel in sports better or worse than average academically?

5. How could you find out if an allegedly 'non-verbal' intelligence test did in fact have verbal component?

6. Does prior acquaintanceship affect group interaction?

7. Are different types of crimes committed significantly more often by different age groups?

8. Is satisfaction obtained from being a member of a group affected by the success and failure of the group in reaching a desired goal?

9. What proportion of people wash their hands after visiting the toilet?
Are any demographic variables (e.g., sex) of particular importance?

10. Does education affect rating preferences?

11. Is the propaganda put out by political parties:
    a. different from language used in other media?
    b. homogeneous, or do the parties differ in style and methods?

12. What, if any, is the degree of similarity between pre-election political aims and post-election performance? Has the relationship been historically constant?

13. Has the socio-economic background of world leaders changed in the last 100, and the last 50, years?

14. Is knowledge of Chinese customs, languages, ideology, etc., in any way related to attitudes towards the Chinese?

15. Are whites more prejudiced against negroes or vice versa?

16. Is there any relationship between the economic prosperity of the country and number of crimes committed?

17. What are the most effective ways of changing attitudes?

18. Is age of weaning associated with neuroticism?

ITEM D I

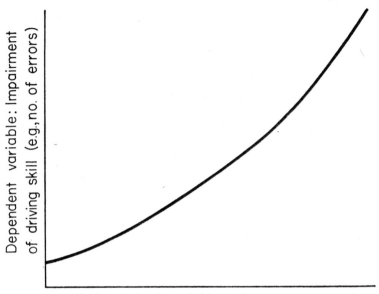

ITEM D2: DIAGRAMMATIC SUMMARY OF TWO BASIC TYPES
OF EXPERIMENTAL DESIGN

Design	*Groups*	*Matching*	*Independent Variable*	*Dependent Variable*
Factorial	Experimental	√	Introduced	Measured
	Control	√	Not introduced	Measured
Functional	Experimental	√	Different values	Measured
	Experimental	√	introduced for	Measured
	Experimental	√	each group	Measured

Exercise 28
Behaviour in the Presence of Others

Introduction

The simplest possible social situation arises when two or more people are aware of each other's presence. Even if no obvious visible interaction occurs, the presence of another person has a considerable influence on the behaviour of each individual. This has been noticed from the very beginning of social psychology. Zajonc (1966) has recently presented a summary of some of the available evidence about the relationship between behaviour and the presence of others. He suggests that the presence of another individual produces social arousal and this produces improvement in some tasks and impairment of other tasks. In particular, the acquisition of new responses (i.e., learning) is hindered by the presence of others, but on the other hand the performance of a previously learned task is facilitated. This statement by Zajonc is a theoretical generalisation on the basis of existing evidence, and some specific predictions arising from it can be tested. It is possible to predict, for example, that learning nonsense syllables will be less efficient by members of small groups than by individuals learning alone. Furthermore, the opposite should hold true for the performance of a simple, well-learned mechanical operation.

Objective

To test by experiment the hypotheses that; *a.* new learning is impaired, and *b.* that previously learnt behaviour is improved, by the presence of others.

Materials

List of Nonsense Syllables for Experiment 1 (Item 28.1).
Multiplication Exercises A (Item 28.2).
Multiplication Exercises B (Item 28.3).
Chart for t-Test (Item 28.4).

Method

SUMMARY OF EXPERIMENTAL DESIGN

Type	Groups	Matching	Independent Variable	Dependent Variable
Functional	Experimental	Matched	In Groups	Performance measured
	Control	Pairs	Alone	Performance measured

Method

1. LEARNING EXPERIMENT

At least six subjects are required. It should be explained that the experiment is concerned with learning, but no mention of competition or comparisons between individuals should be made. All subjects should be asked to learn List 1 (Item 28.1) as follows: Allow the subject to read the list for 1 minute, then using a set of previously prepared index cards with one of the syllables on each, show the first card to the subject and ask him to guess the one that follows. If there is a wrong response or no response within 5 seconds record one error and show the next card. Go through the list of 12 in this way. Repeat until the criterion of *one completely perfect trial* is reached.

For each individual tested there will now be an 'Error score'. On the basis of this select matched pairs whose performances are approximately equal; one of each pair (decide by tossing a coin) goes into the experimental group and the other into the control group. The control group can now be tested individually on List 2 in exactly the same way. These subjects can then be asked to remain as an audience while individual subjects from the experimental group are tested.

2. PERFORMANCE EXPERIMENT

Using different subjects, proceed in the same way using List A of Multiplication Exercises (Item 28.2). Match the subjects for performance and divide subjects into equated experimental and control groups. Test the control group individually on List B (Item 28.3). The experimental group can be tested as a group on List B as long as each subject cannot see what the others are writing. It is important that there should be no deliberate introduction of a spirit of competition because this would be introducing yet another variable.

Treatment of Results

Calculate the mean scores for both tasks in the 'alone' and 'social' situations. Then compare the mean using the t-test chart provided (Item 28.4), i.e., compare means for each task separately.

Discussion

1. Do the results yield any evidence about the value of the original hypothesis that presence in a social group produces an increase in performance and a decrement in learning?

2. In what ways could the experimental design have been improved?

3. Outline other experiments which would be necessary before finally accepting or rejecting the hypotheses.

References

ZAJONC, R. B., *Social Psychology: An Experimental Approach* (Wadsworth, Belmont 1966).

HILGARD, E. R., in Stephens, S. S. (Ed.), *Handbook of Experimental Psychology* (Wiley, N.Y. 1951).

ITEM 28.1: LIST OF NONSENSE SYLLABLES FOR EXPT. I

LIST 1	TAJ	LIST 2	YIC
	ZIN		QOM
	JEC		GEP
	YOX		DUZ
	FUQ		RIJ
	BIP		NAW
	DAK		XOL
	XEW		HUQ
	CUG		TEF
	JOF		ZIF
	QID		VOB
	LEH		PAH

From Hilgard, E. R., in Stephens, S. S., (Ed.) *Handbook of Experimental Psychology* (Wiley, N.Y. 1951), p. 540.

ITEM 28.2: MULTIPLICATION EXERCISES FOR EXPT. 2

Please try and do as many of these multiplication sums as possible. You will be stopped after 1 minute and the number you have computed correctly will be counted as your score. Work as fast and as accurately as possible.

LIST A

| 5242 | 8856 | 7162 | 4308 | 2451 | 8931 |
| 63 | 24 | 84 | 56 | 77 | 69 |

| 4739 | 2445 | 1238 | 7355 | 3367 | 2916 |
| 97 | 18 | 46 | 18 | 85 | 35 |

| 2712 | 9045 | 4563 | 4825 | 8452 | 1936 |
| 89 | 27 | 57 | 37 | 74 | 43 |

ITEM 28.3: MULTIPLICATION EXERCISES FOR EXPT. 2

LIST B

Please try and do as many of these multiplication sums as possible. You will be stopped after 1 minute and the number you have completed correctly will be counted as your score. Work as fast and as accurately as possible.

| 7488 | 6373 | 5681 | 3921 | 1695 | 7049 |
| 73 | 48 | 23 | 94 | 68 | 39 |

| 4955 | 3635 | 1329 | 5126 | 7539 | 6492 |
| 12 | 42 | 95 | 83 | 77 | 73 |

| 1697 | 9534 | 3572 | 7012 | 2643 | 4373 |
| 65 | 58 | 89 | 29 | 18 | 45 |

ITEM 28.4: CHART FOR T-TEST BETWEEN MEAN PERFORMANCE
OF INDIVIDUALS ALONE AND INDIVIDUALS IN THE PRESENCE
OF OTHERS ON NONSENSE SYLLABLE LEARNING

	X	Y	x	y	x^2	y^2
Σ						
$\dfrac{\Sigma}{N}$						

$$t = \frac{\bar{X} - \bar{Y}}{\sigma_D} \qquad \sigma_D = \sqrt{\frac{\Sigma x^2 + \Sigma y^2}{(N_1 - 1) + (N_2 - 1)} \times \left(\frac{1}{N_1} + \frac{1}{N_2} \right)}$$

Look up t in tables for degrees of freedom $(N_1 - 1) + (N_2 - 1)$ (e.g. Connolly and Sluckin pp. 96–9).

Similar chart is needed for multiplication task.

Exercise 29. Restricting Interaction

Introduction

Interaction in a social situation is a very complex process which is very much taken for granted. It is not until there is some deliberate interference with the natural situation that individuals are forced to recognise the many subtle cues they are responding to. The person is in fact behaving like a servo-mechanism, basing the next response on the other person's reaction to the previous one. Just as the motorist is continually changing the track of the car in response to changes in the direction, width and camber of the road, so the individual in a social situation is taking into account the manifest attitude of his social partners and whether they appear interested, bored, amused or displeased. This process is quite unconscious and completely automatic. This exercise and the one following (on social reinforcement) examine respectively the effects of withdrawing feedback cues and of altering them systematically.

Objective

To determine how the accuracy of the individual's perception of a verbal message is affected when 'social feedback' is curtailed.

Materials

The geometric diagrams provided (Items 29.1 to 29.4).
The blank for reproducing one of these diagrams (Item 29.5).
Pencil, ruler and compass.

Method

Summary of experimental design.

Type	Groups	Matching	Independent Variable	Dependent Variable
Functional	Expt. Expt. Expt. Control	same indi- viduals	Degrees of 'feedback' permitted	Performance measured

The task is for one person to describe a diagram to a second and for this latter to reproduce it, the independent variable being the degree of feedback that is permitted. Five subjects are required, four of whom undergo each of the four conditions, the fifth being the individual who describes the diagram in each case (Subject 'X'). The design of the experiment is improved by randomising the order in which the subjects go through the conditions and also by using the four diagrams for different conditions.

Subject X should have the purpose of the experiment explained to him and be given sufficient time to familiarise himself with the diagrams. He should be told that he will have to describe the diagrams to other people under different conditions and that the object of the experiment is to get the subjects to reproduce the diagrams as accurately as possible both in terms of design *and scale*. It must be emphasised that he should never exceed the instructions given and in no circumstances must the experimental subject be allowed to *see* the original diagram.

The four conditions are:

1. Minimal feedback. The subjects sit back to back and Subject X describes Diagram 1 to the other subject who must not say anything or make any other kind of sound. The following instructions should be given.

'You will have a diagram described to you—it is a complicated geometric shape and I want you to reproduce it as accurately as you can both in terms of design and scale. You may not ask any questions or say anything at all. You can use the pencil, ruler and compass provided.'

2. Restricted feedback. Again the subjects sit back to back as in condition 1 but this time the subject is allowed to ask Subject X questions that can be answered by 'Yes' or 'No' only. No other interaction is allowed.

3. Free verbal feedback. The subjects face each other and are allowed to talk and question each other in the normal way but Subject X is not allowed to see the experimental subject's attempt at reproducing the diagram.

4. Control situation. Same as 3 except Subject X can also see the experimental subject's attempt while he is describing the original. He must *not* allow the subject to see the original however.

Randomising. Use the following table for randomising the order in which each subject goes through the conditions.

Subject	Order			
1	1	2	3	4
2	2	4	1	3
3	3	1	4	2
4	4	3	2	1

If the diagrams are always used in the same order, 1, 2, 3, 4, they will serve for different conditions each time. For example Subject 2 will start with Condition 2 (restricted feedback) using Diagram 1. He will then go on to Condition 4 (control) using Diagram 2. The table has been designed to produce the maximum amount of randomisation compatible with the design. Notice that each diagram is only used for each condition once and that no condition is ever followed by the same condition twice. Also any fatigue or practice effects will be perfectly evenly distributed over the different conditions. In any factorial design such as this it is important to bear these considerations in mind. The exact instructions given to subjects will obviously vary depending upon the order of conditions but they should be standardised as far as possible.

Treatment of Results

Each of the four diagrams is contained within a four-inch square. Using tracing paper construct a four-inch square grid which divides the square into 16 one-inch square segments. Score five points for each segment which exactly corresponds on the reproduction to the original and between four and zero if there is some discrepancy but some agreement. The maximum 'agreement score' is therefore 80 and the absolute minimum is zero.

Score each of the reproductions in this way.

At this stage there is a choice of statistical procedures which could be applied. An analysis of variance could be made which would compare all the groups simultaneously with each other and also give an overall estimate of the difference between groups. Alternatively a series of individual t-Tests could be undertaken; where there are four conditions six comparisons would have to be made (between 1 and 2; 1 and 3; 1 and 4; 2 and 3; 3 and 4; 2 and 4).

A chart for the analysis of variance is provided (Item 29.6). Sometimes in practice it is necessary to follow an analysis of variance by individual t-Tests to ascertain exactly where the significant difference is to be found.

Discussion

1. Was there a progression in accuracy scores from the situation with *least* feedback to the one with the *most*?

2. How different would you expect the results to be with other types of material?

References

LEAVITT, H. J., and MUECCER, R. A. H., 'Some effects of feedback on communication', *Human Relations* Vol. 4 (1951), pp. 401–410.

ITEM 29.1

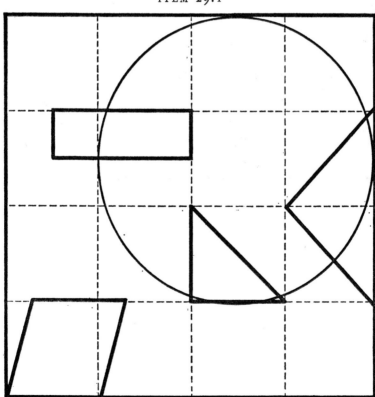

ITEM 29.2

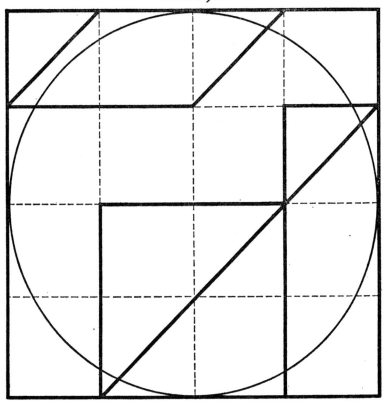

ITEM 29.3

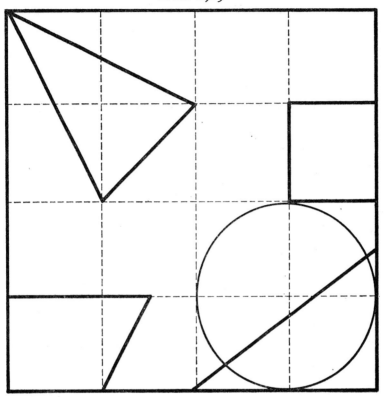

ITEM 29.4

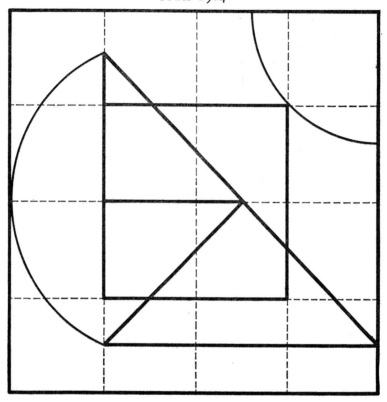

ITEM 29.5: BLANK FOR REPRODUCING DIAGRAMS
AS DESCRIBED

ITEM 29.6: CHART FOR THE ANALYSIS OF VARIANCE

Condition 1		*Condition 2*		*Condition 3*		*Condition 4*	
X_1	X_1^2	X_2	X_2^2	X_3	X_3^2	X_4	X_4^2
$\Sigma X_1 =$	$\Sigma X_1^2 =$	$\Sigma X_2 =$	$\Sigma X_2^2 =$	$\Sigma X_3 =$	$\Sigma X_3^2 =$	$\Sigma X_4 =$	$\Sigma X_4^2 =$
$(\Sigma X_1)^2 =$		$(\Sigma X_2)^2 =$		$(\Sigma X_3)^2 =$		$(\Sigma X_4)^2 =$	

$$\Sigma X = \qquad \Sigma X^2 =$$
$$(\Sigma X)^2 =$$

1. Total sum of squares $= \Sigma X^2 - \dfrac{(\Sigma X)^2}{N}$

2. Sum of squares between groups:

$$\dfrac{(\Sigma X_1)^2}{n_1} + \dfrac{(\Sigma X_2)^2}{n_2} + \dfrac{(\Sigma X_3)^2}{n_3} + \dfrac{(\Sigma X_4)^2}{n_4} - \dfrac{(\Sigma X)^2}{N}$$

3. Sum of squares within groups:

Total sum of squares — sum of squares between groups.

Source of Variation	Sum of Squares	Degrees of Freedom	Mean Square
Between Groups		3	
Within Groups		12	
Total		$15 = (N-1)$	

$$\text{Mean Square} = \dfrac{\text{Sum of squares}}{\text{Degrees of freedom}} =$$

$$F = \dfrac{\text{Mean Square between groups}}{\text{Mean Square within groups}} =$$

Exercise 30. Modifying Behaviour

Introduction

A previous exercise (*No. 28*) on the effect of the presence of other individuals attempted to demonstrate that behaviour is considerably affected by the mere presence of completely passive onlookers. It is evident both from the results of this experiment and from everyday experience that contact and interaction with other people who may deliberately wish to influence behaviour may produce quite important changes in the manner in which a person behaves. Many studies have shown that even apparently insignificant pieces of behaviour such as a nod or a 'hmmm' can produce a significant modification of a subject's verbal responses. Greenspoon (1955) asked subjects to say words completely at random for 50 minutes. Without the subject's knowledge he consistently greeted some words with a 'positive reinforcement'— ('mmmm-hmm') and others with a negative reinforcement ('huh-uh?'). He found that 'mmmm-hmm' increased the frequency of production of that particular kind of word and 'huh-uh?' consistently decreased frequency of production. Other experiments have shown that it is possible to alter not only *how much* a person will say but also *what* he will say. This obviously has important implications in the administration of questionnaires and attitude scales where it is quite conceivable that the interviewer's own bias might influence the responses of his subjects. A disturbing example of this was demonstrated by Singer (1961) and a similar example is replicated here. Singer showed that the kind of items an individual would endorse on the Fascism Scale could be increased to a considerable extent if the interviewer said 'good' or 'right' whenever a subject responded in the chosen direction.

Objective

To assess the effect of social reinforcement on responses made to a questionnaire.

Materials

Eysenck's T-scale and Response Sheet (Items 30.1 and 30.2).

232

Method

Three groups of subjects are required—these can be chosen from a fairly homogeneous student population by matching individuals for age, sex and amount of education (e.g., years in college). As in most social investigations it is desirable to have as many subjects per group as possible. The F-scale as used by Singer is not really suitable for British students mainly because there would be too few authoritarian items endorsed at an operant level of responding. Therefore the Eysenck Tough-mindedness scale is chosen and reproduced at the end of this exercise.

This should be administered verbally to each individual in each of the three groups by reading the item and waiting for the spoken response of 'agree' or 'disagree'. The responses should be recorded on the scoring form provided. For Group 1 subjects' *'tough-minded'* responses should be reinforced with the word 'good'. For Group 2 *'tender-minded'* responses should be reinforced in the same way. In Group 3 (the control group) the answers should simply be recorded and no comment made. The code on the scoring key indicates which responses to reinforce for the tender-minded group. This should be reversed for the tough-minded group.

Treatment of Results

It is predicted that the answers of the two experimental groups will diverge in opposite directions away from the answers given by control groups. This divergence should become more and more marked as more items are answered because more reinforcement of one particular kind of response should have taken place. This is best illustrated graphically.

Group the answers into blocks of four, 1–4, 5–8, 9–12, etc. and calculate the mean number of 'tough-minded' responses in each block for each group. For example, the six members of Group 1 yielded a total of 15 tough-minded answers on the first block of four questions. When divided by the number of subjects (N), i.e., 6, this gives a mean T-score for the first block of 2·5. Repeat for all eight blocks and all three groups. Then plot the number of tough-minded responses per block of four against the successive blocks of four items. There will be three lines on the graph, one for each group which can then be compared.

Discussion

1. How successful was the reinforcement—in what ways could its effect have been increased?

2. Did the subjects realise that an attempt was being made to 'mould' their answers? What were the signs of this?

3. What are the implications of this for attitude scales? What may such scales really be measuring?

References

ZAJONC, R. B., *Social Psychology: An Experimental Approach* (Wadsworth, Belmont 1961).

GREENSPOON, T., 'The Reinforcing Effect of Two Spoken Sounds on the Frequency of Two Responses', in *Amer. J. Psychol.* (1955) 68: pp. 409–416.

SINGER, R. D., 'Verbal Conditioning and Generalisation of Prodemocratic Responses', in *J. Abnom. Soc. Psychol.* (1961) 63: pp. 43–6.

ITEM 30.1: SOCIAL ATTITUDE INVENTORY

(Reproduced by permission from Eysenck, H. J., *Sense and Nonsense in Psychology*, Penguin Books Ltd, 1963)

Instructions to subjects

I am going to read to you a list of sixty statements which represent widely held opinions on various social questions, selected from speeches, books, newspapers and other sources. They were chosen in such a way that most people are likely to agree with some and to disagree with others. After I have read each statement will you please say clearly whether you *agree* or *disagree* or if you cannot decide. I will record your answers. Please answer frankly. Remember this is not a test; there are no right or wrong answers only your own personal opinion. The results of this questionnaire will be completely confidential.

Opinion Statements   *Code*

1. The nation exists for the benefit of the individuals composing it, not the individuals for the benefit of the nation.

2. Coloured people are innately inferior to white people.

3. War is inherent in human nature.

4. Ultimately private property should be abolished and complete Socialism introduced.

5. Persons with serious hereditary defects and diseases should be compulsorily sterilised.

6. In the interests of peace, we must give up part of our national sovereignty.

7. Production and trade should be free from government interference.

8. Divorce laws should be altered to make divorce easier.   T —

9. The so-called underdog deserves little sympathy or help from successful people.   T —

10. Crimes of violence should be punished by flogging.   T —

11. The nationalisation of the great industries is likely to lead to inefficiency, bureaucracy, and stagnation.   T —

12. Men and women have the right to find out whether they are sexually suited before marriage (e.g., by trial marriage).   T —

13. 'My country right or wrong' is a saying which expresses a fundamentally desirable attitude.

14. The average man can live a good enough life without religion.   T —

15. It would be a mistake to have coloured people as foremen over whites.

16. People should realise that their greatest obligation is to their family.

17. There is no survival of any kind after death.   T —

18. The death penalty is barbaric, and should be abolished.   T +

19. There may be a few exceptions, but in general, Jews are pretty much alike.   T —

20. The dropping of the first atom bomb on a Japanese city, killing thousands of innocent women and children was morally wrong and incompatible with our kind of civilisation.   T +

21. Birth control, except when recommended by a doctor, should be made illegal.   T +

22. People suffering from incurable diseases should have the choice of being put painlessly to death.   T —

23. Sunday-observance is old-fashioned, and should cease to govern our behaviour.

24. Capitalism is immoral because it exploits the worker by failing to give him full value for his productive labour.

25. We should believe without question all that we are taught by the Church.

26. A person should be free to take his own life, if he wishes   T —
to do so, without any interference from society.

27. Free love between men and women should be en-   T —
couraged as a means towards mental and physical health.

28. Compulsory military training in peace-time is essen-   T —
tial for the survival of this country.

29. Sex crimes such as rape and attacks on children, deserve more than mere imprisonment: such criminals ought to be flogged or worse.

30. A white lie is often a good thing.   T —

31. The idea of God is an invention of the human mind.   T —

32. It is wrong that men should be permitted greater sexual freedom than women by society.

33. The Church should attempt to increase its influence on   T +
the life of the nation.

34. Conscientious objectors are traitors to their country, and should be treated accordingly.

35. The laws against abortion should be abolished.

36. Most religious people are hypocrites.   T —

37. Sex relations except in marriage are always wrong.   T +

38. European refugees should be left to fend for them-   T —
selves.

39. Only by going back to religion can civilisation hope to survive.

40. It is wrong to punish a man if he helps another country because he prefers it to his own.

41. It is just as well that the struggle of life tends to weed   T —
out those who cannot stand the pace.

42. In taking part in any form of world organisation, this country should make certain that none of its independence and power is lost.

Opinion Statements	*Code*

43. Nowadays, more and more people are prying into matters which do not concern them.   T —

44. All forms of discrimination against the coloured races, the Jews, etc., should be made illegal, and subject to heavy penalties.

45. It is right and proper that religious education in schools should be compulsory.

46. Jews are as valuable citizens as any other group.   T +

47. Our treatment of criminals is too harsh; we should try to cure them, not punish them.   T +

48. The Church is the main bulwark opposing the evil trends in modern society.   T +

49. There is no harm in travelling occasionally without a ticket, if you can get away with it.   T —

50. The Japanese are by nature a cruel people.

51. Life is so short that a man is justified in enjoying himself as much as he can.   T —

52. An occupation by a foreign power is better than war.   T +

53. Christ was divine, wholly or partly in a sense different from other men.   T +

54. It would be best to keep coloured people in their own districts and schools, in order to prevent too much contact with whites.

55. Homosexuals are hardly better than criminals and ought to be severely punished.

56. The universe was created by God.   T +

57. Blood sports, like fox hunting for instance, are vicious and cruel, and should be forbidden.   T +

58. The maintenance of internal order within the nation is more important than ensuring that there is complete freedom for all.   T —

59. Every person should have complete faith in some supernatural power whose decisions he obeys without question.

60. The practical man is of more use to society than the thinker.

ITEM 30.2: SCORING SHEET FOR ATTITUDE INVENTORY

Record the answers of your subjects on this. The purpose of the experiment is to reinforce 'tough' or 'tender-minded' responses according to the group the individual subject belongs to. The 32 items which comprise the 'tough-mindedness' scale are marked with the letter 'T' on Item 30.1. The T-scale is scored in the tender-minded direction. For items marked T + an 'agree' response should be reinforced with the word 'good' for subjects in group 2 (tender-minded) and the 'disagree' response should be rewarded in the same way for group 1 (tough-minded). When the item is marked T — the position is reversed and the tough-minded group is reinforced for agreement and the tender-minded group for disagreement. The other items in the inventory are part of a 'radicalism scale'. See Eysenck (1963). Make sure this is thoroughly understood before beginning the experiment as the reinforcements must appear spontaneous.

Mark the scoring sheet as follows:

Agree = A
No opinion = ?
Disagree = D

Item	Code	Tough-minded Group					Tender-minded Group					Control				
		S_1	S_2	S_3	S_4	S_5	S_1	S_2	S_3	S_4	S_5	S_1	S_2	S_3	S_4	S_5
1																
2																
3																
4																
5																
6																
7																
8	T—															
9	T—															
10	T—															
11																
12	T—															
13																
14	T—															
15																
16																
17	T—															
18	T+															
19	T—															

Item	Code	Tough-minded Group					Tender-minded Group					Control				
		S_1	S_2	S_3	S_4	S_5	S_1	S_2	S_3	S_4	S_5	S_1	S_2	S_3	S_4	S_5
20	T+															
21	T+															
22	T−															
23																
24																
25																
26	T−															
27	T−															
28	T−															
29																
30	T−															
31	T−															
32																
33	T+															
34																
35																
36	T−															
37	T+															
38	T−															
39																
40																
41	T−															
42																
43	T−															
44																
45																
46	T+															
47	T+															
48	T+															
49	T−															
50																
51	T−															
52	T+															
53	T+															
54																
55	T+															
56																
57	T+															
58	T−															
59																
60																

ITEM 30.3: *Chart for Plotting the Effects of Reinforcement on Answers to the Tough-mindedness Scale.*

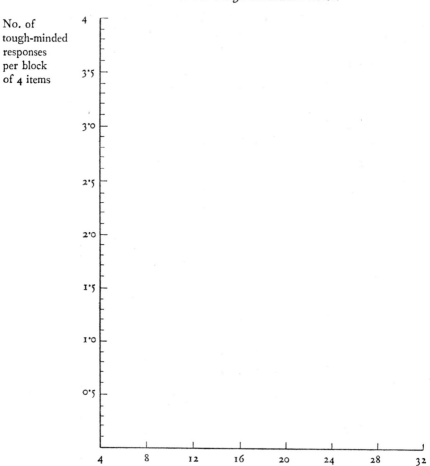

Exercise 31
The Effect of Success and Failure

Introduction

'Intervening variables' are hypothetical processes considered by psychologists as coming between stimulus and response but which cannot be observed directly (e.g., thought, intelligence, memory, motive). The measurement of these variables has always been a challenging problem to experimental psychologists. Subjectively we can be quite convinced that they are affecting all our behaviour. To understand what they are and how they operate is easy when we draw upon our own experience. Emotion, for example, is a universal experience. It is still, however, impossible to talk about it in a completely objective way which permits analysis in terms of type and quantity and which allows the comparison of different individuals and different situations. Recent attempts to define emotion in purely physiological terms have had some success but they are still far from convincing. Intelligence has however fared much better—perhaps because of its educational importance. It is now possible to use the Intelligence Quotient (I.Q.) as a measure of this intervening variable.

Motivation is an extremely important intervening variable since, in theory at least, no behaviour can occur without motivation. The measurement of motivation has however proved extremely difficult. Animal experiments have had a certain amount of success in using duration of food deprivation as an index of motivation, but this is clearly a crude and inadequate measure, even in animals. For human beings deprivation is quite unsatisfactory as a measure, since all kinds of social motives operate and these are very difficult to define.

Kurt Lewin has however had some success in measuring one particular aspect of motivation—'level of aspiration'. In a typical experiment the subject is asked to declare how he expects to perform on a simple repetition task (i.e., his 'level of aspiration'). His actual performance is then measured and the result is told to the subject. The subject is then asked to make a declaration of what he expects his next performance to be.

Objective

To show the effects of success and failure on level of aspiration.

Materials

Stop watch. Test Materials (Items 31.1 to 31.4).

Method

Two small groups of subjects are required: one to form the 'successful' group, the other the 'unsuccessful'. The groups should be 'matched' as far as is possible in terms of age and sex. Ask the subject how many digit symbol transformations he thinks he will make in thirty seconds. In an experiment of this kind the instructions to subjects are crucial, e.g.:

> 'This is part of an intelligence test that we are interested in assessing for your age group. Read the instructions at the top carefully and do as well as you can. I will tell you how you have done after each test.'

After the subject has performed the task and the number of transformations have been counted the subjects in one group must be informed of a fictitious score and told that they have exceeded their estimated score by a few points (the 'successful' group), and the others told they have failed to reach their estimated scores by a few points (the 'unsuccessful' group). It is of course essential that the subjects should not know that the scores they have been told are fictitious. The test should now be repeated (using a new digit-symbol sheet). Before beginning the subject should be asked to guess his new score in the light of his previous results. This should be repeated for four trials each time writing the subject's expected score and 'attained' (fictitious) score on a blackboard where he can see it.

Treatment of Results

For each trial except the first for any subject it will be possible to obtain a Goal Discrepancy Score (G-score) which is the difference between the score the subject believes he made last time and his new level of aspiration (positive or negative).

It is also possible to compute an Attainment Discrepancy score (A-Score) which is the difference between level of achievement set and the true score obtained (although not reported to the subject).

Perform a t-test on the difference between the mean G-scores of the successful and unsuccessful groups (which can consist of one or more individuals having five trials each giving four scores). So three subjects per group yields an N of 12 scores per group. Calculate first the standard error of difference between two means, using Item 31.5.

Discussion

1. What was the effect of success and failure on the individuals' level of aspiration?

2. Are there any reliable individual differences within groups?

3. Is behaviour in this experimental situation likely to be typical of behaviour in everyday life?

ITEM 31.1: DIGIT SYMBOL TEST I

The first row of digits below is paired with a symbol—the task is to go through the test putting the appropriate symbol beneath each digit. You have one minute to do as many as you can. This sheet will then be taken away and your correct score calculated.

1	2	3	4	5	6	7	8	9
⊓	×	○	△	÷	=	+	□	∟

6	5	8	9	2	1	3	9	7	8	9	3	5	1	2	9	2	5	7	6

4	9	2	5	8	1	7	9	5	8	6	7	3	6	4	5	1	2	3	2

6	4	1	3	2	7	5	8	2	9	1	2	9	8	5	6	5	8	5	7

3	2	6	4	5	9	1	8	2	7	5	1	8	4	2	5	2	9	4	6

1	8	5	2	7	7	6	3	5	4	2	9	4	8	6	8	9	3	6	1

ITEM 31.2: DIGIT SYMBOL TEST 2

The first row of digits below is paired with a symbol—the task is to go through the test putting the appropriate symbol beneath each digit. You have one minute to do as many as you can. This sheet will then be taken away and your correct score calculated.

1	2	3	4	5	6	7	8	9
L	□	+	=	△	÷	○	×	∏

6	5	8	9	2	1	9	9	7	8	9	3	5	1	2	9	2	5	7	6

4	9	2	5	8	1	7	9	5	8	6	7	3	6	4	5	1	2	3	2

6	4	1	3	2	7	5	8	2	9	1	2	9	8	5	6	5	8	5	7

3	2	6	4	5	9	1	8	2	7	5	1	6	4	2	5	2	9	4	6

1	8	5	2	7	7	6	3	5	4	2	9	4	8	6	8	9	3	6	1

ITEM 31.3: DIGIT SYMBOL TEST 3

The first row of digits below is paired with a symbol—the task is to go through the test putting the appropriate symbol beneath each digit. You have one minute to do as many as you can. This sheet will then be taken away and your correct score calculated.

1	2	3	4	5	6	7	8	9
÷	O	×	∏	+	=	△	L	□

6	5	8	9	2	1	9	9	7	8	9	3	5	1	2	9	2	5	7	6

4	9	2	5	8	1	7	9	5	8	6	7	3	6	4	5	1	2	3	2

6	4	1	3	2	7	5	8	2	9	1	2	9	8	5	6	5	8	5	7

3	2	6	4	5	9	1	8	2	7	5	1	8	4	2	5	2	9	4	6

1	8	5	2	7	7	6	3	5	4	2	9	4	8	6	8	9	3	6	1

ITEM 31.4: DIGIT SYMBOL TEST 4

The first row of digits below is paired with a symbol—the task is to go through the test putting the appropriate symbol beneath each digit. You have one minute to do as many as you can. This sheet will then be taken away and your correct score calculated.

1	2	3	4	5	6	7	8	9
=	+	△	○	⊓	÷	∟	□	×

6	5	8	9	2	1	9	9	7	8	9	3	5	1	2	9	2	5	7	6

4	9	2	5	8	1	7	9	5	8	6	7	3	6	4	5	1	2	3	2

6	4	1	3	2	7	5	8	2	9	1	2	9	8	5	6	5	8	5	7

3	2	6	4	5	9	1	8	2	7	5	1	8	4	2	5	2	9	4	6

1	8	5	2	7	7	6	3	5	4	2	9	4	8	6	8	9	3	6	1

ITEM 31.5: CHART FOR CALCULATING THE STANDARD ERROR
OF DIFFERENCES (σ_D) BETWEEN TWO MEANS ($\bar{X}$ AND $\bar{Y}$) AND
TESTING THE SIGNIFICANCE OF THIS DIFFERENCE (t)

	'Success' X	x	x^2	*'Failure'* Y	y	y^2
Σ						
Mean						

$$\sigma_D = \sqrt{\frac{\Sigma x^2 + \Sigma y^2}{(N_1 - 1) + (N_2 - 1)} \times \left(\frac{1}{N_1} + \frac{1}{N_2}\right)}$$

$$t = \frac{\bar{X} - \bar{Y}}{\sigma_D}$$

Degrees of Freedom $= (N_1 - 1) + (N_2 - 1)$.

Exercise 32
An Experiment in Communication

Introduction

In 1932 F. Bartlett described a number of experiments on remembering. One of the techniques he used he called 'serial reproduction' whereby some verbal material such as a brief story was presented to one person, who then repeated it to another. This second person then repeated it to a third and so on. Bartlett was concerned with showing that remembering was not simply a restimulation of a 'trace' accurately made and stored up in the mind. If this were true, he pointed out, each individual would have stored up an incredible number of traces corresponding to every event ever experienced. He believed the individual's past to be made up of 'schemas' about the world—active, developing patterns of past reactions and past experiences. In other words, recalling an event involved an imaginative *reconstruction* of that event which is necessarily affected by all kinds of past experiences (which he subsumed under the title of 'schema'). The more nearly a story or an event fits an existing schema the more accurately will it be remembered because it will be changed less whilst being fitted to an existing pattern. It would be expected on this basis that stories which originated in another culture, with presumably very different patterns of thought, would be more markedly changed than stories originating in our own culture.

Objective

To examine what happens to a story from another culture when it is passed along a chain of people by 'serial reproduction'.

Materials

Two stories, one Chinese, one English (Items 32.1 and 32.2).

Method

Two groups of subjects are required with at least six subjects in each group. The subjects should be matched for age, sex and education. All subjects must be British. A coin should be tossed to decide which group uses the Chinese story and which uses the English story. The two groups are then treated identically except that different stories are used.

The first subject should be asked to read carefully the printed copy of the story twice and he should be informed that he will be asked to write it down again after ten minutes. The intervening ten minutes should be filled with any simple pencil and paper task, for example, a personality inventory or a vocabulary test or similar material. The subject should then be asked to write out the story from memory as legibly as possible. This second version is given to the next subject, and so on, for all subjects. The process should be repeated until 6–12 subjects have been tested. The instructions to subjects are important and should be standardised, e.g.:

> 'I am going to ask you to read through twice this version of an anonymous Chinese folk tale and I will ask you to rewrite it in your own words in ten minutes. Please be as accurate as possible.'

After ten minutes:

> 'Are you ready to repeat the story now? Obviously you won't remember it word for word, but please try not to miss anything and be as accurate as you can and write as clearly as possible as someone else will have to read your story.'

The advantages of this method over the original oral method used by Bartlett are twofold:

a. It is not necessary to have all the subjects together at the same time.

b. There remains a complete written record of all stages.

A difficulty may arise from the quality of the handwriting. It may be preferable to perform the experiment verbally, tape-recording the stories so that an accurate transcript can be made later.

SUMMARY OF EXPERIMENTAL DESIGN

Design	Groups	Matching	Independent Variable	Dependent Variable
Factorial	Exptl Control	Individual Matching	Chinese Story Control Story	Changes in the Story

Treatment of Results

Bartlett confined himself to a qualitative analysis based upon inspection and interpretation of changes that occurred together with an occasional word count. This remains, generally speaking, the most productive method of analysis but two useful techniques have been introduced by Paul and these add to an understanding of the changes. Among other measures he used:

a. Word counts—a simple count of the number of words in each consecutive version.
b. Information Unit Counts—the criteria for an information unit being that it should furnish a discrete piece of information that is not redundant (i.e., it is not repeated elsewhere). Each unit which corresponds accurately to one in the story with only minor alterations such as tense or articles scores 1. If the sense is preserved but the words changed the score is $\frac{1}{2}$.
c. Theme score—each theme represents a separate episode or major piece of information and is usually about the length of a sentence. Each reproduction is given a score of 1 for every theme of the original retained, irrespective of the correctness of the details.

These two measures combined give a measure of the degree of literal accuracy and the extent to which the general sense of the story is retained. Obviously they do not give any complete explanation of the changes that occur.

An example of each kind of analysis is included (Items 32.3 and 32.4).

Analyse the changes which have occurred in the two stories, using whichever methods are preferred. The point is to discover whether the two stories have changed in different ways—either in terms of the quantity of change, or the type of changes that have occurred.

Pay special attention to the following points:

1. The fate of detail, proper names, times etc.
2. The overall size of the stories.
3. Is the point of the story retained?
4. Additions, elaborations, or explanations.
5. Aspects of the Chinese story which have been Anglicised.
6. Repetitions and retention of redundant material.

Discussion

1. What kinds of change occurred during reproduction?
2. Did the two stories change in different ways?
3. What is the relationship between changes shown by 'word count', 'information unit count' and 'theme score'?
4. What types of information disappeared first and which remained longest?
5. Did the stories retain their meaning?
6. Has more recent experimental work supported Bartlett's theory?

References

BARTLETT, F. G., *Remembering: an Experimental and Social Study* (London 1932).
PAUL, K., in KLEIN, G. F. (Ed.) *Psychological Issues* (International Universities Press Inc., N.Y. 1959).

ITEM 32.1: THE CHINESE STORY

Ming-Y was the son of a family renowned for its learning and piety and when he was eighteen he became teacher to the children of a man of rank and high station. To fulfil his duties he had to stay in this nobleman's house some miles from his father's home. Before he left his father repeated to him the words of an ancient sage: 'By a beautiful face the world is filled with love; but heaven may never be deceived thereby.'

After two months away Ming-Y desired to see his family again and so with his master's permission he set out on the journey, only to find when he arrived that he had lost his purse. On the return journey he was stopped by a serving maid who told him that her mistress had found his purse and wished to return it to him. So he was led into the deepest and most silent part of the forest where he saw an old and very beautiful house which he had never noticed before.

When he met the mistress of this house he thanked her for returning his silver and learning that she was a widow in mourning wanted to hurry away so as not to disturb her; but Sie (that was her name) did not want him to go quickly. So Ming-Y remained rejoicing secretly in his heart, for Sie seemed to him the fairest and sweetest being he had ever known, and he felt he loved her more than his father and his mother. So he stayed and they talked and sang and drank purple wine and they kissed and the night grew old and they knew it not.

By deceiving his father and his master, Ming-Y was able to visit Sie's house every evening and each night they devoted to the same pleasures which had made their first acquaintance so charming. Until one day there was a chance meeting between the father of Ming-Y and his patron and the deception was discovered.

When questioned by his father the boy was very ashamed and said nothing, so his father struck him violently with his staff and he told his father everything.

Then they all went to the spot deep in the forest where Sie's house was, but when they arrived there the autumn light only revealed an ancient tomb of a great lady of the court who had died six hundred years before. The name on the tomb was Sie.

ITEM 32.2: THE ENGLISH STORY

Helmut and Wilhelm were on their way back to the camp at Peronne 48. They had lost their way and stopped at the Charneau farm to ask for directions. Seeing a half finished bottle of wine on the table, Helmut asked for a drink and was gulping it down when a girl came into the room and started at the sight of the two German soldiers. Her parents were country people but this girl was a little different. Her build was tall and slight and her long dark hair and clear brown eyes gave her a certain elegance. Her expression of surprise turned to hatred as she looked at the two men.

'Isn't it enough for you to take all our food without taking our drink as well?'

Helmut was not used to being spoken to like this by any woman and especially not a French girl. Were not the Germans the conquerors and these the conquered? He lunged towards her. She struggled fiercely and succeeded in drawing four stripes of blood down his left cheek. While Wilhelm stood back rather disturbed by this turn of events and tried to restrain the frightened mother, Helmut swung a blow at the father who had tried to free his daughter which sent him crashing into the table. He dragged Elizabeth outside. Sometime later he returned for Wilhelm and they left together. Duing the following months Helmut returned to the farm several times. He felt slightly guilty because of what had happened and eased his conscience by bringing pieces of cheese and ham. Elizabeth would touch none of it, though after a while her parents accepted it eagerly. It pleased him to think that they were dependent upon him.

On one of his visits Elizabeth was more antagonistic than ever. It annoyed him to think that she could still feel this way despite his gifts. Pulling her sweater tightly over her abdomen she snapped: 'Does this sight make you feel like an heroic conqueror?'

The knowledge that Elizabeth was pregnant shocked Helmut and he returned to his camp dazed. He could not forget that Elizabeth was carrying his child. Unexpectedly this gave him some pleasure and he could not help feeling protective towards the girl. She was still proud and loathed the Germans for what they had done to her country and countrymen. Helmut felt he could change this. He returned to the farm as soon as he could and tried to talk to Elizabeth. After the war, he told her, they would be married and he wanted to teach his son to walk and ride and shoot.

He was unable to return for several months and the next time he arrived there was turmoil at the farm. Elizabeth had started a difficult labour early that morning and her mother had discovered that both she and the baby had disappeared from the bedroom.

A few minutes later the door was flung open: Elizabeth stood there, her face was grey and her clothes and hair were wet and muddy and sticking closely to her body. 'I couldn't bear it,' she sobbed, 'I took him to the stream and held his head under the water until . . .'

ITEM 32.3: EXAMPLE OF THE ANALYSIS

The original version of the story divided into information units:

Ming-Y/was the son/of a family/renowned/for its learning/and piety/and when he was 18/he became teacher to the children/of a man of rank/and high position. To fulfil his duties/he had to stay/in this nobleman's house/some miles from his father's home./Before he left/his father repeated to him/the words/of an ancient/sage:/'By a beautiful face/the world/is filled/with love/but Heaven may never/be deceived thereby.'/

After/two months/away/Ming-Y/desired to see/his family again/ and so with his Master's permission/he set out/on the journey/only to find/when he arrived/that he had lost/his purse./ On the return journey he was stopped/by a serving maid/who told him/that her mistress had found/his purse/and wished/to return it to him./So he was led/ into the deepest/and most silent/part of the forest/where he saw an old/and very beautiful/house/which he had never noticed before./When he met/the mistress/of this house/he thanked her/for returning/his silver/and learning/that she was a widow/in mourning/ wanted/to hurry away/so as not to disturb her/but Sie/(that was her name)/did not want/him to go quickly./ So Ming-Y remained/ rejoicing/secretly in his heart/for Sie seemed to him/the fairest/and sweetest/being/he had ever known/and he felt/that he loved her/ more than/his father and his mother/so he stayed/and they talked/and sang/and drank/purple wine/and then they kissed/and the night grew old/and they knew it not./

By deceiving/his father/and his master/Ming-Y was able/to visit/ Sie's house/every evening/and each night/they devoted/to the same pleasures/which had made/their first acquaintance/so charming./ Until one day/there was a chance meeting/between the father of Ming-Y/and his patron/and the deception/was discovered./

When questioned/by his father/the boy/was very ashamed/and said nothing/so his father/struck him/violently/with his staff/and he told/his father/everything.

Then they all/went to the spot/deep in the forest/where Sie's house was/but when they arrived there/the autumn light only revealed/an ancient/tomb/of a great/lady/of the court/who had died/six hundred years before./The name on the tomb/was Sie./

ITEM 32.4: EXAMPLE OF THE ANALYSIS 2

The original version divided into its constituent themes. Each theme is lettered and named below:

a. Ming-Y was the son of a family renowned for its learning and piety *b.* and when he was 18 he became teacher to the children of a man of rank and high position *c.* to fulfil his duties he had to stay in this noble-man's house some miles from his father's home. *d.* Before he left his father repeated to him the words of the ancient sage: *e.* 'By a beautiful face the world is filled with love but Heaven may never be deceived thereby.' *f.* After two months away Ming-Y desired to see his family again and so with *g.* his master's permission he set out on the journey *h.* only to find when he arrived there that he had lost his purse. *i.* On the return journey he was stopped by a serving maid who told him *j.* that her mistress had found his purse and wished to return it to him. *k.* So he was led into the deepest and most silent part of the forest where he saw an old and very beautiful house which he had never seen before. *l.* When he met the mistress of the house he thanked her for returning his silver and *m.* learning that she was a widow in mourning wanted to hurry away so as not to disturb her but *n*. Sie (that was her name) did not want him to go so quickly. *o*. So Ming-Y remained rejoicing secretly in his heart for Sie seemed to him *p*. the fairest and sweetest being he had ever known and he felt that he loved her more than his father and his mother. *q*. So he stayed and they sang and drank purple wine and they kissed and the night grew old and they knew it not. *r*. By deceiving his father and his master Ming-Y was able to *s*. visit Sie's house every evening and each night they devoted to the same pleasures which had made their first acquaintance so charming. *t*. Until one day there was a chance meeting between the father of Ming-Y and his patron and the deception was discovered. *u*. When questioned by his father the boy was very ashamed and said nothing. *v*. So his father struck him violently with his staff *w*. and he told his father everything. *x*. Then they all went to the spot deep in the forest where Sie's house was but when they arrived there the autumn light only revealed *y*. an ancient tomb of a great lady of the court *z*. who had died six hundred years before. *aa*. The name on the tomb was Sie.

List of Themes

a. Ming-Y's background	*n*. Asked to stay
b. Becomes a teacher	*o*. He remains
c. Leaves home	*p*. Love
d. Father gives advice	*q*. Love
e. The advice	*r*. Deception
f. Desires to return home	*s*. Returns to house
g. Master's permission	*t*. Deception discovered
h. Loses purse	*u*. Father strikes him
i. Meets maid	*w*. Confession
j. Mistress has purse	*x*. Go to house
k. Sees house	*y*. Find tomb
l. Meets mistress	*z*. Six hundred years old
m. A widow	*aa*. Sie

Exercise 33
Channels of Communication in Groups

Introduction

A number of findings have been reported quite consistently from experiments on small groups. A good deal is known, for example, about factors which influence the efficiency of small groups, both from the point of view of getting problems solved (see *Exercise 34*), and from the point of view of giving satisfaction to the individuals within the group. One of the most popular techniques for studying these problems has been to control the number of channels of communication which can be used by individuals within the group. In a five-person group, for example, 20 channels of communication (or ten 2-way links) are possible. An experimenter can, however, easily restrict the number of these he allows—and so discover the effect of this restriction on group behaviour. It has been found in this way that the greater the degree of connection open to members the greater will be their satisfaction, and that the individual member who is most highly 'connected' will derive the most satisfaction. Not only does the 'all-channel net' (the group in which all channels of communication are open) appear to be the most satisfying to its members; it also appears to be the most efficient from the point of view of solving problems and getting work done.

Objective

To study the effects of different group structures on the efficiency of problem-solving and on members' satisfaction by varying the number of communication channels which are open to members of the group.

Materials

The four problems provided (*Items* 33.1 to 33.4).
Index cards and pencils.
Five subjects.

Method

Leavitt (1951) and other workers have generally controlled the number of channels of communication by isolating each individual from each other by erecting vertical partitions around a table—the subjects being allowed to communicate with one another by passing written notes through slots. This is not likely to be practicable for this exercise so the five subjects must be impressed that the point of the experiment will be lost if they permit themselves to communicate in any way other than that prescribed.

The five subjects should be seated around a table and identified with a clearly marked card assigning them a number 1, 2, 3, 4 or 5. The point of the experiment should be explained as being an attempt to discover how efficient are various methods of solving problems. It should be explained that there are certain rules which they must follow. These are:

1. They may only communicate by passing notes written on the index cards provided. Each message must contain only one piece of information, e.g., one question or one symbol.

Each card must be marked with the number of its origin and destination.

2. They must not pass on cards they themselves have already received, and they must not read notes passed between other individuals.

3. The persons to whom they may pass cards are strictly specified and controlled by the experimenter.

4. They will each be given a list of five symbols and the problem they have to solve is to discover which symbols are common to the whole group.

5. The problem will be deemed solved when each individual knows the correct answer.

The lists of symbols are included in Items 33.1 to 33.4.

The four communication nets to be used are described in Item 33.5. The same subjects can be used in each situation. Give each subject a card containing five symbols and instruct them in which pattern is to be followed.

Record the time taken to produce a correct answer and gather up the used message cards. Ask the subjects after each condition to fill in the following rating scales:

1. Please rate on a seven-point scale how efficient you think this group structure is: 1 indicating extreme inefficiency, 7 extreme efficiency, and 4 an intermediate degree of efficiency.

2. Please rate on a seven-point scale how desirable you would find it to work in such a group, 1 indicating that it is completely unsatisfactory, 7 extremely satisfactory and 4 that you would not have any strong feelings either way.

Treatment of Results

For each of the four conditions there will be four sets of results:

1. Time taken to solve the problem,
2. Number of messages passed,
3. Subjective rating of efficiency,
4. Subjective satisfaction.

Plot these graphically on suitable axes.

Discussion

1. Which were the most efficient and which the most satisfactory of the groups?

2. Did your findings support the previous idea that the wheel is more efficient than the full circle even though more channels are open in the latter?

3. In Situation 3 did satsisfaction vary with centrality (i.e., compare 'A' with the others)?

4. Was there any evidence of 'leadership' emerging in any of the situations? Compare who sent most messages and who received most etc.

5. Analyse the *types* of message that were most frequently sent.

6. Was there any evidence of practise effect?

7. What other types of group structure would it be interesting to use?

References

LEAVITT, H. J., 'Some effects of certain communication patterns on group performance', in *Journ. Abnormal & Social Psychol.* (1951) 46: pp. 38–40.

ITEM 33.1: PROBLEM I

Which Symbols are common to all Five Subjects?

| I | ∠ | △ | ♂ | ÷ | Person 1 |

| ÷ | △ | ∠ | 2 | ♂ | Person 2 |

| △ | ÷ | 2 | ∠ | ↑ | Person 3 |

| ∠ | 3 | ÷ | ↑ | = | Person 4 |

| I | ↑ | △ | ÷ | ∠ | Person 5 |

ITEM 33.2: PROBLEM 2

| ◇ | 3 | ? | — | N | Person 1 |

| 3 | N | ◇ | — | ? | Person 2 |

| + | N | ? | ○ | ◇ | Person 3 |

| ? | ◇ | N | ○ | 2 | Person 4 |

| 3 | ? | — | ◇ | 2 | Person 5 |

ITEM 33.3: PROBLEM 3

♂	+	□	K	4	Person 1

K	□	4	♂̶	—	Person 2

□	K	3	4	+	Person 3

□	+	4	—	K	Person 4

+	4	3	—	□	Person 5

ITEM 33.4: PROBLEM 4

○	?	M	5	=	Person 1

M	=	?	5	↑	Person 2

=	M	?	↑	5	Person 3

5	↑	=	N	K	Person 4

○	5	K	=	↑	Person 5

1. *The Circle:* five communication channels open—each individual may only communicate with the individual on his left and no one else.

2. *The Full Circle:* Each individual may communicate with the person sitting on his right and left. Ten communication channels.

3. *The Wheel:* 'A' can communicate with all other members but they can only communicate with each other by going through 'A'. Eight communication channels.

4. *All-Channel Net:* The control situation with all twenty channels open.

Exercise 34. Group Size and Efficiency

Introduction

Small groups have been studied in many different ways. Several research workers have tried to examine the way in which the *size* of the group affects the *efficiency* with which it deals with problems. It is of course difficult to design experiments in which the problems are of the type encountered in real life, and most of the research in this field has used simpler types of problem material. Taylor and Faust (1952) for example presented their groups with problems of the type used in the game of 'Twenty Questions'. They pointed out that a great deal of suitable problem material of this type is available, and that interest and motivation in the subjects is usually high. The exercise which follows is an adaptation of Taylor and Faust's experiment in which they compared the speed with which problem solution was accomplished by: *a.* large groups; *b.* small groups, and *c.* by individuals.

Method

Individuals should be assigned on a chance basis to either: *a.* a group of 4; *b.* a group of 2, or *c.* to work alone. One question-master should also be appointed for each of *a*, *b*, and *c*. The objectives of the game should be briefly explained and question-masters should be instructed that the only responses they may make are 'yes', 'no', 'partly', 'sometimes' or 'not in the usual sense of the word'.

Each question-master should be given a list of 25 objects (Item 34.1) and asked to take his group (or individual) to a separate room for an hour or so. The question-masters are to insist that group members are not to compete with one another but are to co-operate so that the group achieves the answer as rapidly as possible. They are to be told that the efficiency of their group is to be compared with that of the other groups. The maximum number of questions allowed for each object is 30 (not 20). The question-master should keep a record of: 1. the object; 2. time taken per object; 3. success or failure to discover the object, and 4. any other observations on group or individual behaviour. He should also note the passage of time during the experiment by drawing a line across the record form at 15-minute intervals. A suitable record form is shown as Item 34.2.

Treatment of Results

1. Class results should then be combined to show the number of questions per object and the number of man-minutes per problem for each type of situation. (See Item 34.3.) Count failures as 30 questions. A similar analysis should be made of the number of man-minutes per problem.

The significance of the differences between the number of questions per object should be computed (as described, for example, in Connolly and Sluckin, p. 96) for:

a. Individuals versus groups of 2, *b.* Individuals versus groups of 4, *c.* Groups of 2 versus groups of 4.

When critical ratios have been calculated for: *a.* the difference between individuals and groups of 2, and *b.* the difference between individuals and groups of 4, reference should be made to Table XXVI, p. 94, in Connolly & Sluckin to determine whether the critical ratios are sufficiently high in each case to enable us to state at a 5 per cent level of confidence that the differences are significant. The number of degrees of freedom to be used (df) is $(N_1 - 1) + (N_2 - 1)$, where N_1 is the number of objects examined by individuals, and N_2 the number of objects examined by groups (i.e., 25 in each case). If the value of t given in the table is exceeded by the CR obtained then the difference is significant.

2. Repeat for the average number of man minutes per problem.

3. The effect of the passage of time should be demonstrated graphically as shown in Item 34.4.

Discussion

1. How was efficiency in problem solution related to group size,

a. in terms of questions per object,
b. in terms of man-minutes required to solve problems,
c. in terms of failures?

2. Did efficiency change with the passage of time? Did groups improve at the same rate as individuals?

3. In what circumstances and with what types of material is individual problem solution desirable and in what circumstances is group solution desirable?

4. How could the experimental design have been improved? Could groups have been matched?

References

TAYLOR, D. W., and FAUST, 'Twenty Questions: Efficiency in Problem Solving as a Function of Size of Group', *Journ. Exp. Psych.* (1952), pp. 360–8,
and quoted in HARE, A. P., BORGATTA, E. F., and BALES, R. F., *Small Groups* (Knopf, N.Y. 1955).

ITEM 34.1: LIST OF OBJECTS

1. Man Friday	14. Seal
2. Railway carriage	15. Brick
3. Tablecloth	16. Screwdriver
4. Cloud	17. Daffodil
5. Blackcurrant	18. Stiff upper lip
6. Potato	18. Tape-recorder
7. Sewing machine	20. Paper-clip
8. Caviare	21. Polar bear
9. Peaches and cream	22. Overcoat
10. Electric light bulb	23. Ton of coal
11. Australia House	24. Fish and chips
12. Crab	25. Wish
13. Nelson's Column	

ITEM 34.2: RECORD FORM FOR QUESTION-MASTER

Name of question-master. . . . .

Size of group. . . . .

Object No.	No. of Questions needed	Time taken	Success(√) Failure(×)	Notes
1				
2				
3				
4				
5				
6				
7				
8				
9				
10				
11				
12				
13				
14				
15				
16				
17				
18				
19				
20				
21				
22				
23				
24				
25				
26				
27				
28				
29				
30				

Total No. of   Total time   Total successes =
questions   taken on   Total failures   =
asked =   successful
                 problems =
                     mins.

Total man-minutes   Total time on successfuls
spent achieving   = multiplied by size of
successful solutions   group

Therefore, man-minutes per successful solution $= \dfrac{\text{Total time} \times \text{size group}}{\text{No. of problems solved}}$

ITEM 34.3: SIGNIFICANCE OF DIFFERENCES BETWEEN MEANS

Objects	*Individuals*			*Groups of 2*			*Groups of 4*		
	Questions Required	d_1	$d_1{}^2$	Questions Required	d_2	$d_2{}^2$	Questions Required	d_3	$d_3{}^2$
Σ									
Means									

d = deviation of score from mean of that column

$$\sigma = \sqrt{\frac{\Sigma d^2}{N}} \qquad \sigma_D = \sqrt{\frac{\Sigma d_1{}^2 + \Sigma d_2{}^2}{(N_1 - 1) + (N_2 - 1)} \times \left(\frac{1}{N_1} + \frac{1}{N_2}\right)}$$

$$t = \frac{\text{Mean 1} - \text{Mean 2}}{\sigma_D}$$

Degrees of Freedom $= (N_1 - 1) + (N_2 - 1)$

ITEM 34.4: EFFECT OF PASSAGE OF TIME ON QUESTIONS
REQUIRED PER PROBLEM

No. of

Questions

per

Problem

Individuals . . . .

Groups of 2 — — —

Groups of 4 ————

| | 1st ¼ hour Period | 2nd ¼ hour Period | 3rd ¼ hour Period | 4th ¼ hour Period |

Exercise 35
Leadership and Group Decision-Making

Introduction

This is an experiment on the relationship between leadership and the formation of opinions and decisions. It is very likely that the results of an experiment of this kind would be upset if the participants were aware of the true nature of the dependent and independent variables. For this reason it is suggested that consideration of the theoretical issues be deferred until the experiment has been performed. A postscript has accordingly been added at the end of this exercise which should not be read at this stage.

Materials

Survival kit for aircraft crossing Andes (Item 35.1).
'Instructions to Leaders Type A' (Item 35.2).
'Instructions to Leaders Type B' (Item 35.3).

Method

1. All subjects should be asked to study carefully the contents of Item 35.1 and then to rank the items in order of importance. Individuals' rankings should then be collected.

2. The whole class should now be divided into groups of five individuals. The individual whose surname begins with the earliest letter in the alphabet should then be designated 'leader' of the group.

3. Half the 'leaders' should be given a copy of the 'Instructions to Leaders A', and half of them a copy of 'Instructions to Leaders B', and they should be asked to study these carefully on their own.

4. Each leader should then take his group of four to a separate location and encourage the group to arrive at a consensual opinion on the most appropriate ranking of the contents of Item 35.1. The group judgement should then be recorded by the 'leader' but by no one else.

5. The groups should then disperse and after a short break individuals should be asked to rank the contents of Item 35.1 yet again.

6. Interview briefly two people who have completed their experiment in an A group, and two from a B group. Make a note of their comments. In particular try to find out to what extent your subjects were satisfied with the group decision they arrived at.

7. All individuals should then be given back:

a. their original ranking (Ranking 1)
b. a copy of their own group's ranking (Ranking 2), and
c. their latest individual ranking (Ranking 3) which they already have.

8. These three rankings should then be tabulated by each individual as shown in Item 35.4.

9. Each individual should then study the two sets of instructions to leaders (A and B) and note the major differences between these two types of leadership.

Treatment of Results

1. Using the chart provided in Item 35.4, each individual should now calculate Spearman's coefficient of rank correlation (ρ) (see Connolly and Sluckin, p. 150):

a. between rankings 1 and 2 giving ρ_1
b. between rankings 2 and 3 giving ρ_2, and
c. between rankings 1 and 3 giving ρ_3.

2. Each individual should examine his own results and consider the following possibilities:

a. Does ρ_1 indicate in any way the influence that he personally has had on the group decision? What is the implication of a high value for ρ?
b. Does ρ_2 indicate the effect of his group on his final individual decision?
c. Does ρ_3 indicate the extent to which the individual has been affected by the intervening experience in the group?

3. An attempt can now be made to compare the effect of the two different leadership patterns (A and B) by collecting together class results. One way of doing this is indicated in Item 35.5 in which six mean values of ρ are calculated.

Discussion

1. What do you consider from an inspection of the 'Instructions to Leaders' were the main differences between Leadership Type A and Leadership Type B?

2. Does an inspection of *a.* your own, or *b.* combined class results

suggest whether leadership-type affected the amount of opinion change?

3. What methods are available for assessing the significance of difference between correlations? Outline a method for more rigorous analysis of the result of an experiment such as this.

4. Do the class results show any notable difference in individual susceptibility to the intervening leadership experience?

Postscript

(Not to be read until the experimental observations have been made.) Small social groups have been studied from many different points of view. A particular problem which has attracted many researchers has been the way in which opinions are arrived at or problems are solved by small groups such as committees. Such decisions are sometimes reached by democratic discussions in which each member's opinion is carefully weighed and examined. Sometimes, however, the leader takes a disproportionately large part in the decision-making process. His role has been that of a 'supervisor' rather than that of a 'patient participator' in the discussion. Studies have been made of the effect of 'supervisory leadership' as against 'participatory leadership' in producing *changes* of opinion among group members. Preston and Heintz (1949), for example, were able to show that participatory leadership was more effective in changing opinion than was supervisory leadership. The experiment in this exercise has been based on the original experiment of Preston and Heintz. The dependent variable is the amount of opinion change, measured by the rank correlation coefficient between first and last rankings. The independent variable is the type of leadership applied to the group.

References

PRESTON, M. G., and HEINTZ, R. K., 'Effects of Participatory versus Supervisory Leadership on Group Judgement', *J. Abnorm Soc. Psychol.* (1949) 44: pp. 345–55.

HARE, A. P., 'Small group discussions with Participatory and Supervisory Leadership' in HARE, A. P., BORGATTA, E. F., and BALES, R. K., *Small groups* (Knopf, N.Y. 1955).

ITEM 35.1: SURVIVAL KIT FOR THE ANDES

1. Tin of grease
2. Knife
3. Tin of corned beef
4. Compass
5. Antiseptic
6. Tin of Elastoplast
7. Volume of Shakespeare's works
8. Tin of water
9. Ball of string
10. Bible
11. Spade
12. Tin opener
13. Sunburn lotion
14. Dried fruit

ITEM 35.2: INSTRUCTIONS TO LEADERS TYPE A

You are to regard yourself as the source of authority in the group. Make sure that you explain firmly and clearly the nature of the task which the group, under your chairmanship, is to solve (i.e., to arrange the items in List Item 35.1 in order of importance for survival in the Andes following a crash landing). Do not let any member of the group monopolise the discussion and interrupt if necessary. If any group member is making no contribution, ignore him. Make sure that your view prevails which (for the purposes of this experiment) is that the Bible is the most important item since spiritual survival is of paramount importance. For this reason too, the volume of Shakespeare's works is of high importance.

ITEM 35.3: INSTRUCTIONS TO LEADERS TYPE B

Your task is to encourage as much discussion as possible by group members, to arrive at a common view on the order of importance of the ten items in the survival kit assuming that the plane has to make a forced landing in the Andes. Try to suppress your own opinions. It is the group's opinion which is to be established. Try to involve all members of the group in the discussion but say as little as possible yourself.

ITEM 35.4

Object	Rankings			Differences					
	1 Indiv	2 Group	3 Indiv	1–2 d_1	$d_1{}^2$	2–3 d_2	$d_2{}^2$	1–3 d_3	$d_3{}^2$

$$\rho = 1 - \frac{6\Sigma(d^2)}{n^3 - n}$$

	Initials of Leader	Individuals	ρ_1	ρ_2	ρ_3
Type A Leaders	1.	1			
		2			
		3			
		4			
	2.	1			
		2			
		3			
		4			
	3.	1			
		2			
		3			
		4			
	4. etc. . . .	Mean ρ_{1A} =		Mean ρ_{2A} =	Mean ρ_{3A} =
Type B Leaders	1.	1			
		2			
		3			
		4			
	2.	1			
		2			
		3			
		4			
	3.	1			
		2			
		3			
		4			
	4. etc. . . .	Mean ρ_{1B} =		Mean ρ_{2B} =	Mean ρ_{3B} =

Exercise 36
Forming Impressions of Persons

Introduction

Whereas many of the earlier experiments in social perception were concerned with the determinants of accuracy of social judgements, there has more recently been a shift of emphasis towards the study of the actual *processes* which occur when impressions are being formed. Some of the experiments on impression formation have used real people as stimuli, others have employed cine or still photographs, and yet others have employed verbal descriptions of persons. This exercise is based on an experiment using such verbal descriptions which was made by A. S. Luchins in 1957.

The object of the experiment is to find the effect of different types of information on impression formation. Further discussion of the experiment will be deferred until later, however, since the subjects in the experiment should not be fully aware of the nature of the variables. The purpose of the exercise will be discussed therefore in a postscript to this exercise, which should not be read until the practical work has been done.

Objective

To study the effect of different types of information on impressions formed about people.

Materials

Description E (Item 36.1).
Description I (Item 36.2).
Description EI (Item 36.3).
Description IE (Item 36.4).

Method

1. The class should be divided into four approximately equal groups: Group E, Group I, Group EI and Group IE.

2. Duplicated copies of Description E should be given to Group E, copies of Description I to Group I and so on for all groups.

3. All subjects should then read their description carefully until they have a clear impression of the individual described.

4. They should then write a short description (about 100 words) which conveys their own impression of the individual they have just been reading about.

5. All subjects should be asked to make a note of any difficulties etc. experienced in writing the description.

6. Each subject should then rate the individual described on each of the following scales:

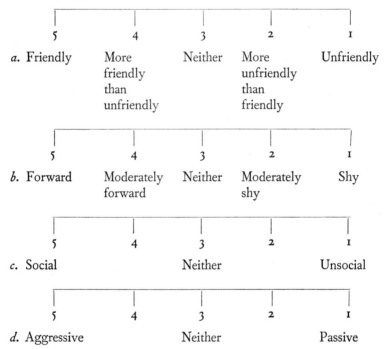

5	4	3	2	1
a. Friendly	More friendly than unfriendly	Neither	More unfriendly than friendly	Unfriendly

5	4	3	2	1
b. Forward	Moderately forward	Neither	Moderately shy	Shy

5	4	3	2	1
c. Social		Neither		Unsocial

5	4	3	2	1
d. Aggressive		Neither		Passive

Postscript

The main purpose of Luchins' original experiment was to determine whether it was the *initial* information that was given about the person or on the other hand the *most recent* information which was given which made the greater impression on the judge. In this experiment Group E were given a verbal account which stressed Jim's *extraverted* characteristics. Group I, on the other hand, received an account which described Jim as very much an *introvert*. Group EI were given a somewhat conflicting account whose first paragraph described him in the same extraverted terms as before, and then proceeded to describe him in the same introverted terms as before and vice versa for Group IE.

The question we have to try to answer is whether, in the case of the EI group, the E characteristics (the first information presented) made the most impact ('primacy'), or whether the I characteristics (the latest, i.e. the most recent) made the most impression ('recency'). If the extraverted paragraph made more impression, then the numerical score in Section 6 above will be high since the left hand of each of the scales represents highly extraverted characteristics (or so we assume here). By contrast, if it was the more recent introverted information which contributed most to the total impression then the numerical score would be low. Analysis of the numerical scores for each group will therefore demonstrate whether primacy or recency is dominant in impression formation.

Treatment of Results

1. A total score should be computed which consists of the sum of all the separate scores $a + b + c + d$. The maximum possible score is 20 and the minimum is 4.

2. The mean of these total scores for all the subjects in each of the separate Groups E, I, EI and IE should then be computed.

3. The differences and the significance of the differences between the means of the four groups should be computed according to the following schedule.

	To compute the difference between
Group E	E and I E and EI
Group I	E and IE I and EI
Group EI	I and IE
Group IE	EI and IE

Tables similar to those in *Exercise 34* should be used in computing the significance of the difference between means.

4. An attempt should be made to 'score' the 100-word accounts for expressions of extraverted and introverted characteristics. A comparison should then be made between the strength of extraverted impression created in each of the four groups.

Discussion

1. Did any subjects report any difficulties arising from the conflict between the two halves of the EI and IE accounts?

2. Did the results support Luchin's conclusion that primacy rather than recency determines impression formation?

References

LUCHINS, A. S., 'Primacy-recency in impression formation' in HOVLAND, C. I., (Ed.) *The Order of Presentation in Persuasion*, Vol. 1 (Yale University Press, New Haven 1957).

BRUNER, J. S., and TAGIURI, R., (Harvard University) 'The Perception of People' in LINDZAY, G., (Ed.) *Handbook of Social Psychology* (Addison-Wesley, Mass. 1954), Ch. 17.

ITEM 36.1: DESCRIPTION E

Jim left the house to get some stationery. He walked out into the sun-filled street with two of his friends, basking in the sun as he walked. Jim entered the stationery store which was full of people. Jim talked with an acquaintance while he waited for the clerk to catch his eye. On his way out, he stopped to chat with a school friend who was just coming into the store. Leaving the store, he walked towards school. On his way out he met the girl to whom he had been introduced the night before. They talked for a short while, and then Jim left for school.

ITEM 36.2: DESCRIPTION I

After school Jim left the classroom alone. Leaving the school, he started on his long walk home. The street was brilliantly filled with sunshine. Jim walked down the street on the shady side. Coming down the street towards him, he saw the pretty girl whom he had met on the previous evening. Jim crossed the street and entered a candy store. The store was crowded with students, and he noticed a few familiar faces. Jim waited quietly until the counterman caught his eye and then gave his order. Taking his drink, he sat down at a side table. When he had finished his drink he went home.

ITEM 36.3: DESCRIPTION EI

Jim left the house to get some stationery. He walked out into the sun-filled street with two of his friends, basking in the sun as he walked. Jim entered the stationery store which was full of people. Jim talked with an acquaintance.while he waited for the clerk, to catch his eye. On his way out, he stopped to chat with a school friend who was just coming into the store. Leaving the store, he walked towards school. On his way out he met the girl to whom he had been introduced the night before. They talked for a short while, and then Jim left for school. After school Jim left the classroom alone. Leaving the school, he started on his long walk home. The street was brilliantly filled with sunshine. Jim walked down the street on the shady side. Coming down the street towards him, he saw the pretty girl whom he had met on the previous evening. Jim crossed the street and entered a candy store. The store was crowded with students, and he noticed a few familiar faces. Jim waited quietly until the counterman caught his eye and then gave his order. Taking his drink, he sat down at a side table. When he had finished his drink he went home.

ITEM 36.4: DESCRIPTION IE

After school Jim left the classroom alone. Leaving the school, he started on his long walk home. The street was brilliantly filled with sunshine. Jim walked down the street on the shady side. Coming down the street towards him, he saw the pretty girl whom he had met on the previous evening. Jim crossed the street and entered a candy store. The store was crowded with students, and he noticed a few familiar faces. Jim waited quietly until the counterman caught his eye and then gave his order. Taking his drink, he sat down at a side table. When he had finished his drink he went home. Jim left the house to get some stationery. He walked out into the sun-filled street with two of his friends, basking in the sun as he walked. Jim entered the stationery store which was full of people. Jim talked with an acquaintance while he waited for the clerk to catch his eye. On his way out, he stopped to chat with a school friend who was just coming into the store. Leaving the store, he walked towards school. On his way out he met the girl to whom he had been introduced the night before. They talked for a short while, and then Jim left for school.

Appendices

Appendix 1

Glossary of Statistical Terms

This very short list of statistical terms is intended simply to assist the initial orientation of the student meeting these ideas for the first time. The definitions are certainly not complete, and are followed by specific chapter references to five standard introductory texts, where fuller definitions and further explanations will be found.

These books cover virtually the same ground, though in rather different ways, and the choice the student makes for his own working text-book should be very much determined by his personal preference for the style of presentation and exposition of one particular book. It will be seen, as these books are examined, that they differ not only in style but in level of mathematical sophistication.

The following abbreviations are used to refer to specific texts:

C & S: Connolly, T. G., and Sluckin, W., *Statistics for the Social Sciences* (Cleaver Hume Press, London 1957).

A: Allen, R. G. D., *Statistics for Economists* (Hutchinson, London 1951).

F: Ferguson, G. A., *Statistical Analysis in Psychology and Education* (McGraw-Hill, N.Y. 1959).

I: Ilersic, A. R., *Statistics* (H.F.L. Publishers, London 1959).

L: Loveday, R., *Statistics, A Second Course* (Cambridge University Press, Cambridge 1964).

'C & S 9' refers to 'Connolly and Sluckin: Chapter 9'.

Chi-Squared (χ^2)

A statistic which enables us to decide whether an actual observed frequency distribution is what we should have expected on theoretical grounds. For example, a genetic theory might have suggested that people with blonde hair should also have blue eyes, and people with dark hair, brown eyes. Computation of chi-squared from a simple contingency table showing the frequency of cases in each possible category would show whether the actual observations confirmed or refuted the original hypothesis (which is known as the null hypothesis).

C & S 8; A 9: F 13; I 10; L 7.

Contingency Table

A table used to record the association of two attributes, such as sex and left-handedness, in a particular population (such as a school). The observed frequencies are entered into each cell of the table. In this particular example there would be four cells in the table: left-handed males, right-handed males, left-handed females and right-handed females.

F 13; L7.

Correlation Coefficient

A statistical measure (ranging from $-$ 1·0 through 0 to $+$1·0) of the extent to which two variables fluctuate together. Thus the height and weight of school children would be found to increase together, i.e., to be positively correlated to one another. On the other hand, there would be a negative correlation between the number of people contracting typhoid in different towns and the number of people who had been inoculated against typhoid.

C & S 9–10; A 8; F 7; I 12; L 10.

Critical Ratio

The ratio obtained by dividing the difference between two means by the standard error of the difference between them. If the ratio is sufficiently high then it is probable that there really is a difference. (Exact methods are available for deciding just *how* probable.)

C & S 7; A 9; F 11; I 10.

Degrees of Freedom (df)

The number of degrees of freedom is the number of values that are free to vary in a particular investigation. It varies with the number of restrictions imposed upon the data. It is used when consulting tables to assess the significance of values of chi-square, t, etc.

C & S 7; A 9; F 4; I 10; L 6.

F. Ratio

This is a test applied at the conclusion of an analysis of variance to determine the significance of the ratio of two variances, i.e., whether they differ. The F. ratio is always greater than unity because the larger variance is divided by the smaller. A significance level for the F. ratio can be determined by consulting appropriate tables.

C & S 11; A 7; F 18.

Frequency Distribution

A tabulation in which observed values of a variable are paired with the frequency with which they occur in a population. For example, a table might list heights in steps of one inch and the frequency with which these heights occur in a class of children.

C & S 3; A 5; F 2; I 7; L 1.

Frequency-Polygon

A diagram or graph which shows vertically the number of cases occurring in each of several different categories which are marked horizontally. Each point on the graph is connected to the next to create a many-sided area. It has the advantage over the histogram that several frequency-polygons can be superimposed on the same diagram to allow comparisons between different groups of data.

C & S 1; A 3; F 2; I 5; L 1.

Histogram

A diagram which shows as vertical columns or bars the number of cases occurring in each of several categories. These categories may be qualitative (e.g., men, women, children) or quantitative (e.g., age below 10, age 11–20, age 21–30, etc.).

C & S 1; A 3; F 2; I 5; L 1.

Levels of Confidence

Unfortunately we cannot measure whole populations but only small samples. The level of confidence in a specific case tells us the range of values within which we can be confident an actual total population value lies when our estimate has been based on only a small sample. For example, we can be 95 per cent confident that the correct population mean lies within 1·95 standard errors of our sample mean value (provided the population is normally distributed).

C & S 6; A 9; F 10; I 8; L 8.

Mean

The arithmetical average of a set of individual values. It is obtained by dividing the sum of all the values by the number of values present.

C & S 2; A 5; F 3; I 6; L 1.

Median

The middle value of a series of observations arranged in ascending order. Thus if the heights of five children in a class were 48″, 49″, 52″, 55″ and 56″, the median height would be 52″.

C & S 2; A 5; F 3; I 6; L 1.

Mode

The most frequently-occurring value in a series of observations. Thus, if the heights of a small class of schoolchildren were 48″, 49″, 49″, 50″, 52″, 53″, 53″, 53″, 54″, 55″, 56″, 56″, the mode would be 53″.

C & S 2; A 5; F 3; I 6; L 1.

Normal Curve

Many biological, psychological, social and physical phenomena yield measurements which, when plotted as a frequency distribution graph, show a bell-shaped curve which has a remarkably constant shape whatever the subject matter. Thus the curves for both height and intelligence in the general population show the same basic distribution curve. This bell-shaped curve is known as the 'normal curve'. A good deal is known about the mathematical properties of the normal curve and consequently some important inferences and predictions can be made about a phenomenon once it is known that it happens to be normally distributed.

C & S 5; A 9; F 6; I 7; L 1.

Percentile

If n per cent of a population have a score less than a particular value, then that value is the nth percentile point. If, on an intelligence test, 75 per cent of individuals score less than 90 then 90 is the 75th percentile point. Percentiles are frequently used in the standardisation of psychological tests. The 25th, 50th and 75th percentiles are respectively known as the lower quartile, median and upper quartile.

C & S 4; A 4; F 16; I 8; L 1.

Point-Biserial Correlation

A measure, ranging from zero to unity, of the relationship between a continuously variable measurement (e.g. height) and a two-categoried or dichotomous variable (e.g. sex). The coefficient is expressed in the same way as the product moment coefficient (and is in fact a special case of product moment correlation).

C & S 9, 8; A 8; F 15; I 12.

Random Numbers

A collection of numbers, selected in a haphazard way so that there is no relationship or connection between successive numbers. Each number is equally likely to occur. Useful in helping us to decide which people shall be selected from a numbered voters' list when we want to be quite sure that our selection is unbiased.

C & S 6; F 9.

Sample

A limited selection of cases taken from a large group or population. The question arises as to how well this sample reflects the characteristics of the whole population, and this depends on the method used to select the cases. Sometimes 'random' selection is used, and sometimes 'systematic'. The greater the number of cases selected, however, the greater will be our confidence that we have avoided bias and that our sample is truly 'representative' of the whole population.

C & S 6; A 9; F 9; I 9; L 10.

Standard Deviation

Expresses how concentrated, or how dispersed, are a collection of separate observations or scores. Thus, all the children in a particular class might be within one year of each other in age, and the standard deviation for age would be small. On the other hand, in an adult education class, the standard deviation for age would probably be large.

C & S 3; A 5; F 4; I 7; L 1.

t-Test

A statistical calculation which allows a decision to be made as to whether an apparent difference, such as that between the mean height of 12-year-old boys and girls measured in a particular school really allows any firm conclusion to be drawn about the differences in height of 12-year-old boys and girls generally.

C & S 7; A 9; F 11; I 10; L 8.

Appendix 2

Notes on Using the Charts Provided to Help with the Statistical Computations

Special charts have been provided in many exercises to make simpler the computation of the various statistics recommended. No advanced statistics are ever employed but with even the simplest computations the arithmetic sometimes becomes tedious. Neatness and clearness are essential. Nothing is more frustrating than to face several pages of figures without knowing which deviations are linked to which set of raw scores. The charts are intended to help here—everything is clearly labelled and everything is in rows and columns. At least one chart for each type of statistical operation is included somewhere in the exercises. Copies of these can readily be made for use in other exercises where a chart is not provided.

It is also recognised that many people approach statistics for the first time with considerable apprehension. We have included none of the mathematical rationale behind the statistics and we have attempted to break each computation down into the smallest possible steps. It is surprising how quickly one becomes familiar with the processes of statistics after performing a few examples. Certain conventions of notation are used. Unfortunately these are not universal but we have used the most common of the notations. It is customary to represent raw scores by capital letters (usually X and Y) so that a column of figures headed by a capital X means that this is a list of raw scores. The mean or average of the raw scores under X is given the symbol $\bar{X}$. The deviations of the raw scores from their mean is given as x, i.e. $X - \bar{X} = x$.

The Greek capital Sigma (Σ) means that all the scores under the symbol it accompanies are added together, therefore ΣX means that the column of raw scores must be summed. Similarly Σx means that all the deviations of the raw scores about their mean must be summed.

Apart from basic mathematical conventions such as X^2 (X squared), $\sqrt{X}$ (square root of X) and XY meaning X multiplied by Y there are no other symbols used unless they are explained in the text.

An example: $\sqrt{\overline{\Sigma(xy)^2}}$ means that the following calculations have been made:

1. The column of figures under the heading (x) has been calculated by obtaining the deviations of the raw scores (X) from their mean (X̄).

2. The column of figures under (y) has been obtained in the same way.

3. The cross products have been calculated by multiplying each (x) by a corresponding (y).

4. These cross products have been squared to give $(xy)^2$.

5. The resultant $(xy)^2$ have been summed to give a total at the bottom of column (6) which is $\Sigma(xy)^2$.

6. The square root of the total is found.

ITEM STAT. I.

Raw Scores		Deviations		Cross Products	Squared Cross Products
X	Y	x	y	xy	$(xy)^2$
4	3	−4	−2	+8	64
12	5	+4	0	0	0
11	7	+3	+2	+6	36
9	2	+1	−3	−3	9
3	9	−5	+4	−20	400
7	4	−1	−1	+1	1
10	5	+2	0	0	0
Σ 56	35	0	0	−8	510
Symbols ΣX	ΣY	Σx	Σy	Σ(xy)	$\Sigma(xy)^2$

N (number of cases) = 7

N_x (number of cases under X) = 7

N_y (number of cases under Y) = 7

$\bar{X} = \dfrac{\Sigma X}{N_x} = \dfrac{56}{7} = 8.$ $\bar{Y} = \dfrac{\Sigma Y}{N_y} = \dfrac{35}{7} = 5$

$\Sigma(xy)^2 = 510$

$\therefore \quad \sqrt{\Sigma(xy)^2} = \sqrt{510} = 22 \cdot 58.$

Explanation of Statistical Symbols Used

The symbols used throughout this book and which are listed below are widely used in statistical texts.

N   Total number of cases

n   Number of cases in a defined sub-group

$\left.\begin{array}{l}X \\ Y\end{array}\right\}$ Capital letters used to indicate raw scores

$\left.\begin{array}{l}\bar{X} \\ \bar{Y}\end{array}\right\}$ Arithmetic means of the scores listed under X and Y

X^1 Predicted value of X

$\left.\begin{array}{l}x \\ y\end{array}\right\}$ Lower case letters indicate the deviation of a raw score X from the arithmetic mean $\bar{X}$ therefore can be positive or negative

Σ Greek Sigma: the sum of

σ^2 Variance: the sum of the squared deviations from the mean divided by N

σ Standard deviation: the square root of the variance

σ_D Standard error of the mean

r_{xy} The product moment correlation between the variables X and Y

X_{mid} The mid point of a class interval

O   Observed scores

E   Expected scores

ρ Rho: Spearman's Rank Order Correlation Coefficient

d   The difference in rank of items in a pair

χ^2 Chi-squared.

Useful Equations

Refer to the glossary of symbols on the preceding page.
The mean ($\bar{X}$)

$$\bar{X} = \frac{\Sigma X}{N}$$

Standard Deviation (σ)

$$\sigma = \sqrt{\frac{\Sigma(X - \bar{X})^2}{N}}$$

Standard Error of the Mean (σ_D)

$$\sigma_D = \frac{\sigma}{\sqrt{N}}$$

Product Moment Correlation (r)

$$r_{xy} = \frac{\Sigma xy}{\sqrt{(\Sigma x^2)(\Sigma y^2}}$$

or if the standard deviations have to be found for other reasons the following equation may be used:

$$r_{xy} = \frac{\Sigma xy}{N\sigma_x\sigma_y}$$

Rank Order Correlation Coefficient (ρ)

$$\rho_{xy} = 1 - \frac{6\Sigma(d^2)}{N^3 - N}$$

Appendix 3

The Use of Machines in Computation

Investigations in the social sciences frequently yield data in *numerical* form —such as test-scores or frequencies of cases in particular categories. These numbers rarely speak for themselves and statistics must be used to summarise them, to compare them and to analyse their meaning. Very large numbers of cases are frequently involved and often many different variables are studied simultaneously. It is not uncommon, for example, for an opinion-poll to collect responses from 2,000 people, or for an intelligence-test standardisation to be based on a sample as large as 1,700 people. Such large quantities of data cannot be processed without mechanical assistance—even if only the very simplest statistical calculations are to be made.

There are four main types of machine-aid available: (1) the adding machine; (2) the desk calculator; (3) the computer and (4) the card-sorting machine.

1. *The Adding Machine.* This is the simplest type of mechanical aid and is easy to use. For simple computations—such as calculation of means—it saves a great deal of time. (Though more complicated calculations *can* be undertaken with the adding machine, the procedures tend to be tedious and it is usually better to employ more sophisticated machines for the computation of such quantities as square roots. Multiplication and division *can* be undertaken by obeying some very simple procedural rules—but again these are much more easily calculated on larger machines.) Addition and subtraction are quite straightforward. It is simply necessary to press the keys corresponding to the numbers to be added and then to press the handle (or lever or key) which transfers these numbers in turn to the 'product register' at the top of the machine. Most machines also have a counting-indicator of some kind which shows how many different numbers have been transferred to the top register and added. This is, of course, extremely useful when calculating a mean. Special keys are provided for clearing all the indicators and registers of the machine—and it is essential to make sure the machine has been properly cleared before beginning a new calculation.

Multiplication can be undertaken on an adding machine. To multiply a number by 2 it is necessary simply to add it to itself, i.e., to enter it twice in succession into the product register at the top of the machine. This is accomplished by pressing the keys corresponding to the number and then operating the handle or lever *twice*. To multiply by 20 it is simply necessary to proceed as for multiplying by 2 but with the movable carriage of the machine deliberately pushed one space sideways. To multiply by 200 the carriage must be pushed two spaces sideways. To multiply by 250 we proceed as for 200 and then move the carriage back one space and press or wind the handle five times. To multiply by 253 we proceed as for 250 but then move the carriage back yet another space and turn the handle three times. The counting register will show at a glance whether we have in fact turned the handle the correct number of times in each carriage position. The final answer is clearly seen in the product register.

Just as multiplication can be considered in this way as a series of separate additions so can *division* be treated as a series of subtractions. Dividing 200 by 5 simply means finding how many times 5 can be subtracted from 200. Most adding machines have a handle which can be rotated to transfer a number from the keyboard to the product register. Rotating this handle forwards gives 'addition';—rotating it backwards subtracts the number on the keyboard from the number already on the product register. Hence our problem is simply to find how many times we can 'unwind' the handle before the number on the product register is entirely removed. We can subtract 5 from 200 forty times; hence we should need forty back windings of the handle to empty the product register. That would be a laborious process; in fact by shifting the movable carriage one space sideways before doing the unwinding we need only unwind the handle *four* times. Much more complicated divisors and dividends can be used of course—using the same principle of successive subtraction. Care should be exercised in moving the carriage sideways and in placing the decimal point. (Most machines have special markers to show the position of the decimal point.) The counting register serves as a check on the number of rotations of the handle which have been made—and this is the required answer: the quotient. An alternative way of undertaking division is by using reciprocal tables. The number to be divided (the dividend) is simply multiplied by the reciprocal of the divisor.

2. *Electronic Desk Calculators*. These machines can perform addition, subtraction, multiplication, division and often more complicated quantities, such as square roots, quite automatically. In addition some of these machines have what is termed 'storage facilities'. This means that the machine may 'remember' certain numbers which happen to be required for later stages in the calculation. They hold this information in suspense on dials or indicators while the main part of the machine carries on with the next stage in the calculation. The 'memory store' of small, compact desk-top machines is of course necessarily limited. Electronic desk calculators are extremely powerful tools for the statistician or researcher. Their great virtue is that they are usually very easy to operate, and require little previous training.

3. *Computers*. These are in many ways similar to the electronic calculator. They are not however limited to the four operations of addition, subtraction, multiplication, and division—but are capable of a great number of quite different operations as well. The main reason for this extra capacity is that they have very much greater 'memory stores'. A computer can 'remember' not only numbers but also an extremely long and difficult list of instructions. When it has been prepared or 'programmed' by the operator it can apply these instructions many hundreds of times per second to new raw data which is supplied to it. Thus the operator can 'programme' the computer to get itself ready to go through all the stages of extracting a mean from a set of numbers. The numbers can then be fed into the machine and the mean of these will be immediately computed in a few millionths of a second. Though computers are very hard and rapid workers they are of course completely unintelligent and they do require the most precise and painstakingly-given programming by the operator. The programme instructions must be broken down into the minutest possible stages—for example to make a computer find the mean of a set of numbers the following instructions are required:

1. Start
2. Read the data tape. Store numbers on tape
3. Add all the numbers on that tape
4. Call this product X
5. At the same time count the number of additions
6. Call this number N
7. Divide X by N, correct to 5 decimal places
8. Print out the result
9. Stop

Producing these instructions in a form which the machine can understand is known as 'programming' and can be a lengthy process and calls for a good deal of expertise. The programmer usually 'writes' the programme on a tape punch which resembles a typewriter in many ways except that the output is in the form of a tape in which holes have been punched across a column of five or seven spaces. Each digit or letter is represented by a special configuration of holes and blanks. The 'programme' when written consists of a roll of tape in which a sequence of hole arrangements have been punched. This is fed into the computer through a 'tape reader' which can sense the holes in the tape very rapidly. The programme tape is followed by the data tape and then the computer begins to work. The machine puts out the required transformations or answers in one of many different forms—usually on tape again. This is read though a tape reader which is connected to a teleprinter and this prints out the results.

It is necessary to use a special code or intermediate 'language' to convey instructions to the machine. In the earliest computers each different machine had its own special language code and this had the unfortunate result that programmes written for one machine could not be used on another. Nowadays, however, there are a number of 'universal' languages which can be used on many different makes of equipment. Two of the most successful languages are 'ALGOL' and 'FORTRAN' and most new computers will accept both of these. The social scientist need not learn the principles of programming or the use of these 'languages' since most computer-centres employ specialist staff for this purpose (and many programmes already exist in 'programme libraries' for the more common statistical operations, and these rolls of tape can be used over and over again). The social scientist must, however, know the most useful ways of presenting his raw data for processing by the staff of the computer centre.

4. *Card-sorting machines.* These enable us to examine a large amount of diverse data (such as that obtained from surveys) very rapidly, and to locate cases with the particular features we happen to be interested in at any given stage of the analysis. A very large amount of data about one individual can be recorded on a punched card since each card has as many as 80 columns and each of these columns has spaces for up to nine different entries. Thus, 80 × 9, or more than 700 units of information, may be recorded on a card no bigger than a postcard. The investigator must decide on a simple code. He might decide, for example, to use the first column on the card to represent the sex of the individual studied, thus a hole punched in the first space of column 1 might indicate a 'male', whereas a hole in space 2 would indicate a 'female'. The second column might be used to record age group: the top space indicating 'below 20', the next lower space in the same column '21–40', the next space '41–60' and so on. We have still 78 more columns left for more information to be recorded if necessary. Once the information about each individual has been punched on a separate card a large bundle of these cards can be taken to the card-sorting machine which can then be 'instructed' to throw out for example 'all males' (Column 1, hole 1). When these have been automatically thrown out (in a matter of a few seconds) the machine can then be emptied of all cards. A second sorting of the male cards already thrown out could then take place. Thus the machine could be instructed to select from the previously selected males 'all those people between 21 and 40 years of age' (Column 2, hole 2). In this way, in a matter of a few seconds we could locate from a very large population of perhaps 2,000 people those relatively few people who happened to be both 'male' and also 'between 21 and 40'. Not only does the machine select cards in this way but it also 'classifies' cards for any particular feature such as 'age'. Thus it can simultaneously divide a large population into different age piles representing 'those under 20', 'those between 21 and 40', 'those beween 41 and 60' and so on. Simple statistical calculations on large populations can be very much assisted by a card sorter. Finding the mean score of 12,000 individuals on a variable with nine alternative values would be a very tedious operation if performed by

hand or with a calculating machine, but if the data is put on to punched cards the machine will very quickly sort the cards into batches representing the nine positions and give a frequency count as well. The mean is easily obtained by multiplying the frequency of a particular score by the score itself, summing and dividing by the total number of individuals $\left(\dfrac{\Sigma f x}{N}\right)$. The preliminary stages in the calculation of a coefficient of correlation and other similar statistics are also considerably speeded by allowing the sorting machine to do repetitive counting. All these items of equipment enormously increase the range, power and speed of computational work in the social sciences. They are to be regarded as extremely energetic but completely unintelligent slaves. The methodological argument, however, and the statistical reasoning and the conclusions drawn depend completely on the training and good judgement of the social scientist himself.

Appendix 4

Writing a Report

An experimental report has a standard structure which varies very little between different disciplines. It is standardised to allow easy comparison and to ensure that essential information is not omitted. The amount of detail included is to some extent determined by the purpose for which the report is prepared but it should never leave any step in the design, execution and analysis of the situation unclear or ambiguous. Ideally enough information should be given so that the exercise could be replicated by a reader with a high degree of accuracy—this facilitates comparison of both data and conclusions.

Title
This should express concisely the nature of the study.

Objective
This is a statement of the purpose of the experiment in the form of a working hypothesis. It should include a clear statement of what is being proved or tested.

Materials
An accurate description of all apparatus and equipment used is required. If the apparatus is standard, for example, a stopwatch, no further description is necessary.

Method
A precise description of the method used in collecting the data with adequate details of design, matching, number of subjects and nature of raw data. Where applicable a verbatim copy of instructions to subjects should be included.

Results
Where convenient a summary of the raw data including preliminary analysis (such as means) should be presented in tabular form. It is not necessary to include all computations but the exact nature of any statistic used should always be made clear.

Discussion

The findings should be discussed in the light of the original hypotheses. New and original interpretations of the data may be made at this stage. Possible explanations of interesting, inconsistent or indicative points in the original data, tables or graphs should be pointed out. An attempt should be made to relate the exercise to previous work, and where relevant, theoretical implications should be discussed. The author may say what further work is indicated as being fruitful, and may make suggestions for improvements in the design of the experiment. The 'discussion' is in fact the most important part of the report and since it includes all the original and creative analysis made by the investigator most attention should be devoted to it.

Conclusions

Usually these are best presented as numbered summary statements of the results and of the fate of the original hypotheses.

References

Full details of any work mentioned in the discussion must be given in addition to general references to work done in the same area. The following format is used:

KRECH, D., CRUTCHFIELD, R. S., and BALLACHEY, E. L., *Individual in Society* (McGraw-Hill, N.Y. 1962).

TAFFEL, C., 'Anxiety and the conditioning of verbal behaviour', in *Journ. Abnorm. Soc. Psychol.* (1955) 51: pp. 496–501.

(*Note:* Use italic or underlining for titles of books, journals and periodicals; quotation marks for titles of articles within them.)

Index

Index